AMBASSADOR to the PENGUINS

Clifford Ashley's painting entitled "A Dead Whale or a Stove Boat!" shows the Daisy *hove to with her boats down and around a sperm whale in its flurry.*

AMBASSADOR to the PENGUINS

A Naturalist's Year
Aboard a Yankee Whaleship

by ELEANOR MATHEWS

DAVID R. GODINE · PUBLISHER · BOSTON

First published in 2003 by
DAVID R. GODINE, Publisher
Post Office Box 450
Jaffrey, New Hampshire 03452
www.godine.com

LIBRARY OF CONGRESS CATALOGING-IN-PUBLICATION DATA

Mathews, Eleanor.
Ambassador to the penguins : a naturalist's year
aboard a yankee whaleship / Eleanor Mathews.
p. cm.
ISBN 1-56792-246-5 (alk. Paper)
1. Murphy, Robert Cushman, 1887—Travel Antarctica.
2. Antarctica—Description and travel. 3. Daisy (Whaling brig)
4. Naturalists—United States—Biography.
I. Title.
G8501912.M8 M38   2003
508.98'9—dc21   2003013721

First Edition, 2003
Printed in the United States of America

CONTENTS

Robert Cushman Murphy.

PROLOGUE

THE STORY here has already been told by the man who experienced it.

In 1947 my grandfather, Robert Cushman Murphy, published *Logbook for Grace* (Macmillan). In it he offered an edited version of the letters he had written my grandmother, Grace Emeline Barstow Murphy, while on his first scientific expedition thirty-five years earlier and at the outset of their marriage. While she waited out the year, he criss-crossed the Atlantic Ocean in a wooden whaleship that took him to the rim of the Antarctic and back. As a museum curator, he was in search of specimens from the wild world. The captain's goal was blubber.

Logbook received lavish praise. At my mother's urging, my grandfather reissued his popular book in 1965 (Time Reading Program). Neither edition, however, included any of the photographs he made during the voyage. In 1967, with readers' increased interest in whales and whaling, he published *A Dead Whale or a Stove Boat* (Houghton Mifflin), a collection of some seventy of his photographs that are felt by many to be among the best documentation of the New England tradition.

The two books were not published as companions, however. Many readers of one were unaware of the other. Yet the narrative and the photographs are a natural pairing. It has long been my hope to bring them together in a single volume. Furthermore, *A Dead Whale* focuses solely on the whaling aspect of the voyage. Though innately curious as to how the operation worked, my grandfather's primary purpose was elsewhere. He was a biologist—a more delicately inclined blood-and-guts man than the captain and crew of the *Daisy*. His real goal was to reach penguin territory. A working ship was the only way to get there, and while he was along for the ride he took pictures of the goings-on. That was his nature.

My grandfather was much lauded for his writing style and flair for language. His voice rings clear in my memory: imposing, scholarly, and precise. For me to take on an already well-told story was no small matter. In expanding his work, I had some measuring up to do.

There may be those who think I have trespassed on another's literary territory. To them I apologize. The only legitimate way to expand my grandfather's account with details not previously published was to move it out of his telling into my own less intimate, third-person prose. By doing so, however, I was able to include more about the man than the man had revealed about himself. I have also brought my grandmother into greater focus. She was, after all, the person who convinced him to make the trip and for whom he passionately described what he saw, feared, yearned for, and felt the entire year, including details of what he ate and wore, possibly now of greater interest than in 1947.

More than the rambling attempts of an admiring granddaughter rifling through the family attic, I hope what follows still makes for a rip-ping good yarn. Independent of personal links, my feeling is that it is a tale that warrants being kept alive. It is history. It is American muscle and meat.

My grandfather wrote hundreds of articles and was a terrific keeper of papers and clippings. Readers may wonder why some of the quotes and excerpts here do not match word-for-word what is in *Logbook*. Any dis-similarities stem from my having referred to his pre-edited manuscripts and other sources in which the voyage of the *Daisy* was described, and, of course, from having heard his accounts directly. Nowhere have I know-ingly altered his words, but I have drawn upon a variety of sources to find them. Some passages are paraphrased, but those sections do not appear as quotes. Additionally, the order of events here is not a precise match with *Logbook*. Though he wrote copiously while on the voyage, my grandfather could not experience the storms and the hunts and the drama and write of them simultaneously. Consequently, his notes describe some events after the fact. In an effort to straighten those chronological kinks, I have placed things as they occurred, thus making, I hope, a clearer sequence.

This work is one of nonfiction; all the people named once lived. If any of their descendants feel their relatives are unfairly portrayed, I apologize. My grandfather's reports are the best I have to go on. Though he strived to be accurate and fair, he, like anyone, held his own biases and was subject to the beliefs of his day.

THIS BOOK is the result of a sort of vast partnership. In particular I am indebted to Robert Cox, manuscript librarian at the American Philosophical Society; Jill Wright, curator at the Whaling Museum in Cold Spring Harbor; Anne Canty, senior director of Media Relations at the American Museum of Natural History; and Matthew Pavlick, media assets archivist, also of the American Museum of Natural History. The existence of these institutions, the archives they house, and the assistance of the people who maintain them have elevated the quality of my work. By researching a man much admired where his journals and photographs are kept, I have benefited by association. The encouragement and support of Patrick Preston, Judy Hume, Carolyn McConnell, Robert Kaye, Judy Lightfoot, Edith Rhode, Bonny Becker, Eve Khiem, and Jill Anderson helped me through the writing process. Thanks also to Steve White and Laurel Schultz for helping to mine the microfilm of a lost journal. Special thanks go to my editor, Elsbeth Lindner, for advice, patience, and tact, to David Godine for finding her and for his faith in the "Murphy Project". To Gary Kroll, scholar and historian, I am also grateful. Would that he could have met my grandfather.

For Carl Youngmann, there are not enough words.

—ELEANOR MATHEWS
Seattle, Washington

INTRODUCTION

A DISTINGUISHED ORNITHOLOGIST, oceanographer, and conservationist, Robert Cushman Murphy was above all an old-school natural historian in the best sense of the term. In an age of dizzying specialization in the sciences of biology, zoology, and ecology, he remained a steadfast generalist who rarely allowed any natural or cultural phenomena escape record from his ever-scribbling pencil. Whether he was examining the guano deposits on Peruvian islands, a moa skeleton in New Zealand's Pyramid Swamp, or the Long Island Sound from his home in Old Field, New York, Murphy appreciated the world as a product of historical forces long in process. His impeccable reputation in the fields of ornithology and conservation was founded on his historical sensibilities and his extraordinary attention to detail.

He spent his life oscillating between the field and his office at the American Museum of Natural History, publishing books and articles both scientific and popular, delivering papers, and speaking out on behalf of environmentalists dismayed at humanity's encroachment upon the fragile natural world. Indeed, he may be best remembered today for his role as plaintiff in a suit against the U.S. Department of Agriculture to halt the spraying of the pesticide DDT over Long Island—a case that Rachel Carson followed very carefully.

All this was captured in microcosm on Murphy's voyage on the *Daisy* to the tumultuous oceans of the South Atlantic. Akin to a youthful Charles Darwin some eighty years earlier, Murphy was keenly aware of the importance of his first far-flung expedition. Recently graduated from college, he was working at the Brooklyn Museum of Natural

Science in 1912 when he was offered the opportunity to spend a year on the hermaphrodite brig *Daisy* that was plying the South Atlantic waters for sperm whale and sea elephant oil. Murphy's scientific objectives were simply to observe, catalog, map, and collect the life of the region, especially the oceanic bird life so abundant in the sub-Antarctic ocean. He succeeded with a deftness that would eventually lead to the publication of his magnum opus *Oceanic Birds of South America* (1936), a monograph that is still recognized as an authoritative source in ornithology and represents an early treatise on the biogeography of the ocean. Perhaps the most important outcome of the expedition was that it framed in his mind an environmental ethic that was as applicable in the world's oceans as it was on land. Despite the fascinating range of his many environmental campaigns, Murphy continuously warned his audience that the ocean was not a trove of inexhaustible resources. In this, Murphy was a visionary, for only lately have humans begun to own up to the over-harvesting of the ocean's natural resources. But the historical significance and the human drama of Murphy's 1912–1913 expedition to South Georgia and the sub-Antarctic are not captured in his persistent environmental messages nor in a naturalist tome on ocean birds; we need to look elsewhere.

A consummate naturalist, Murphy was rarely without pencil and notebook. He routinely had his notes transcribed and bound into volumes that corresponded with various expeditions. The journals are currently held at the American Philosophical Society, and by all indication, Murphy rarely paused in his life-long practice. The "Diary of the Expedition to South Georgia," however, was no ordinary notebook. It is a daily log written to his new bride and is fittingly redolent of the passion and longing that one might expect from a young man undertaking a year-long expedition several months after marriage. With senses highly attuned, Murphy breathed a literary life into this expedition that invites comparison to *Voyage of the Beagle* and *Moby Dick*, both of which he enjoyed from the quarterdeck of the *Daisy* in the off-hours. At once, Murphy's diary is a testament to New England-style whaling then in its final days, a chronicle of the human drama of nautical life, and a portrait of the hardened but beautiful natural history of the sub-Antarctic world. It is also a commentary on the nature of human kindness and compassion, and even a bit of a diatribe on the fate of nature at the hands of human ingenuity.

Both Murphy and his wife Grace knew that the "Diary" was something unique, but it was not until thirty-four years later that an edited version of the text found its way into bookstores, re-christened as *Logbook for Grace*. It was favorably reviewed, but the most poignant commentary I have found comes from Murphy's father.

> It's truly up to the style of your best letters to us, and I've told you before that I would use those masterpieces—which always delight us—as a criterion. . . . If I boiled everything I have to say about your book down to a single drop I would say that it has all the learned mastery of your usual writings—sure—but in addition a most wonderful amount of warmth, and it is the latter which makes it seem different from your other opuses, and like your letters. You've always used humor, but it seems to me never before with such sensitiveness; you've always been keen in observing and describing people and phenomena, but I think never before with such empathy (in your writings, I mean). I get the feeling in reading *Logbook* that you have consciously tempered your penchant for sharp wit so as to allow plenty of room for a warm humor, and in my opinion this is the factor that will make it a sellout.

It is a great privilege to see the story of Murphy's first expedition resurrected through the talented voice of his granddaughter, Eleanor Mathews. *Ambassador to the Penguins* hews closely to *Logbook* but is enriched with fascinating historical details that only add to Murphy's vivid travel narrative. Most importantly, Mathews captures the human drama of Murphy's experiences with an attention to detail that seems characteristic of the Murphy lineage, while at the same time maintaining the "warm humor" that makes this tale of science and adventure such an incredible joy to read. *Logbook* is a forgotten classic of American nature writing and travel literature—a book not only significant in the annals of natural history, but also a treatise on the nature of history. *Ambassador to the Penguins* bestows new form on a story whose relevance is only too clear.

—GARY KROLL, Ph.D.
History Department
Plattsburgh State University

SECTION I
The Offer

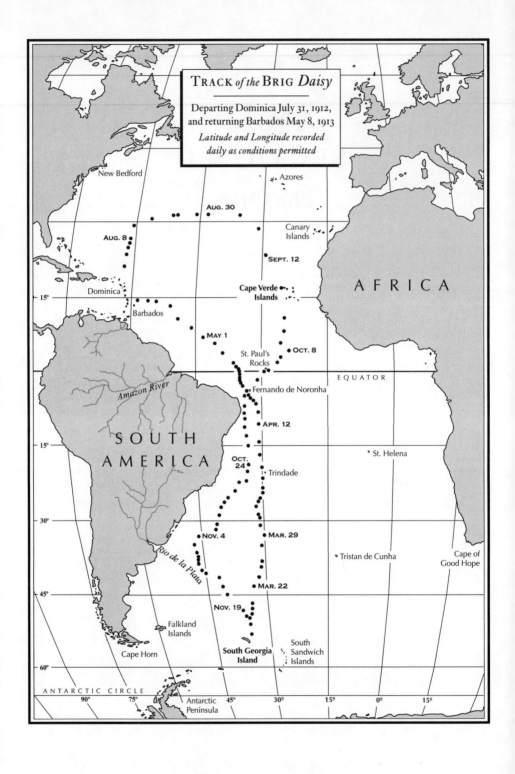

TRACK *of the* BRIG *Daisy*

Departing Dominica July 31, 1912,
and returning Barbados May 8, 1913

*Latitude and Longitude recorded
daily as conditions permitted*

New Bedford

Azores

AUG. 30

Canary
Islands

AUG. 8

SEPT. 12

Cape Verde
Islands

AFRICA

15°   Dominica

Barbados

MAY 1

OCT. 8

St. Paul's
Rocks

EQUATOR

Amazon River

Fernando de Noronha

APR. 12

15°   SOUTH
AMERICA

OCT.
24

St. Helena

Trindade

30°

NOV. 4

MAR. 29

Rio de la Plata

Tristan de Cunha

Cape of
Good Hope

45°

MAR. 22

NOV. 19

Falkland
Islands

Cape Horn

South Georgia
Island

South
Sandwich
Islands

60°

ANTARCTIC CIRCLE

90°   75°   45°   30°   15°   0°   15°

Antarctic
Peninsula

Chapter One

History could not have stirred a more unlikely mix: two museums, a blubber hunt, an irascible captain, a steward with an actual peg leg, several million birds, and Robert Cushman Murphy reading Shakespeare on deck during his spare time. It was 1911. Old-style seafaring was dying out; Murphy's career was just getting going. Having grown up on Long Island's shore, he knew a bark from a sloop from a brig from a ship, but he had only fantasized that he would ever go to sea himself. He was fresh out of Brown University and eager to begin his biology career with a bang. A trip to the Antarctic would surely do that.

The scientific world buzzed with news of polar exploration. U.S. Navy Admiral Robert Peary and his men had reached absolute North. Robert Falcon Scott and Roald Amundsen were in a race to conquer the bottommost point on Earth.

Ten years earlier Scott had set out for the far south on the *S. S. Discovery* with a goal of collecting penguin eggs. Studying the eggs, some felt, might reveal the answers not only to what penguins were but might help explain the development of birds altogether. Early seafarers had described penguins as part beast, part bird. Others thought them to be fantastic air-breathing, feathered fish. Some scientists believed they were an evolutionary precursor to birds.

Men came back from early expeditions bursting with stories of icebergs towering above their ships. They reported on albatrosses spreading wings wider than a country lane and soaring beside the sails for days at a time. And, of course, they described the penguins not flying at all but using their paddle-like wings as flippers under water, more like the seals they shared the beaches with than the birds they really were. All the while the seals themselves were being clubbed to death by the thousands for the softness of their fur.

Explorers and hunters. These were the people heading to the frozen south.

The Brooklyn Museum of Natural Science and the American Museum of Natural History felt the excitement. The two institutions had teamed up in hopes of sending one of their own to collect whatever specimens could be brought back. They would need someone trained as an observer of the natural world, adept at scientific record keeping, skilled in making accurate measurements, and hardy enough to endure an icy year at sea. They would also need a vessel and its crew to get him there and back. Exploration teams aside, the only way to reach the white frontier was to cooperate with whalers or sealers.

Whether the museums approached the owners of a New Bedford whaling ship or the owners of the ship proposed the idea to one of the museums is no longer known. Either way, a deal was struck: in exchange for subsidizing the voyage of a brig named the *Daisy*, the museums would secure passage for one to the Island of South Georgia and cargo space for the specimens he would bring back. The museum directors' first choice turned them down, so they approached a promising young scientist, Bob Murphy, who worked in taxidermy and had recently begun as Curator of Birds and Mammals at the Brooklyn Museum.

He possessed the right temperament for the job. Perpetually full of wonder and with a rare combination of formality and mirth, he was as likely to recite Walt Whitman as Dante or to break into a verse or two of *Blow the Man Down*. Though respectful of accomplishment, he was neither cowed by social status nor scornful of the lower classes. This would endear him to the captain and the crew alike.

Even today the Antarctic zone is difficult to reach. In Murphy's time, it was much harder. When the offer to hitch such a ride was made, it must have struck him as more thrilling than a trip to the moon—except nothing grows on the moon. Living things had been this man's passion from the start. At age seven, in a boy's best penmanship on ruled paper, he began recording what he found in the woods, the fields, the marshes. One early entry describes how he had come upon a nest of chickadees hatching in the hollow of an apple tree and how he broke away a large slab of bark for a better view. This allowed him to monitor nesting behavior, hour-by-hour. But a heavy rainstorm erupted, and the chicks died of exposure. Murphy was devastated.

As an adult he continued to keep meticulous notes and to catalog his observations. By agreeing to take the museums up on their offer, he had two purposes in mind: first, to contribute to the scientific advancement his employers sought, and second, as his own project, to document the details of a dying era. The American whaling industry was about to come to an end. Petroleum and electric lights were replacing marine mammal oils for lubrication and illumination. That Murphy wanted to describe what remained of Yankee seafaring traditions was admirable. That he could carry it off with color and precision would be a bonus.

The old windjammer that Murphy would be setting out on had already seen forty years of service and was decidedly a working vessel. By coincidence it had been christened only four and a half miles from Murphy's boyhood home. Taken out of context, it might seem implausible that the brig *Daisy* and the man had started out independently in such proximity. However, for more than a century, Long Island Sound had practically defined shipbuilding as an industry. Anybody within shouting distance of New York's Port Jefferson, Setauket, or Stony Brook was familiar with the ring of adzes as they

Murphy was the oldest of eleven children, nine of whom lived to adulthood.

shaped native trees—already bent by coastal winds—into curved deck beams and framing members. Even the tiny settlement of Mt. Sinai where the Murphys lived, east of Port Jefferson, had seen shipwrights regularly easing sloops and schooners down the ways and into the sea.

The *Daisy* was built by Nehemiah Hand and launched in Setauket Harbor in 1872, fifteen years before Murphy's birth. Hand had framed her in white oak and chestnut. For her planks he brought up long-leaf pine from the Carolinas. All was copper fastened. The vessel was two-decked and 123 feet long. She was two-masted: square-rigged on the foremast for speed but with sails fore and aft on the mainmast for safety and ease. Technically, that made her a half brig, or hermaphrodite, but she was registered simply as a brig. Originally, she had sailed as a merchant ship, loading and unloading cargo in the Baltic and Mediterranean seas and putting in at American ports from Boston to Buenos Aires. Her strength and speed made her handle well. Her capacity made her profitable.

In 1907, a New Bedford group bought and refitted the *Daisy* as a whaler, adding accommodations for a crew four times larger than she had required when operating as a merchant ship. As a property she was split into thirty-two shares, with Captain Benjamin Cleveland holding the most at nine shares and his wife owning one. Assorted sea captains, tradesmen, manufacturers, a schoolteacher, a carpenter, and a seedsman, all from Massachusetts and Connecticut, held the remaining shares.

Along Long Island's shore, when a ship was completed, the launching would be a gala event. Murphy had attended such celebrations. In 1902, when he was fifteen, he wrote in his diary of how he had witnessed the launching of the *Martha E. Wallace*, a four-masted schooner. The boy in him responded to the lure of faraway ports. The scientist in him wanted

The Daisy *was launched in 1872 to serve as a merchant ship.*

6

to identify all the specialized components of the schooner's elaborate rigging.

Now, however, transportation was becoming modernized; wind on canvas was no longer counted on as the only impetus for moving a vessel forward. Steam and steel were taking over. Murphy had attended school with Nehemiah Hand's descendants and had grown up among the children and grandchildren of other yard bosses. The thought of boarding the *Daisy* for a year must have struck him as living in something of a museum itself. Her blubber-hunting crew would be in search of whales and sea elephants. Murphy would be in search of birds, fishes, plants, insects, mammals, mollusks, winds, clouds, temperature readings, soundings—anything and everything he could put on record, history included.

Chapter Two

WHEN THE OFFER FIRST CAME, Murphy's initial response was, "I can't." He explained that he was engaged to be married. It would never have occurred to a man like Bob Murphy to break a promise—certainly not to his fiancée—no matter how dazzling the opportunity, no matter how passionately he wanted to see the twelve-foot wingspan of an albatross in flight.

From the very start there was something about birds that had captivated Bob. The summer he was sixteen he wrote, "I noticed a late set of song sparrow's eggs in a nest in the Poulson's honeysuckle . . . after a swim I saw a scoter and a great blue heron . . . had a long chat with Gustavus Tooker, a lifelong resident of Mt. Sinai, about changes in the status of fish, and more especially, birds in this area. He says that purple martin, Baltimore oriole, bluebird, blue jay, indigo bird, cedar bird, crow–blackbird, and tanager have steadily decreased in his lifetime, whereas hummingbird, kingbird, wood thrush, bob-white, house wren, and the obnoxious English sparrow have increased. He and his father call the high-hole or flicker a 'clape.' "

But Bob's interest extended beyond simply seeing and naming the species. He also wrote about their behavior, "explored the alder swamp adjacent to our home and tried in vain to find a yellowthroat's nest. Notes of alarm near a catbird's nest led me to investigate, and I found a large blacksnake among the branches, the parent catbird uttering distracted cries. . . . Before breakfast my setter, Dewey, brought me a yellow-throated vireo. He carried it gently, without hurting it. While I held it, the parent bird flew around with a caterpillar in her bill, and when the young bird perched on my finger the mother flew down to it. But instead of feeding the youngster she teased and coaxed it into flying to a bough, and only then was it rewarded . . . up at five o'clock and went to Brooklyn with Mama, Augusta, and the baby . . . preserved a sea-robin (fish) in alcohol . . . heard the first katydids of the summer . . . found a young chimney swift in our fireplace; put it back up the chimney. Arthur Helme offered to give me a lesson in taxidermy, so I took my gun and looked for a suitable bird. The crows were too wary, but I shot a green heron . . . skinned the green heron . . . saw an indigo bunting . . . saw scoters, old-squaws, and plovers . . . in the evening, I saw a night-hawk."

Bob's focus, however, was not limited to birds. He was a born observer of whatever moved across his path, whether it was the one leading to the beach or the sandy lane that wound its way toward town and the ship-yards and into the wider world. Growing up in the country and near the shore he probably investigated more clam holes and anthills than most, though never to the aimless detriment of the clams or ants. And he took the time to write down what he saw.

Unlike some young boys, his was not the curiosity of random destruc-tion; it was simply a healthy wonder at the workings of the world. He returned beetles and snakes to the ground intact, the better to study their habits. If he found a tortoise he would count the growth rings of its shell plates before carefully replacing the hard beast to earth, trying to imag-ine how those bony plates had grown in the first place. Studying a popu-lation of fiddler crabs, he noted that, "each male possesses one great claw, larger than himself, with which he can give an unpleasant pinch. . . . If held long by the claw, they will separate themselves from it."

Somewhere in those early years Bob taught himself to whistle the same open twist of notes the thrushes made in the meadow and he found their nests among the oaks and counted their eggs. He watched. He saw the natural world around him. The boy burned to know what made it pulse.

All the while there was the sea and its beyond, with its mysteries and implicit distances. He saw the sailing ships go past. Though Bob had

The Murphys at home in Mt. Sinai. Bob stands at the back.

rowed, swum, paddled, fished, and sailed Long Island Sound, he could only fantasize crossing an ocean.

His father had trained as a lawyer but when the work did not appeal, he had become a secondary school principal. His mother was also educated—and, apparently, thrifty. In an early letter, she wrote, ". . . such a delightful book store where you may sit in a comfortable chair and read a book through and go out without buying if you wish."

Thrift was key. Bob was the oldest of nine children. A schoolmaster's salary afforded the family few advantages. Theirs was a simple, country life supported by a spine of New England values: hard work, decency, and self-reliance. At sixteen, Bob wrote, "July 25, 1903, arose at half past four and went out after bluefish in Captain Davis' sloop-rigged, flat-bottomed sailboat. . . . July 27, My father's fiftieth birthday. Worked on the chicken-house all morning, and stayed home in afternoon while the rest of the family went to the Sound beach for a swim. . . . Aug. 3, Sawed wood, took a swim, and made a bow of red cedar. Caught a fledgling olive-backed warbler."

Bob's fascination with birds eventually took him to the museums of New York City, in particular the Brooklyn Museum and the American Museum of Natural History. There he made connections with the staff and after high school graduation was hired to proofread galleys for a book entitled *Warblers of North America*.

His earliest hope as a small boy had been that one day he could go to work in a museum. He had dared to think that being a guard in such a place would be the fulfillment of a fine ambition—with the institution's scholarly staff, its enormous and comprehensive collections, its world-wide programs for research, and its incomparable exhibition halls. He saw any museum as a sort of Mecca for naturalists. With the proofread-ing job, his dream began to come alive.

His family had always called him Rob, but the larger world began to identify him more formally as Robert Cushman Murphy with him invariably emphasizing the middle name and his connection through his mother, Augusta Cushman, to an ancestry that had arrived in the New World on the *Mayflower* and a subsequent ship in 1621. The Irish influence from his father's side, however, was evident in a different way. The Murphys of Mt. Sinai were Roman Catholic.

Bob, as the oldest of nine, was first to leave home. He was also first to quit the Church, possibly because the beliefs did not coincide with his scientific analysis of the world and its origins. Whatever the reasons, dis-missing Catholicism did not sit well with Bob's father. For a period of time the oldest son was not welcome inside the Mt. Sinai home.

Fortunately the proofreading assignment led to more work and a modicum of independence. With a high school diploma and a job in New York City, Bob felt ready to make his own choices. Earning forty dollars a month, he found himself a "hall bedroom" for rent near the museum. He lived on what he could afford at the corner shop, bread and buttermilk, which he ate while sitting on the edge of his bed. Toward the end of one salary period, he ran out of money and had nothing but water at mealtimes. He had been working nights reading scientific proofs with a Dr. Jonathan Dwight.

As he bid good night, Dr. Dwight said, "I owe you for several evenings. Shall I pay you now?"

"Just as you please," said Bob, trying to sound as casual as he could. But once he had pocketed the ten dollars and walked sedately down the steps, he ran lickety-split to the nearest hot meal.

Friends at the museum continued to find him work in the bird collection. They saw potential in the fact that Bob was earnest, sharp, focused, and eager. "That boy should have his chance to go to college," they said, which was exactly where he himself wanted to go. With eight siblings still at home and with tension lingering between him and his father, he had no hope of his family helping him make his way.

The director of the American Museum, along with its curator of birds, Frank Chapman, whose galleys Bob had proofread, pulled whatever strings they knew how to pull and somehow arranged a full scholarship to Brown University. Bob packed his bags.

During his freshman year he slept on a cot in the old Biological Laboratory. Whether he was on duty as a guard of some kind or was given this free space by professors who wanted to help him out is not known. Beyond that he tutored a little, took odd jobs, and accepted loans from several people.

In June 1911, Bob graduated with a Phi Beta Kappa key jingling on his watch chain. This was an enormous achievement for a country boy who started out with no Ivy League connections. Chosen valedictorian, he spoke at graduation of the value of Latin and Greek in the college curriculum. Years later, he would return to his *alma mater* to receive an honorary doctorate, his second.

During his days at Brown, Bob had met Grace Emeline Barstow, third and last child of a successful cast-iron stove manufacturer who had died when Grace was fourteen. Mrs. Barstow, however, remained very much alive and welcomed her daughter's friends with ease.

After a time, whenever people could not find Bob on campus, they invariably located him at the Barstows' house. It had become such a comfortable second home for him that one day when he came across two dead skunks while tramping past a farm, he took them to Mrs. Barstow's to skin. His mother-in-law-to-be was said to have gasped audibly at the sight. Bob said he would take them to the cellar and assured her, "But, Mrs. Barstow, there will be no odor, as it is contained in a sac that I'll take out whole." She acquiesced. His knife slipped. The stink erupted.

Grace dashed up the back stairs, the mother down the front stairs. Bob sprinted to the drugstore for odor-killing candles and injured his leg in the rush. This all happened on New Year's Eve. He and Grace had accepted an invitation to a formal dance. Bob wore gloves, even during supper.

Grace Emeline Barstow.

Chapter Three

WHEN GRACE BARSTOW WAS TEN years old, her parents took her to an ear specialist to discuss her apparent hearing loss. Soon after, a doctor arrived at the house to remove her adenoids. This was a different era when even loving parents thought it best not to prepare children for painful procedures. Grace sensed something and ran terrified and screaming up the second flight of curving stairs. They carried her to her mother's room, laid her flat and held her down. Sunshine flooded rose-covered wallpaper, but the ugly memory of ether would remain vivid all her life, and the harsh operation did nothing to arrest the hearing loss.

Grace expected to be sent to Smith College as her sister had been, but when the time came, her mother denied her any further education because of the advancing deafness. Instead Mrs. Barstow announced, "I am taking you to Europe for one year."

Grace had already been abroad. The year of the adenoid horror, she had gone with her mother by steamer to Ireland. Later, her father had taken his daughter to England, Holland, Switzerland, and Italy.

Architecture, cathedrals, the French language, symphonies, and opera were all very fine, but Grace felt unjustly treated. She wanted to continue her schooling. After the European trip and the homecoming celebration at New York's Waldorf Hotel at which Grace tasted her first champagne, she struck an agreement with her mother and was allowed at least to earn a certificate at Pembroke College.

· None of this prevented Grace from emerging into the social world. The time arrived for her coming out party. Engraved invitations, caterers, extra servants, ball gowns, and formal lunches were her *entrée* into the adult world.

She had grown to be a tall, upright young woman with slender ankles and a direct gaze. Full dark hair was pulled off her face to show a long, alabaster neck. Her laughs came easily to the surface, like music, and her hands moved in the air when she spoke. Long fingers had been trained to the discipline of her violin, to which she clung desperately in the confusion of diminished hearing. Music was everything to her.

It was during a June weekend party held by another debutante that Grace first saw Bob. College men had been invited to an outdoor lunch. She noticed him as a tall good-looking fellow reciting Dante to another girl. Grace had been in Dante's city. The dark-eyed girl had not. Grace wanted that young man to sit with her.

The following winter that same tall fellow put on his evening clothes to call on the dark-eyed girl. She was not at home. Not wanting to "waste his tails" he decided to call on Grace instead. Invited to sit on a carved rosewood settee, polished to a fine gleam and upholstered in mohair, he seemed immediately at ease in the opulence of the Barstows' parlor. Not only was Robert Cushman Murphy six foot three, he had a polished look himself, with a fine straight nose seeming to punctuate quick, deep-set eyes. Dark hair obeyed a side part and lay close to his head. Even in repose, his face looked ready to break into a smile. Grace especially noticed his hands, manicured and nimble; they appeared to be capable of almost anything. When he spoke—and his voice rang clear—he drew up his height as if to deliver an oration, as if to convey some terribly important and fascinating fact, something delightful that his listeners would treasure and remember. He took command; he entertained.

Without necessarily intending it, Grace's father had created in his daughter a ready attraction to any man who loved the natural world. Mr. Barstow—whom Grace adored—had taken her on long and frequent wildflower walks, starting with the first skunk cabbages in spring and on to the pussy willows and bird's foot violets of May, pointing out the delicacy of their color and the deep-cleft leaves that really did look like birds' feet. Her father would hire a buggy to take them far afield, driving along a country road, the horse's heels clicking pebbles. Then he would slow the horse to climb a hill, maybe to stop at columbine in bloom, or gold-enrod or fringed gentians, buttercups, daisies, trailing arbutus, dog-wood, or a stand of lady-slippers.

Bob took Grace on nature walks, too, but on these it was the birds—and not the flowers—that he pointed out. Soon the two had fallen deeply in love, and Bob presented Grace with a pearl and sapphire pin to mark their engagement. Grace was twenty-one; he was twenty-three. They planned to marry one year after his graduation.

Toward the end of his time at Brown, Bob received the offer to be curator of birds and mammals at the Brooklyn Museum. Apparently, his earlier diligence at the American Museum was paying off. The recom-mendation letter from Frank Chapman read, "regarding young Murphy, I . . . was favorably impressed by him. I understand his record at school is *good* and he looks as though he was built on the right plan. Hope you will be able to give him a chance to demonstrate."

The job was his. He reported for work the summer of 1911. George V had been crowned King of England. New York City had hired its first black policeman. The Panama Canal was receiving its finishing touches. The world was moving forward, and he felt its momentum.

By winter Murphy had received the offer to travel to South Georgia Island, twelve hundred miles east of Cape Horn. At first, he did not indulge himself in the ecstasy of what a trip like that would mean. Parts of the globe remained unexplored, unmapped, unreachable. That little brig could take him to the homes of new species—birds and other ani-mals yet to be scientifically observed, some never before photographed, and most of them not part of any museum collections anywhere. It could be a pilgrimage of sorts. He could study the birds' patterns of behavior, their calls, their habitats, what they ate, the eggs they laid. He could be among the first to get there.

But Bob had made a promise, and he was a man of his word.

"I'm going to be married in June," he said.

Rather than asking his fiancée to postpone the wedding, he thanked the museum directors but respectfully declined.

Who knows why he thought to tell all this in a letter to Grace? Maybe it was simply his habit to report to her on whatever occurred in his daily life. More likely, he wanted to convey the strength of his devotion by letting her know about the sacrifice he had been willing to make for her. Whatever his reason, he wrote of the rejected voyage.

She responded by immediate return telegram, delivered in the middle of the night. Her instructions were: HOLD OPEN THE SEAFARING OPTION STOP COME BY EARLY TRAIN TO PROVIDENCE FOR FURTHER DISCUSSION.

He was barely out of the station and inside Mrs. Barstow's house before Grace came right to the point, stating firmly that she refused to stand in his way and let him turn down such a chance. She reported years later that she had said, "It's a wonderful start for an ornithological career. You'll be like Darwin sailing around the world in the *Beagle*. I'll marry you now."

A wedding celebration in their society was no small event and needed time to plan. A rush to vows would raise suspicion. Furthermore, Mrs. Barstow had at first welcomed Bob as a man who might easily become an asset to her family. Now, she was aghast to think her daughter would hurry up a marriage to someone who would shortly thereafter desert her. And going to South Georgia was dangerous; men lost their lives to whales, to storms, to the sea. It was not unusual for a ship to leave its harbor and simply never be heard from again. Grace's new husband might not return.

Grace went to her family members and convinced them, one at a time, that the captain of the brig was experienced, that the trip would be a safe one, and that it would benefit Bob's career and, ultimately, their future together. With family blessings at last, a modest ceremony took place February 17th, after which Grace took up residence with Bob in New York. She began to brace herself for the loan of her husband to the sea. She also began to anticipate the success that would follow his return.

Grace and Bob found an apartment in New York as temporary housing until his departure date. Part of Grace's preparation for their long separation was to go around to family and friends, secretly collecting a year's worth of letters and mementos. She tied these up in a large bag, along with her own letters—also written in private and which accounted for most of the bulk—to be taken on board the *Daisy*. There would be no spot on the brig for Grace—not even as cabin boy in disguise, though she was probably willing—but she could at least accompany her husband on paper.

Chapter Four

THE DAISY HAD LEFT NEW BEDFORD for the West Indies in October 1911. The two-part voyage had been scheduled so the vessel would put in at Barbados in June 1912, to transship her first load of oil and to pick up Bob and Benjamin Cleveland, who would be master of the ship for the second part of the voyage. Grace and Mrs. Cleveland were able to accompany their husbands from New York as far as Barbados.

Traveling to that Caribbean rendezvous was something of a second honeymoon for Bob and Grace, the first having been only a few short days in the Connecticut hills, which she later described as the two of them "watching nuthatches walk headfirst down pine trunks" and enjoying "everything that lived and grew in the loveliness of the snowy countryside."

Along with Captain and Mrs. Cleveland, the Murphys departed New York City by the steamship *Guayana* on May 25th. Their route followed the arc of the Lesser Antilles across the Caribbean Sea. Beginning at St. Thomas, the *Guayana* put in and lingered at St. Croix, then St. Kitts and Montserrat, where the Murphys had time to climb the slopes of a volcano before moving forward to Antigua and Guadeloupe. Then on to Dominica, Martinique, and St. Lucia and finally reaching Barbados.

With Grace's participation, Bob studied and collected along the way. Right from the start, a dozen crabs escaped their box on the floor of the tiny stateroom, pincers on alert in all directions, sending Grace into a good-natured leap for the upper berth. In St. Thomas, above Charlotte Amalie's harbor, full of laughing gulls and brown pelicans, they climbed a hill where little boys appeared and showed them how to catch flabby-skinned green lizards using nooses made of grass. Land crabs scuttled into holes under palms. An old, old woman asked Grace, " Be ye his wife or his sweetheart?"

Grace delighted in the details—flying fish and colorful birds, people with soft lilting voices that had been influenced by French, Dutch, and African languages, open fields full of sparrow hawks hunched on low rocks and ready to make short flights for prey, spirit crabs the color of sand scuttling in either direction but always at top speed and to no apparent goal.

Grace's brother, Palmer, had teased before the ceremony that there would be no room in their house for wedding presents. "Bob will have pickled snakes in jars across your mantelpiece," he had predicted. To some degree her brother had been correct, but the snakes were not always pickled. In Dominica, Bob tied up a small—but live—snake in his good linen handkerchief then carefully placed it on top of the tester of the four-posted bedstead while they slept beneath. Later, in that same room, a tarantula looked out from under a chest. Where most people would have moved immediately to kill the spider, Bob caught it, studied it for his notes, and preserved it in alcohol.

Barbados lies off to the side toward the end of the West Indies archipelago. The steamer reached that southernmost port June 8th. At their little hotel by the water, Grace asked the hostess about tasting a flying fish.

"We're having them tonight at dinner," the hostess said.

"What luck," Grace answered, not knowing they would be having them every night at dinner and, it seemed later when looking back, at midday and breakfast, too.

Their room was white with cool thin curtains blowing in the tropical breeze. In the evenings, several sizes of bats flew above the narrow, walled streets, in and out among flamboyant trees. Using a borrowed horsewhip, Bob knocked three down, elated to see these airborne mammals up close and commenting with curious glee at their *vibrissæ*, sensory bristles growing between the toes. He seemed to care about any detail that would set one species apart from another.

From Barbados, Mrs. Cleveland and Grace were able to board the *Daisy* for one short sail before they and their husbands would set off in opposite directions. After that, the women would reboard the *Guayana* on its return to New York. Captain Cleveland, who seemed to make a point of gruffness, showed surprising generosity by lending the Murphys his gimbal bed for the twenty-eight-hour run back north to Dominica. The motion of a sailing ship was new to Grace, and despite having steamed to Europe and back and now having traveled the Caribbean, she and Bob were both sick, he even losing a precious fountain pen out of his pocket and over the rail in one of his sudden dashes.

Yet, Grace thrilled at the overall experience. All canvas was set as they rushed through clear blue-purple waters. She knew no one in her stratum of society who had ventured onto a whaleship and, by her telling, took pride in having embraced such daring.

The *Daisy* dropped anchor at Portsmouth, Dominica, where Bob and Grace went ashore. Captain Cleveland needed time to find local replacements for thirteen crewmembers who had deserted. They had broken their agreements to tough out the entire two-part trip.

Methods of whaling had not changed much for almost a century, but Yankee crews had dwindled. With the exception of Captain Cleveland, Murphy, and one other, the *Daisy*'s men were equatorial—Cape Verdeans, from that peppering of islands off the big bulge of Africa's west coast, West Indians from Martinique and St. Eustatius, and now, Dominicans.

In Portsmouth town, also, the population was black. Except for two French priests and a doctor who lived up in the hills, the Murphys were the only white people in evidence. Every move they made seemed to attract attention. Several times when entering their plain little room at the hotel above the village store, nameless people slid along the wall and slipped silently out. Each time possessions were ever so slightly rearranged, apparently examined, though none ever missing.

Finding good meals was a problem, but hospitality was not. The Murphys were invited to be part of an island wedding celebration only to be

Inside the three-hundred-year-old powder magazine at the French fort, roots and damp vines clung to the walls. A seemingly mucilaginous gecko known as a "wood slave" or "mabouya" clung to the ceiling.

shocked that the large, tiered cake was alive with red ants—the same as they had skimmed from their tea after mistakenly having stirred them in along with sugar from an open bowl. The locals, however, took the ants in their stride.

Intrigued by talk of birds and bats, the town merchant asked the Murphys along on a picnic trip with his wife and children. Everyone was rowed to an island by hired men. They all scrambled to a summit amid the ruins and rusting cannon of an old French fort. After exhausting the food hampers, Grace and her host lost themselves in a discussion of English literature, which was always a welcome topic as far as Grace was concerned.

Birds were everywhere in Dominica's densely luxuriant vegetation. Near a small, rocky stream, hummingbirds by the score fed and danced among blossoms. But Bob wanted more bats. Locals directed him to the belfry of the church where an island native predicted he would find plenty of "bats and other insects." Later, honeycreepers attracted Bob's attention, thrusting their brush-like tongues into flowers over and over.

In the afternoons, to the sheer amazement of the village populace,

Grace joined Bob swimming. People watched from the bank, mystified to see a woman in the water. They thought at first Grace would surely drown.

The end of all this adventure and exploration drew near, however, and Grace began to see their impending separation as a "rain-wall creeping toward sunshine from across the sea." It came time to part.

"We will be together in our thoughts all the time that I am gone, but oh! I'll miss you, Grace," said Bob.

Murphy and Captain Cleveland accompanied their wives by sloop from Portsmouth at the top of Dominica to Roseau at the bottom, where they would say good-bye. In Roseau, they found a little boardinghouse run by a Miss Jolly, who served fricassee of "mountain chicken," the big island frog. But Grace found it difficult to feel jolly. Time was closing in and their year apart about to begin.

Their last touch was a handshake, she on the steamer's step, he in the little boat to be rowed ashore. They smiled thin smiles.

"I love you enough to give you up," Grace said. "I want you to be one of the biggest scientists in the world."

Murphy's written account of his day-to-day experiences and observations begins, "The *Guayana* has faded from sight and even her smoke no longer hangs over the northern horizon. Behind my eyelids I still see you, standing straight, and tall and proudly smiling, with the small figure of the skipper's wife beside you on the *Guayana*'s glorious deck."

Bob had already stowed Grace's letter bag on board the *Daisy* with his sea chest. She had

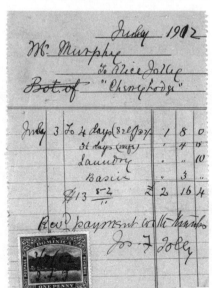

Receipt from Miss Jolly's Cherry Lodge.

marked each envelope with the date when it was to be opened. He would be on his honor not to read ahead, regardless of how much he might long to see Grace's tender communications or feel connected to people at home.

In response to her letters and with deep gratitude toward his new bride for having accommodated the voyage, he kept a separate journal especially for her, a year-long letter home in place of those he could not send. Along with the copious scientific notes he made, each day he averaged more than one thousand written words, regardless of cold or pitching waves.

Murphy's notes were in no way the official record—on most such voyages that would have been the first mate's responsibility—but the *Daisy*'s first mate could write no English. In this case, her skipper kept the log. Captain Cleveland's entries dealt with such matters as wind and weather, the status of the crew, navigational readings, and the commercial progress of the voyage. The latter was a subject in which everyone on board took more than a casual interest, since as soon as the *Daisy*'s barrels would be filled once more with oil, she would set her sails for home, hence the old sentiment that wives and sweethearts would wish their whaling men as they went off to sea: Godspeed and, "a short and greasy voyage."

Continuing to describe the *Guayana*'s departure, Murphy wrote, "I have waited for the skipper to say the first word, pretending not to notice his brimming eyes, but thus far his only sound has been a murmured, 'My soul and body!' Parting is an old, old story to a whaleman, born and bred. And yet, the prospect of a year's absence, perhaps without

Benjamin Dunham Cleveland.

Continued June the 3th, 1846

First seen by the Cooper
Dead

Wednesday the 3th 1846

First part light breezes from W b S W Steerd by
the wind to the westward at 3 Pm saw a shole of
sperm whales loard the boats at 4 W B struck and
Irn drew at sundown the boats came board the wha
les going N E b E middl part light wind headed to S ward
ward under short sail latter part pleasant in the morning
made all sails at 7 AM tackd ship to westward Saw
finbacks so ends Manoel and Micky sick poor ten
lame finger Lat 28..54 N Lon 175 34 E

Thursday the 4th first part light winds from W 3 N
and pleasent steerd W by S at sun down shortnd the
sails and wore ship to the E S E middle part at 12 wore
ship to the S W latter part winds from E S E sterd W S
so ends Lat 28.52 N Lon 175 09 E

Friday the 5 th

First part light winds from S S E in pleasent
steerd W at sundown shortnd sail and left to the
wind and headed to S ward middle part light winds
latter part fresh winds from W S W steerd N W by W
3 men sick Bromly with Consuption so ends
Lat 29 08 N Lon 174 18 E

Saturday the 6 th

first part fresh winds from S W and pleasent steerd
N W by W at sundown took in light sails, and rieft
top sails hold up courses headed to W southly
middle part at 12 wore ship latter part in the morning
headed W b N W wind from S W at 7 AM saw whales
heading to windward lowerd boats but got none whales
going to fast so ends Lat 29.51 N Lon 173 14 E

Mr. Stantons

Sunday the 7 th

First part strong winds from S W at 12 boats came
board and beept forward futing to the windward at 5 PM
saw a shole of whales head going to leeward at 6 loard 2
boats and got within 2 boats leanth they turn S flooks stam
down the boats came board headed S eastward under short sails
midle part the wind sheift to the N E light rains and fogy
at 6 AM steerd W at 9 saw Whale going to windward
we saw him but 2 riseing So ends Lat 29 56 N
Lon 173. 48 E.

Bromly and Davis sick

ABOVE: *Margins were reserved for descriptions of the hunt. Spouts and flukes indicated sightings, and an attempt was made to show the arrangement of whales, ship, and lowered boats. Openings in the whale silhouettes were for the first mate to write in the number of barrels that tried out from each captured animal. Some captains used stamps to show various whale species.*

FACING PAGE: *Some captains kept elaborate records like this page of the 1846 logbook from the* France. *The entry for Sunday the 7th reads, "First part strong winds from S.W. at 12 boats came board and —? foward beeting to the windward at 5 P M saw a shole of whales head going to leeward at 6 lowared 2 boats and got within 2 boats length thay turned flooks at sun down the boats came board headed S eastward under short sails middle part the wind sheeft to the N E light rains and fogg at 6 AM steered W. at 9 saw Whale going to windward we saw him but 2 riesing 'so ends Lat 29 56 N. Lon 173.40 E. Bromly and Davis sick."*

communication, must carry a very different portent to him at sixty-seven than to me at twenty-five."

The *Daisy* remained at anchor near Portsmouth; Captain Cleveland and Murphy were on foot in Roseau, twenty miles to the south where they had gone to see their wives off. The skipper had it in mind to telephone and send for one of the *Daisy*'s whaleboats to collect them, but he was not able to make a connection. Failing that, he arranged for passage on an unpainted, ramshackle sloop.

They left Roseau at nine o'clock the evening of July 3rd. The *Lily Laurie* was piled high with fifty barrels of flour, forty-five cases of oil, twenty more cases of fish, limes, and vinegar, along with the luggage of her fifteen other passengers bound for the northern tip of the small but mountain-steep island. The sloop's boom barely cleared the water's surface for the weight of her load.

It was a glorious, tropical night with big stars blazing and lively sea chanteys from the foredeck and even a rendition of "My Old Kentucky Home" with a Caribbean cadence. Her passengers included several men whom Captain Cleveland had booked to crew the *Daisy*, three women, and a small girl, Diana. One old woman smoked a clay pipe and claimed she could always tell a married man from a single one at a glance. Put to the test, she got everyone's status correct, including Murphy who was delighted to be identified as no longer a bachelor. "Single men," the old black woman said, "always have a wil' look."

The *Lily Laurie* sailed into Portsmouth at six o'clock in the morning on the Fourth of July. "I found in your packet for this date the flag and the fan," wrote Murphy to Grace. "The flag is going to swing above your picture all year. As for the bundle of firecrackers, I banged 'em off to the tolerant amusement of the British Colonials."

He also celebrated Independence Day by obtaining yet another zoological oddity, a Dominican Hercules beetle for which he and Grace, in their zeal to collect any and every biological curiosity of the region, had hunted in vain before leaving for Roseau. The offer came to him via a boy who appeared to recognize Murphy on shore.

The boy said, "A lady have a spin-saw insect she wish to sell you, sir."

"How much?" Murphy inquired, knowing the *Dynastes hercules* to be the world's biggest beetle and member of the scarab family. He had already heard an explanation for the common name, stemming from the colorful belief that the insects would clamp their notched horns on tree branches and let the breeze spin them around like whirligigs until the branches were sawed off.

Back went the boy and returning again, "One pound sterling, sir."

"Tell the lady," Murphy said, "that I will gladly pay thruppence for her astounding natural phenomenon."

Once more the boy made a round trip to report, "The lady reply that she cannot deliver the insect for thruppence, but she will be happy to accept sixpence, sir."

By this point the haggle had progressed so well Murphy asked the boy to fetch the lady and her imposing bug so he might assess the situation directly. Males of the species can grow to eight inches; this one turned out to be not quite six. Nevertheless, Murphy decided to pay a whole shilling, one twentieth of a pound sterling and equal to twelve pence.

No doubt that very bug ended up in a glass case at the American Museum of Natural History one year later. And no doubt Murphy submitted a reimbursement voucher for the U.S. equivalent of one shilling. Never a stingy man but a keeper of pinpoint accounts his entire life, he even noted the one shilling and four pence he paid for the twelve dozen bananas he bought to take aboard ship.

Eventually, land-based adventures and good-natured negotiations in the open-air market came to an end. There would be no more fresh fruit, no more palm trees to sit beneath, and no more white-curtained hotels, quaint or otherwise. It was time to get underway. Captain Cleveland had gathered enough Dominicans to fill out the crew, and water lapped at the *Daisy*'s waiting hull. The wooden brig was about to become their home. She had no engine, no communications gear, no navigational gizmos, no Marconi wireless, no knobs and dials to speak of, nothing to whir or click.

A compass, sextant, and timepiece would be how they would know their position beneath the sun and the stars. For a voyage that would probably last twelve months but which was guaranteed not to exceed thirty, any contact with family or home would be by luck and by letter.

Even at that, postings would be uncertain. To predict general delivery addresses in the strew of Atlantic islands would be impossible. Murphy could only guess at where the ship would be and when it would be there. Tristan da Cunha? St. Helena? Ascension? Ports and dates would be determined by winds and whales and the speed with which the barrels filled.

This much was certain: the captain's word would rule. His manner was brusque and his opinions strong. It would be up to Murphy, the Latin scholar and genteel scientist, to make himself fit in. He would be living tight with rats and roaches, four pigs, a mongrel dog, and thirty-three other men of widely disparate backgrounds, some of the men not fluent in English.

Once they hoisted their sails in Portsmouth, there would be no turning back.

SECTION II
Outward Bound

Chapter Five

THIS VOYAGE WAS NOT THE FIRST on which Captain Cleveland had made an effort to advance the cause of science. A newspaper article promoting him as "the famous whaling master of New Bedford" and "skipper naturalist" made much of the fact that he knew well the bottom parts of the world, saying he had greater knowledge of the habits of the "giant and savage elephant seal than any scientist." He was also alleged to know as well as any man living the conditions under which Amundsen and Scott labored in their race for the southern pole. Five times, Captain Cleveland had visited Kerguelan in the southern Indian Ocean. In 1909, commissioned by the American Museum of Natural History, he returned from that volcanic and storm-swept island with the nucleus of one of the "largest and most valuable collections of the animals, vegetables and minerals of the south seas that had yet been made." His plan for the 1912 South Georgia venture was to study and collect penguins, albatrosses, sea leopards, and sea elephants, which he described as reaching thirty feet in length and sometimes yielding as much as seventy gallons of clear and odorless oil from a single specimen. The flesh—especially the tongue and liver and steaks—was considered excellent eating by whalemen, who, however, "should not be accepted as criterions of choice dainties, for they relish the tough steaks from the huge whale." Captain Cleveland also described the sporting fight often encountered when attempting to slaughter the animals for their blubber.

One can only assume that the heart of Benjamin Cleveland's interest was more as hunter than scientist.

Whatever his true motivation, the skipper had committed himself to

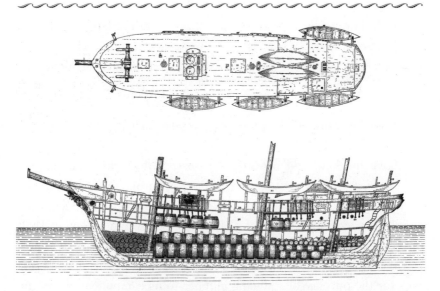

Schematic of the Alice Knowles, *a whaleship similar to the* Daisy, *showing the locations of her whaleboats, the spare boats, her trypots, and her cargo of oil.*

museum work once again by accepting Murphy as a passenger and taking a subsidy for the voyage. To that end, a great amount of storage space was dedicated to the specimens Murphy would collect. In the *Daisy*'s hold were casks and barrels destined to be packed with bone and skin and feather rather than the profitable whale and seal oil of an ordinary voyage. Additionally—where a second spare whaleboat might have been stored across the stern of the ship—the *Daisy* carried a little dory especially assigned to Murphy's purposes as weather and conditions would permit.

As well as scientific paraphernalia, the hold was a warehouse of sorts. Spare sails, rigging, flour, salt beef, hard bread, beans, and tobacco were all headed up in casks of various sorts that crammed the greater part of the hold, that belly of the ship below the forecastle and the officers' quarters. Those casks that would otherwise be empty in anticipation of oil were filled with fresh water, which kept them tight and sound and maintained the vessel in ballast trim. The water would be pumped overboard when storage of oil became a necessity.

The hold was a dim and moldy-smelling place. The largest casks had the capacity of fourteen barrels. These were packed with smaller casks in between, which in turn, were mingled with even smaller, slender oaken pipes called "wryers." In addition to the finished casks were plenty of shooks and hoops from which the cooper would fabricate even more when the time came. Throughout, cordwood dunnage was wedged, both as storage and to keep anything from shifting.

Above the hold and beneath the weather deck the forecastle (or fo'c's'le as it is often written since the word is pronounced *fok*-sel) had been altered to accommodate a larger crew than when *Daisy* had been simply receiving and discharging cargo up and down the Atlantic. Abaft of the foremast were the brick tryworks, built over a water-bath to protect the deck, where a fire would be made beneath a pair of rendering pots for the purpose of reducing blubber to its component oil, steam, smoke, and scrap.

No rendering could take place until the crew had secured a dead whale to the ship, however. Four whaleboats were at the ready on their davits with a spare upturned beside Murphy's dory. The extra whaleboat would be used only if one of the four would be stove.

A Yankee whaleboat was outfitted like none other. Each was supplied with the essentials of the hunt and nothing more: a mast and sail; six oars—five for pulling and one for steering—and ranging in length up to twenty-three feet; paddles, should the boat's crew find it necessary to move noiselessly on a calm ocean; barbed harpoons for fixing boat to prey and unbarbed razor-sharp lances to accomplish the kill. Waifs and wig-wags were stowed to mark the location of a (floating) dead animal with a flag and to send status signals to the lookouts at the mastheads of the ship, which might be several miles in the distance by the time the kill had been accomplished. A piggin was provided as a bailer. A keg of fresh water was kept full for the crew, since the hunt was often long and arduous. Each boat had a lantern keg containing flint, steel, a box of tinder, a lantern, candles, bread, tobacco, and pipes (in case the boat should be caught out at night), a line tub with 100 fathoms of manila line, and

Murphy's oil painting of the Daisy's *larboard bow boat coming in after a hunt.*

another with 200 fathoms, one of which would be "bent" onto an iron (harpoon) as soon as the boat would leave the ship. Finally, the boat was supplied with a drogue (pronounced *drug*), a shallow tub of heavy oaken staves that could be lashed onto a runaway whale to act as an anchor and impede the animal's ability to run.

Each whaleboat had its own pre-assigned crew of four oarsmen, one officer—or mate—and one boatsteerer. In addition to pulling the forward oar, he would be the one to plant the harpoon. Later, he would take the steering oar while the mate moved forward for the kill. Captain Cleveland would remain with the ship at all times, along with nine others, these being the shipkeepers, or ship tenders.

With the exception of the "idlers" (cook, steward, cooper, and Murphy) all officers and crew would be assigned to four-hour watches around the clock. The hierarchy of men went from Captain Cleveland, down through the four mates, to boatsteerers, to greenhands, to cabin boy. Among those who had deserted the *Daisy* after she had shipped her first load of oil at Barbados was a Bermudian boatsteerer. That was unusual; the other runaways were all greenhands.

With seventeen new men on board, the *Daisy*'s anchor was catted up to the hoarse strains of a chantey on July 5, 1912. She drifted out of Portsmouth's roadstead, the safe water near harbor and shore. The first official business was to fill the vacancy left by the former second mate, Antão Eneas, who had been killed by a sperm whale before reaching Barbados. Captain Cleveland advanced Vincente Lunda, the twenty-nine-year old third mate. Similarly, fourth mate João Almeida, a twenty-eight-year old Cape Verdean with a fiery red beard, became the third officer.

Since Lunda was unable to read, write, or sign his name, Murphy was asked to witness the document. It read, "I have this day promoted Vincent Lunda from 3rd officer to the second mate's berth, and for his services he is to have the one-thirtieth lay of the net proceeds for whatever oil and bone may be taken from this date forward. Signed, Benjamin D. Cleveland, Master and Agent of Brig 'Daisy.'" Beneath an X is written "Vincent Lunda, his mark," and to the left, "Witness, R. C. Murphy."

Murphy had signed himself on to the voyage not as "Scientist"—there was no such title—but as "Assistant Navigator." Murphy was no navigator, but every man on board needed a title to be recorded in the articles. Assistant navigator was a catchall, traditionally applied to a captain's wife, should she decide to go along, and was thus a source of ribbing. Of course, Murphy stood out as a natural target already. Neither whaleman nor seaman, he had no official duties or corresponding skills.

No one on board would be paid wages. Everyone worked for a share of the profits when all was tallied up at the end of the voyage. The greenhands, for example, signed on at 1/185 of the lay. This share would be paid out after having been debited for taking anything out of the ship's stores such as clothing, tobacco, knives, or needle and thread.

Murphy's was the longest lay of all at 1/200, something of a formality, since he would not be required—or even expected—to contribute to the

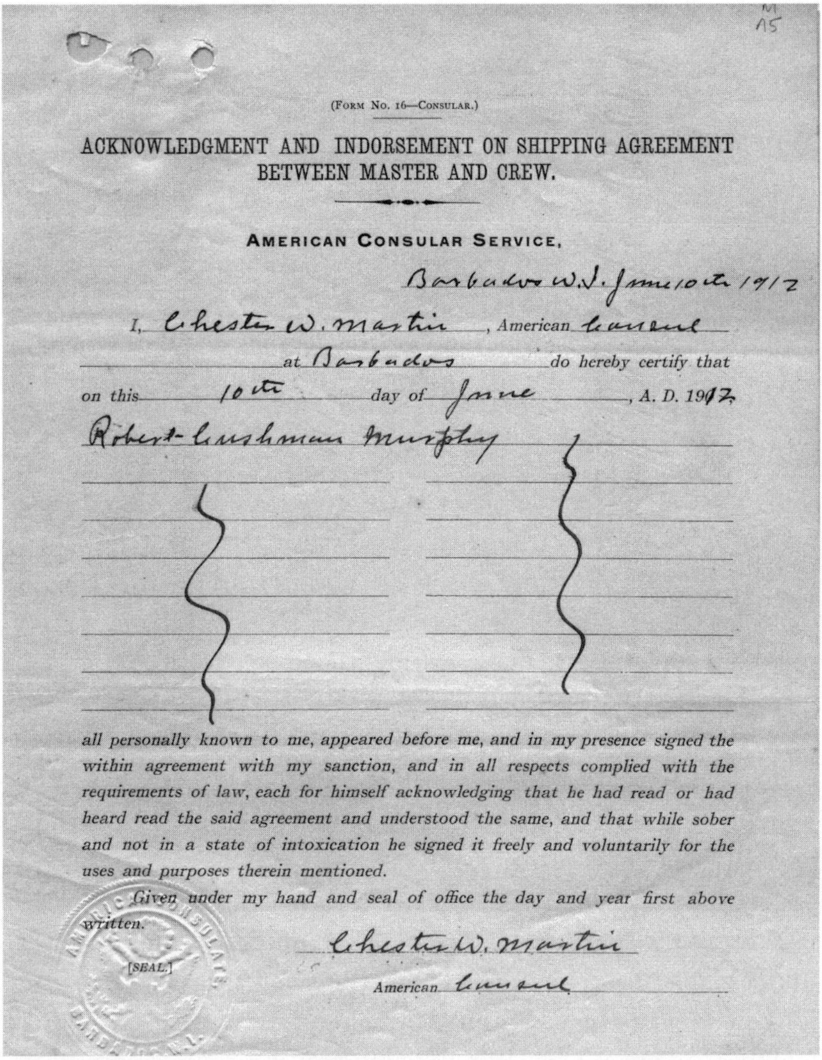

(FORM No. 16—CONSULAR.)

ACKNOWLEDGMENT AND INDORSEMENT ON SHIPPING AGREEMENT BETWEEN MASTER AND CREW.

AMERICAN CONSULAR SERVICE,

Barbados W.I. June 10th 1912

I, *Chester W. Martin*, American *Consul*

at *Barbados* do hereby certify that

on this *10th* day of *June*, A. D. 191*2*

Robert Cushman Murphy

all personally known to me, appeared before me, and in my presence signed the within agreement with my sanction, and in all respects complied with the requirements of law, each for himself acknowledging that he had read or had heard read the said agreement and understood the same, and that while sober and not in a state of intoxication he signed it freely and voluntarily for the uses and purposes therein mentioned.

Given under my hand and seal of office the day and year first above written.

[SEAL.]

Chester W. Martin

American *Consul*

Murphy thought it was the height of bureaucratic redundancy to acknowledge that he had "read or had heard read the said agreement and understood the same, and that while sober and not in a state of intoxication," signed freely and voluntarily.

37

work of filling any casks with oil. This, too, was cause for good-natured teasing.

Murphy got along with his shipmates, but he did not blend in. His speech reflected his education. Captain Cleveland was entertained by Murphy's language and was fascinated by technical words in general. He frequently asked to be told the scientific name of a particular bird or fish. In this vein, the skipper waited until all officers were present at table that first day with the new crew when he made it a point to order the steward to make up some griddlecakes.

"Griddlecakes?" asked the diminutive grub slinger. "What's them?"

"Griddlecakes," explained the captain, "is the *scientific* name for flapjacks."

THE DISTINCTION between crew and officers was a sharp one. Murphy, of course, associated with the officers—and in particular, the captain himself. He even joined in Captain Cleveland's cruel fun by asking the cabin boy one day while he was serving a dinner of clam chowder, macaroni, and apple pie, "Johnny, tell me something. Do macaroni trees flourish in the Cape Verde Islands?"

"Plenty, two beeg ones grow by my fader's house."

The captain winked at the cooper, and Murphy had a chuckle. They were the only three white men on the ship. No one else saw anything unusual about this exchange.

New men were on board, but some of them had been merely picked up at Roseau and Portsmouth and not yet "shipped," meaning the paperwork had not been completed. Captain Cleveland had yet to sign on the full crew. The new ones were hired to replace those who had disappeared into the shadows of Dominica. Running away was considered a serious offense. The local police had searched but turned up no one. Not that the skipper or the officers felt any great loss; the men who had decamped were thought to be among the *Daisy*'s least desirable.

One of the new recruits from Portsmouth was a coal-black youth of seventeen by the name of Conrad Peters. His older brother had delivered him to the ship and for some unknown reason had assigned him to Murphy's special care, possibly having mistaken him as owner, first mate, or captain. "He's a good Latin scholar, he is," said the brother, and, in fact, the earnest fellow did indeed speak English extraordinarily well. Conrad wore a silver crucifix around his neck and was quick to make the sign of the cross at the slightest sight of lightning, whether near or far off on the horizon.

Maybe it is just as well that the ship drifted before a slender wind that first day while the new ones learned the ropes and adjusted to the peculiarities of being at sea and of being under a strict chain of command. As it was the ship remained within sight of Morne Diablotin, Dominica's tallest peak at 4,747 feet, until the setting sun turned its capping cloud pink.

Chapter Six

WIND CAME UP during the night. Murphy's berth, which had been converted from the cabin settee, ran athwart ship, across rather than with the length of the vessel. Whenever the ship tacked, he found it necessary to change ends of the bed to assure that his head would be comfortably above the level of his feet. He likened the experience to sleeping in a butter churn.

By the following morning, land had slipped below the horizon. Lookouts were posted at the two mastheads. These were small platforms atop the mainmast and foremast, a hundred feet or more above the deck, where pairs of men scanned the sea for signs of whales.

Lookouts were the eyes of the ship. They stood two-hour watches in rotation from dawn to dusk, armed with foggy French-made binoculars and motivated by the promise of five pounds of tobacco for the first man to raise a whale that would be subsequently captured. Perched on these platforms above the sails and contained by no more than a single iron hoop at chest height, it was likely an uncomfortable post except on the glassiest of seas. Any motion at the waterline would be augmented dramatically by the towering mast, and the men would careen around above groaning rigging.

Access to the lookout stations was via the tarred, horizontally-fixed ropes attached to the shrouds and known as the ratlines. Conrad was ordered to the foremast head for his first stand as lookout. The poor fellow had never imagined going aloft. He gulped and started up the ratlines with a boatsteerer following close behind and encouraging him with a rope's end fanning his rump. But when Conrad reached the futtock

LEFT: *Lookouts stood 2-hour watches throughout the daylight hours. Conrad Peters eventually made it up to the masthead without fear. He stands on the right.*

BELOW: *A captain's settee like this one across the stern of the ship was converted for Murphy's use. The water closet through the louvered door at the left, was accessible only to Murphy and Captain Cleveland. Notice the medicine chest on the shelf.*

Standing on the main masthead, it seemed as if the sway and rock of the ship were magnified one hundredfold. Without the lookouts' elevation, however, whales would not have been as easily seen.

shrouds partway up, his nerve gave out, and he clung like a Dominican gecko to the foreyard, the lowest and largest spar fixed to the mast. Because the spar was wooden, it gave more stability than the quivering ropes, shaking beneath his rattling knees and feet. The boatsteerer's improvised whip had no effect. Neither coaxing nor dire threats budged poor Conrad, so John Paul, a greenhand from Barbados only one year older than Conrad but more confident, was sent up to relieve him.

Having witnessed the action Murphy wrote, "Feeling it high time to show my own nonchalance and to give the impression of a long seafaring background, I shortly afterwards made my own maiden climb to the mainmasthead. It was accompanied by much concealed sympathy for Conrad, because the distance was ten times as far looking down as looking up. The motion was extremely disconcerting, particularly the sentient and malevolent snap at the end of each roll by means of which the vessel endeavored to catapult me off into the sea. However, there were already three men up there, two at the fore and one at the main, and with outward casualness I finally crawled through one of the rings of the lookout hoops and calmly (?) surveyed the horizon. The deck looked small and queer, and usually far off to one side, but the strangeness soon wore off and I began to enjoy my vantage point above the shimmering ocean."

A hard-worked whaleman could easily grow drowsy and tend toward dozing while in that precarious station. One can only imagine a calm afternoon, sun-drenched and rocking gently on a smooth sea. The lookout had nothing for protection but that single iron hoop. Melville wrote, "For every swing we made there was a nod from below from the slumbering helmsman. The waves, too, nodded their indolent crests; and across the wide trance of the sea, east nodded to west, and the sun overall."

Just after supper, a cry from above bellowed, "Porpoises!" and everyone crowded toward the bow, where they could watch the beautiful play of long gray and white bodies under the stem. Mr. Vincent climbed into the martingale stays—rigging beneath the bowsprit, fixed to a strut that reinforced the jib boom—where he stood above the rushing sea to dart a harpoon at one of the graceful animals. But he missed and frightened away the entire shoal.

The Old Man, as the skipper was called behind his back, emitted a volley of oaths. This was a talent he concealed while on shore. On board he stated a strong distaste for profanity—*from others*. As far as his own language was concerned, he apparently saw no reason to curb it when vexed. Murphy observed that the skipper was, indeed, a "soul who is always deeply repentant of other peoples' misdeeds."

West Indian blackfish or pilot whales frequently swam with porpoises, sometimes indiscriminately mixed, sometimes in apparent stampede, often in shoals of seventy-five to a hundred. New Bedford whalers had hunted these small cetaceans around Portsmouth for years. One schooner reported taking forty animals in just a few days. These animals grow to twenty feet or more. They were hunted in particular for the two-and-a-half to five gallons of oil contained in their melon-shaped heads. This is known as the "junk." In 1912, a gallon of melon oil was valued at $15 as compared to 53¢ for the product of body blubber.

It was also common practice for sailors to cut the meat into strips and salt it. This would be traded on shore for fruits and vegetables.

But blackfish were wary, appearing to avoid the ship with conscious skill. They were hard to catch. Story had it that they would often tease the rowers in their lowered boats into a hopeless and tiring chase. Boats would draw near, harpoons at the ready, and the animals would "let go," sinking straight down.

Murphy watched blackfish from the masthead. They lowered themselves with no appreciable alteration or inclination of the body until becoming indistinct shadows in clear water. Within a few minutes they reappeared a short distance away. After the maneuver, they would raise their hind ends above the water and beat the surface a dozen times with the flat of their flukes, making loud reports.

If a blackfish were successfully harpooned, members of the herd would gather around, making it comparatively easy for the other boats to select and strike more victims. Once fast, however, the struggle was only begun. Blackfish were strong fighters, sometimes tearing themselves free from deeply planted irons. Their typical pattern was to pull straight for a short distance, and then dodge sharply, yanking the boat from side to side or spinning it end to end. As the animal exhausted itself, and the boat drew close, the blackfish lashed back and forth in final flurry with terrific jerks. Lancing could be accomplished only with swift and skillful action.

As part of the settling-in process, Captain Cleveland and José Correia, the cooper and ship's carpenter, helped put up shelves to hold Murphy's library of some thirty books. Murphy wrote, "While the skipper was nailing up the shelves, he waxed reminiscent. As a lad of fourteen, he, Ben Cleveland of Martha's Vineyard, shipped as cabin boy on his first voyage in a whaleship of which his elder brother was master. One day during a gale, a great wave piled over the quarterdeck and swept the captain overboard. The sea was so wild that lowering a boat was out of the question. Young Ben, who was standing his trick at the wheel with another man to lay hold when the hard kicks came, could not even look astern where his brother drowned."

A sobering story by which to unpack the works of Melville, Darwin, and Shakespeare! The complete library included:

Cambridge Natural History,
   volumes on Fishes, Birds, & Mammals
Comparative Anatomy of Vertebrates, Wiedersheim
Zoology, Parker and Haswell
Physiology, Howell
Mammals Living & Extinct, Flower and Lydekker
Book of Whales, Beddard
Orders of Mammals, Gregory
Review of the Delphinidae (Porpoises), True
Moby Dick, Melville
A History of the American Whale Fishery, Tower
History of the American Whale Fishery, Starbuck
A Voyage towards the South Pole, Weddell
Catalogue of Birds of the British Museum

(on albatrosses, petrels, gulls, and terns)
Journal of the Right Hon. Sir Joseph Banks,
    during Captain Cook's First Voyage on HMS "Endeavour"
Nomenclature of Colors, Ridgeway
Notes on the Vertebrates of South Georgia, Lönnberg
Voyage of the Beagle, Darwin
Notes by a Naturalist on H.M.S. "Challenger" Narrative, Moseley
New Testament
Divina Commedia, Dante
Pilgrim's Progress, Bunyan
Carmina, Horace
Oxford Book of English Verse
The Oxford Shakespeare
Age of Mammals, Osborn
Physiological Chemistry, Hawk
Typewritten summaries and translations about South Georgia
from Guyot, Cook, Forster, Sparrman, Bellingshausen, Klut-
schak, Szielasko, von den Steinen, and others
Various notebooks to be filled in as the trip progressed

HANGING AND LASHED beside the shelves was the round cloth sack in
which Grace, by incredible labor and wile, had arranged the dated files of
letters, sketches, and other communications from herself, friends, family, and associates. There was something for her husband to open nearly
every day of the long year ahead.

Weather continued calm with only occasional cats paws to ruffle the
surface. Murphy familiarized himself with the chronometer while the
Old Man barked out the instant of his sight, and together they worked
out the longitude. A steady breeze came up late in the day, and they
pointed optimistically toward Guadeloupe. Noddies, a kind of small
tern, flew past. Someone from the forecastle brought out a guitar, and
someone else, a bugle.

Chapter Seven

SUNDAY WAS MARKED by the first of what would become weekly distributions to each forecastle hand of a bucket of fresh water for washing his clothes. Murphy made arrangements with Johnny, the twenty-two-year-old cabin boy, to take care of his laundry. For this service, Murphy agreed to pay a rate of a dollar a month for the duration of the voyage. Johnny had a coffee-and-cream complexion and hailed originally from Brava in the Cape Verde Islands. More recently, he claimed Falmouth, Massachusetts, as his home. Their common connection to New England threw Murphy and the cabin boy into a sort of instant affiliation, despite the dichotomy between Murphy's scientific orientation to the world and Johnny's, whose whole world seemed to be one of make-believe.

The afternoon continued calm. Lack of wind and an adverse current prevented any progress up the coast of Dominica. They stood approximately where they had begun. Some of the men grew edgy. They complained about the food.

The captain listened to the grievances before going forward and tasting what the crew had to eat. He evaluated each dish and pronounced them all excellent—except the bread, which he agreed was soggy. This, he promised to have improved.

But the green West Indians turned up their noses at good, old-fashioned New England baked beans and did not cotton to soup or stew. Several of the men inclined toward impudence. The captain brandished a pair of handcuffs. Feddy Lundy cried out to the Lord to provide for him, saying he was "in a way to starve." He also claimed his mother was "a proper cook," and that "she even own a cookbook, she do." The captain assured Lundy that he would be sent back to his mother damn quick if he did not stop bellyaching.

Elise St. Rose, who, like the others, was accustomed to plenty of Dominican fruit, fish, and cassava, was even more outspoken. He asserted his rights as a freeborn British subject and even went so far as to shout to Captain Cleveland, "I shall tell my king of you!" as he dove for cover at the forecastle scuttle.

The well-timed appearance of a school of skipjacks (bonitos) provided a diversion. The cook baited lines with white rags and paid them out from bowsprit and stern while the ship moved slowly along. Several five-pound fish were soon being scaled and gutted on deck. A supper of their solid, beef-like flesh put everyone in a more agreeable mood and helped the new men forget their troubles.

In conclusion of all the uproar, Murphy observed, "It appears to go against the principles of the Old Man to be amused, in which respect he has good Victorian precedent. Nevertheless, he is not without his tolerant streaks. During the evening he once again became reminiscent and told me of the proverbial difficulty of keeping the large crew of a whaleship in a cheerful mood during the long periods that often pass between the sighting, taking, and cutting-in of whales." Murphy listened intently.

That night he wrote to Grace of the brief tangle between captain and crew, "Why, after all, should these equatorial children take delight in the experiences that will somehow carry me through until you and I are once again together? Their comfort is far less than mine, their work more arduous, their privacy nil. In the face of unfamiliar food, they remember only their palmiest days ashore. Hope of money, all too likely dim with experience, is their sole lure. Their thoughts and desires are centered on whales—whales and a port. They follow the calling not for its own sake, but only for what it may bring—the lay, one-hundredth, one hundred-and-fiftieth, one two-hundredth, or whatever the humble cut may be. They are poor observers of things in general. Living creatures interest them when they can eat them or boil them down to oil, but they are as unconcerned with the dazzling plunge of a tropic-bird as with the glowing, luminescent waters of a Caribbean evening. Sunsets, and the constellations of night skies, they do not appear to see. Perhaps their first thought of a star will come when the *Daisy*, her hold filled, turns her bow away from the southern ocean. Then we shall all be gazing nightly toward the line until changeless Polaris pops up to guide us home."

By first light, that now-familiar lump of ground, Dominica, was still in sight. The Old Man claimed rarely to have been in such a hole, drifting without enough wind for the rudder to hold steerage.

But where would he have wanted to get to? As it happened, the skipper was killing time, waiting the surprise arrival of a final crew member. John da Lomba was on his way from New Bedford and due to join the *Daisy* as a sort of super mate. Da Lomba was experienced in sea elephant hunting (also called elephant seals). He would be useful once they all reached South Georgia Island.

To make use of slack waiting time, they "broke out ship," meaning the men cleared rubbish from below decks and sorted and restowed supplies. The skipjacks returned, this time with a school of albacores in pursuit. Out went the *Daisy*'s lines again, and while her deck was aslop in fish cleaning activities, the water below turned red. Whatever skipjacks escaped being hooked survived only to be bitten in half by the huge albacores, evidence that it was a fish-eat-fish world out there.

Captain Cleveland didn't expect Mr. da Lomba to arrive before July 17th, at which point he would send a boat ashore to collect him. Until then, there was time to kill. Murphy set up his canvas chair atop the poop, the aftermost deck and above the quarterdeck, where he could be out of everyone's way and lose himself in the pages of Dante's *Paradiso*.

The morning of the 12th blew in a squall. At half past five, waves whitened the water and lifted the ship's stern. She pitched as Murphy had not yet seen. To the starboard, Mont Pelée, which had erupted as recently as 1902, waved a long flag of clouds from Martinique. Dominica loomed ahead with its highlands enveloped in weather. Presently, the sun came up. Murphy wrote, "A more beautiful daybreak has never been known since Creation. Flying fish—not by the dozens as I have seen them before—but by the tens of thousands, scudded along with the spume, shining like happy souls in the heaven of the sun, of which I had been reading last evening:—*Quant' esser convenia da sè lucente, Quel ch'era dentro al Sol dov' io entra'mi Non per color, ma per lune parvente!* How shining must that be which in the sun, whereinto I had entered, reveals itself not by hue but by light!"

Though not seasick *per se*, some of the men had trouble adjusting to ship's food and tight accommodations. Murphy took a dose or two of castor oil, which solved his problems. Mr. Alves, the elderly and slow first mate who had been run over by a cart in Barbados, suffered a more severe attack of indigestion. Despite repeated warning cramps, he continued to stuff his belly at mealtimes, and he ended up in such a violent grip of pain, the skipper feared the poor man would pass out or even expire altogether. Captain Cleveland and the cabin boy woke Murphy during the night, rattling about in the medicine drawers. Murphy assisted the skipper in ministering to the ailing officer, after which Murphy noted, "Even we, as his doctors, failed to kill him!"

The squall continued. The ship knocked around between Dominica and Martinique, a distance of fifteen and a half miles. They ran close to shore more than once; they headed off as many times.

When coming about the *Daisy* seemed to breathe like a sentient being. "Ready about! All hands on deck," bellowed the Old Man from the quarterdeck. All mates echoed the order. Boatsteerers and sailors echoed it back. "Keep her off a bit and let her go," the captain shouted to the helmsman, and the brig spurted ahead as the sails caught full.

"Helms alee!" soon followed. The ship was "in stays," meaning her bow was pointing into the wind. Square sails quivered. If she "missed stays" she would fail to complete the tack and find her next direction.

"Tacks and sheets!" The forecourse lines were cast loose. The lowest square sail flapped freely. The vessel swung around and headed to the wind. The fore-and-aft mainsail boom was eased over, and the great canvas filled. Then, "Foresail let go and haul!" and the *Daisy* rapidly gained momentum while the perspiring crew relaxed.

Those moments of urgency were exciting, but they did little to break the monotony of waiting and getting nowhere. Murphy's attitude was, "Bring on your whales!" He was impatient to see what it was all going to be about. He wrote,

> 'Tis a boresome game to watch a cockroach crawl
> Across the somersaulting *Daisy*'s cabin wall.
> 'Tis dubious joy to rove the many-sounding seas
> With the wild, uncouth, though baptized, Aborigines.
> 'Twould be bliss (for us) a keen harpoon to whack
> Into a sparm whale's blubbery, unexpectant back.

The following Sunday, they were still off Dominica, this time the windward coast, where cliffs and headlands piled up more boldly than on the eastern shore.

Without warning, a crackling snap sounded overhead. A sail had torn and blown out just like that. Skillfully and quickly, the mates set to work with their spikes and leather sewing palms, and soon had the square fore-topsail mended.

Later, the crew had to reef—or shorten—the mainsail. This reduced the amount of canvas exposed to the wind, but it slowed the ship little. The *Daisy* pitched and rolled clear down to her gunwales—or upper sides—and the waves overtook the stern in long curls. Chairs had to be lashed in place, and in the officers' mess they found it necessary to balance their plates with their hands. Soon enough, a driving rain followed.

Sitting still became an effort in itself, trying to keep up with and compensate for the wild action of the sea. Eventually, the wind calmed, but the sea continued in heavy swells. With no wind to hold up the masts—that is, to stabilize the ship against the motion of the swells—the ship pitched and rolled the scuppers under. Scuppers were the deck-level side drains that allowed rain or storm water to run off, so she was taking water in with a roll to one side and pouring it out the other on the next. By this time the deck boards were so slippery that men were sliding from rail to rail. Murphy, on the other hand, amused himself by eliminating vermin from the ship's population: five Norway rats and countless cockroaches went over the rail.

They had seen a lone grampus the day before—a small whale also known as a Risso's dolphin. Now, the mastheads reported a shoal of blackfish—or pilot whales—about a mile off. The brig crowded sail and headed in the direction of the blackfish shoal, back toward Martinique. The captain ordered two whaleboats lowered as they went.

A ship under full sail did not—and could not—come to any sort of stop for the mere purpose of lowering boats. Those had to be launched while under way. Two mates, Mr. Almeida and Mr. Vincent commanded the two boats. Once afloat and released, they skimmed in among black and shiny backs. Fins cut the water. Rowers pulled with force enough to flex their stout oars. The boatsteerer in Mr. Vincent's boat darted his iron two times but missed on each try. Mr. Vincent took over and immediately plunged the harpoon into the back of a bull. Murphy wrote, "A free ride followed, the blackfish pulling the ocean chariot in circles until the victim became exhausted and could be pierced horribly through and through the body with the knifelike lance."

They drew the animal up to the ship and hoisted its full fourteen foot length on board, the bulk exceeding that of three large oxen, all this to be cut up and boiled down to the finest jewelers' oil money could buy.

Processing the blackfish put the skipper in high spirits and a garrulous frame of mind, less for the value of the catch than the fact that everyone was busy. Murphy liked being included in the captain's conversations. He wrote, "The skipper and I get along famously, thus far. Before breakfast he is inclined to be grumpy, as he admits, but for the rest of the day he is as gentle as a lamb, unless something riles him—bawdy language among the men, for example. That usually leads to a gentle admonition to all concerned that he'll be goddamned if he'll stand for one such word from any Christless bastard on board, afore or abaft the mainmast," meaning crew and officers alike. The entry continued, "After supper I jolly him into a talkative mood, and he yarns about the sea, islands of palm or ice, whales, porpoises, birds, fish, and mighty sea-farin' men."

There was always an officer and his crew on deck manning the ship. To avoid having the same group on watch the same four hours each day, the evening was broken into two two-hour periods known as the dog watches. After supper Murphy fell into chatting among the mates and the idlers, all of whom worked during the day and therefore were never required to stand watch. Occasionally, during the dog watches, Murphy would be asked to read a newspaper or magazine article aloud. Other times, if someone were writing a letter home, Murphy would be asked to spell out a word. Other times still they would simply swap stories, such as the officers describing how they and the boatsteerers had gathered in the evenings on Dominica below the Murphys' window for the sheer pleasure of hearing Grace play her violin, an image that no doubt made the bridegroom more than a little homesick.

Chapter Eight

By July 17th the men of the *Daisy* were ready to be finished drifting around Dominica. John da Lomba was due to be in Portsmouth, waiting to be picked up.

But it seems Dominica was not finished with the *Daisy*. And Mr. da Lomba had not yet arrived from New Bedford.

Not knowing any of this, Murphy and Captain Cleveland went ashore with a boat's crew and spent the night at Miss Jolly's Cherry Lodge. The crew were put up at a boarding house "of lower order."

Mr. Alves, the first mate and therefore second in command of the *Daisy*, was left behind as the shiptender. The captain had instructed him to lie offshore while the boat's crew investigated da Lomba's status. If Captain Cleveland and the boat had not returned by nightfall, Mr. Alves was commanded to stand off and on—sail out and back—until the following morning. Of course, there would be no communication from shore to ship.

In Roseau, letters made it clear that da Lomba was still in New Bedford. Captain Cleveland cabled an order to come to Dominica at once. Even at that, his delayed arrival would mean a minimum of ten days' more waiting.

In the meantime, the *Daisy*'s thirteen deserters had shown up in Portsmouth. They had emerged from the shadows soon after the ship's departure, July 5th. Little did the fugitives know that Cleveland's vessel would be circling back. As soon as the *Daisy*'s boat showed up at Roseau's waterfront, Dominican authorities began to round up the runaways.

The deserters had drawn up a petition to the United States Consul, stating that during the "week's sail" from Barbados to Dominica (which, in actuality, was less than twenty-four hours) they had been served only dry bread and salt meat, that they "had suffered untold agonies from the captain's cruelties," and that the mate had informed them they would be shot and cast overboard when they were once well out to sea.

All that afternoon, squads of black policemen seemed to be marching one or another of these malcontents to the lockup in Roseau's old fort. By the end of the day, five were behind bars. The others had either escaped back to Portsmouth or had been clever enough to ship out on other vessels.

Captain Cleveland had no desire to have any of these five unfortunates reinstated on his crew. Dominican proceedings had been set in motion, however, and it became necessary to see the process through to a conclusion. Never mind that the sun would soon be setting or that the brig lay ten miles offshore, and that it would be a long pull to make before dark.

Amused by the formalities, Murphy sat back and watched the show. "British Colonial decorum is not conducive to speed," he wrote. "First His Excellency, the Royal Inspector of the Leeward Island Police, was called. He was a quizzical, deliberate gentleman whom I had met before. Next the Sergeant-at-Arms, the American consular representative and his secretary, the Magistrate of Roseau, the Master of the *Daisy*, and the fort guard of ten uniformed and heavily armed men, were all officially sent for, and seated in state in the small courtroom before the magistrate, who was the bodily representative of His Majesty George V, by the Grace of God of Great Britain and Ireland King, Emperor of India, Defender of the Faith, etc."

The five haggard deserters were ushered into court before a line of Enfield rifles. Their names were verified as those listed on the Consul's shipping papers for the *Daisy*. The magistrate gazed long and hard at the scruffy collection of sailors before him. Captain Cleveland repeated a request that the proceedings be hastened, stressing the urgency of having left his vessel in the care of a man who was not an accomplished navigator, and it was of utmost importance that he, the master, reach the ship before dark.

Although the magistrate could clearly see—and count—the men before him, he asked for the second time how many deserters there were.

"Five men, Sir, Your Honor," said the secretary of the American consular representative.

"You are sure there are five of them here?" said the magistrate as if to throw new light on the subject.

"Five of them here, Sir."

"Who is the master of this vessel, the United States whaling brig *Daisy?*" said the magistrate, although he had been introduced to Captain Cleveland by six different people already.

"I," said Cleveland.

"You are the master?"

"I *am*, sir," said Cleveland, clearly trying to hide his vexation at the formality, the repetition, and the red tape.

"A Bible is required," said the magistrate, and a New Testament was passed along.

Murphy could not have been more entertained if he had bought a ticket to the theatre. He watched as Cleveland placed his hand on the Bible and swore aloud for the benefit of the court but also swore under his breath to relieve his frustrations. The two oaths were not the same. He laid the book down only to be instructed to take it up once more for the purpose of kissing it, after which the proceedings could commence in accordance with the rules. Finally, the captain was given the opportunity to tell his brisk story: that he had left his ship in the Portsmouth roadstead and that the men had departed without leave.

He did not want the men back. But the law required him to take them, thus saving the United States the expense of transporting the men to the ports from which they had shipped.

Next, the deserters were questioned. Their story soon fell to pieces under the magistrate's elaborate and exhaustive questions. The runaways did not want to return to the ship, they said, for fear of "being shot."

Nevertheless, a document was drafted that ordered them all back on board.

Everyone was just about to wrap it up when one of the five suddenly found himself ill. His legs went weak; his knees, he claimed, had troubled him for months—brutal work on the *Daisy* had injured them, perhaps for life. If he walked to the boat now, he said, the exertion might bring about a condition that would surely necessitate amputation.

The British justice system, if nothing else, is inclined to be thorough. His Majesty's Magistrate sent for a reputable surgeon. Forty-five minutes later, a doctor hurried in, and the pace of things picked up. This pleased Captain Cleveland. He had, after all, left his brig offshore—in the dark—and in the charge of a timid old mate who had never so much as looked through the vane of a sextant, let alone done the necessary calculations to determine his position.

The "sick" man was stripped, examined, and pronounced sound, if not downright healthy. As punishment for deception and in partial payment of the physician's fee, he was relieved of two shillings and thruppence—his entire worldly wealth. The balance of the fee had to be borne by the United States Treasury, an additional six and ninepence.

By then it was pitch dark. All thought of returning to the ship was abandoned. The five offenders were escorted back to their cells and given a supper, also courtesy of Uncle Sam. Cleveland quartered his boat's crew at the already crowded cabin of a matron in town and repaired, with Murphy, to the comforts of the Cherry Lodge.

Murphy took advantage of being on land by sending to Grace, by registered mail, the first installment of his diary for safe keeping. In the accompanying letter, he wrote, "The one vast consolation in this delay is that I am now assured of hearing from you before our departure from Dominica, perhaps by the courier service of John da Lomba who, by all accounts on board, must be a Homeric hero among whalemen."

The *Daisy* lay quietly in the offing. With plenty of daylight and therefore a lessened need for haste, Cleveland negotiated with police authorities and selected several new recruits from a group of minor criminals languishing in the Roseau jail. They were just as glad to leave their cells for a forecastle, and the authorities were happy to be rid of them, even putting on paper that Cleveland would have the option of returning to jail any of the new recruits who might be "unruly or otherwise undesirable members of the troop" by the time he entered the port to pick up da Lomba.

Almost awash with the extra men, they loaded the cheerful felons and erstwhile deserters into the boat and set to rowing. The latter were somewhat sheepish and tired from the debauchery they had indulged in prior to their apprehension and seemed glad to escape the public's gaze, having been conducted in irons to the Roseau dock.

The boat joined the brig about two miles off the coast. The captain was heartened to learn that all had gone well under Mr. Alves' command. With obvious irritation, he entered in the log that their extra night ashore had been a forced put, but he closed as he always closed, "and so ends."

Chapter Nine

IT WOULD BE ALMOST TWO MORE WEEKS before a steamer delivered John da Lomba from Massachusetts, making it one full month between the time the *Daisy* had supposedly weighed anchor for the southern hemisphere and the day she would actually set out in earnest. Murphy was no closer to a penguin than when he had bid Grace farewell at the waterline of the *Guayana*.

Tracing and retracing the same tropical waters mattered little to the crew or officers. They were at sea for the sake of being at sea rather than getting to any port. Unlike a merchant ship with a clear destination, the business of a blubber hunt was to locate, kill, and process whales. And kill they did.

Rather than bogging down in impatience or vexation at not getting underway, Murphy characteristically found the bright side. Sticking close to civilization carried the promise of further contact with Grace. He wrote to her, "I am really glad of this delay for many reasons, despite the fact that it is a bit tedious. I can . . . assure you that I am comfortable and happy on ship-board. . . . I am having a month's rest in a perfect climate; I am learning much about birds and other animals; and I am collecting."

With plenty of slack time when not engaged in watching tropic-birds or frigate-birds or macerating and measuring blackfish heads, whose skulls would be packed away in barrels, he jumped at the chance to curry favor with the captain. Having overheard Cleveland say he was in need of a match scratcher, Murphy quickly painted a wooden plaque with the image of a sailor boy facing away. On the boy's rump Murphy fixed a square of sandpaper and wrote around the edge, "Scratch your matches on my patches." Another time, during an especially hot stretch of weather, Murphy covered his canteen with wet felt and hung it in the night wind, causing rapid evaporation from the felt and thereby cooling the water within. When Murphy produced a chilled drink, the Old Man seemed delighted and astonished.

The closest Murphy came to having any routine tasks was keeping his clock wound. He had unpacked all his gear. A shotgun and two rifles hung neatly in a gun rack overhead in his cabin where he could put them to service on a moment's notice, should the right bird appear. The captain's arsenal of four heavy rifles and a shotgun were mounted in a similar rack in his own quarters. Murphy had also stowed an assortment of knives and specimen jars, laboratory glassware, formalin, cheesecloth, two cameras, photographic chemicals, and a safe light—an oil lamp fitted with a ruby red chimney. As luxuries, Grace had given him a canvas chair to take along and use on deck, a pair of binoculars, and a white pith helmet to protect him against tropical exposure.

Stowed between decks for preserving specimens was a barrel of bonded alcohol on which the words STRYCHNINE and POISON were lettered in red paint, separated by a skull and crossbones. These fabricated warning labels had been applied in Barbados at the suggestion of an older museum colleague, Dr. Bashford Dean, who had cautioned Murphy that sailors "would cheerfully drink the rum or alcohol in which the captain's body was being shipped home from the China Sea!" Captain Cleveland was the only other man on board who knew what the barrel actually contained. He accompanied Murphy on his first trip to draw off alcohol, the two of them commenting loudly at the danger of the fluid being handled.

Murphy was also outfitted with a Swampscott dory, a rowing boat like those traditionally used in the New England cod fishery and an unusual accessory aboard a whaler. But this would facilitate investigating and collecting at water level. It hung on its own davits where a spare whaleboat would have gone, to be used at Murphy's option. In keeping with the design's Nova Scotian origins, he painted the double-ended craft the classic buff of all proper dories. He ran a black stripe around her upper strake—or hull plank—and he painted her name, the *Grace Emeline*. "So I shall often be down on the great waters alone in your namesake, just as you will be alone in my heart, during the long year ahead."

As for tarrying in Dominica's waters, Cleveland divulged no plan, and the others knew not to ask. Murphy could only guess at where they would be going next and when they would be getting there. The da Lomba connection came up as a complete surprise, after all. Murphy did manage to inquire tactfully as to when Cleveland anticipated the voyage would conclude. Shipping papers guaranteed they would not be at sea longer than thirty months, regardless of progress or profits. Cleveland *hoped* to be back in a year but offered no promises. Everything would depend on the catch and the winds.

Whenever that home stretch might be, Murphy would have the option of splitting off from the *Daisy* and finding his way to New York by steamer, if they put in at a convenient port. He wrote to Grace that he had had the thought of her coming down to meet him at the end. It might be possible to send word ahead from St. Helena, should they touch on that island in the middle of the South Atlantic, but he had no idea when that would occur. Moreover, the captain could not say what his route back to New Bedford would be. Murphy did not like the idea of asking Grace to wait weeks or even months in the Caribbean, so they had no choice but to endure uncertainty.

At hand were the particulars of the here and now. His third Sunday finally felt, indeed, like a Sunday, marked by baked beans for breakfast, and clam chowder and apple pie for dinner. The clams were canned and the apples dried, but the cook did a good job with them, so they tasted like the fresh articles. The steward had taken care of the laundry, prompting Murphy to write Grace, "It is a pleasure to wear his unstarched, unironed shirts. I try to keep everything neatly sewed, and my socks darned, or rather, mended, for I use white linen thread."

Through the late afternoon Murphy occupied his canvas chair on deck and enjoyed the sweet pleasure of a tropical breeze on the lee side of the mainsail. A couple of the officers sat on the carpenter's chest and read in a Portuguese Bible; some of the greenhands clustered around a crude drawing of a compass dial at the foredeck; the captain sported a new blue shirt and a panama hat. A Sabbath calm pervaded. "The temperature is the most delightful that I have ever felt and the air the most caressing. It is like Eden, just right for no clothes. Every sense is delighted, and I expect to 'hear old Triton blow his wreathed horn.'"

Earlier that day, from half past six until mid-afternoon, Murphy had worked hard at specimen preparation. The crew had killed four blackfish the day prior and had enthusiastically returned with three of the severed heads. The men had failed, however, to determine the sex of the animals before detachment, so the skulls were of no scientific value. The fourth animal was still intact, a cow, and it so happened Murphy wanted a cow. He made careful measurements overall, including the twenty-five-centimeter embryo he extracted from the carcass.

But he also wanted more skulls. As did the crew. Already the six blackfish captured had yielded twenty-five gallons of head oil. At $15.00 a gallon, and at Murphy's 1/200 lay, he calculated his net worth to have risen by one dollar and eighty-seven and a half cents.

The next day, after Captain Cleveland explained to the crew the importance of Murphy being able to document and catalog his specimens, they brought in another kill, this time a bull blackfish. Murphy tried to make a plaster cast of the head before cutting flesh away from bone, but the plaster did not set well when mixed with warm salt water. He wrote, "The results were slightly better than a failure," and he found the putrescence of blackfish lingered long on his hands and forearms in the absence of ample soap and water.

Of the various inconveniences of being ship-bound, Murphy was most bothered by the matter of water. With thirty-five men on board, of course, they had to be careful to conserve the supply. Murphy had already learned to bathe in half a basin full. And the basin was a small one at that. That the drinking water was not only warm and stale, but often "bilgy" helped in its conservation. Moreover, the forecastle hands obtained their water with a long tube known as a thief, which was inserted through the bunghole and drawn out by means of a lanyard, or short piece of rope. The amount of time and labor involved discouraged wastefulness. Bilgy water was the result of the tight bungs employed to minimize evaporation. Gases, the natural product of microscopic decomposition, had no escape. When the vent of the cask did not have sufficient air passing through it, the water stunk horribly. Murphy went thirsty as long as he could stand, then he would hold his breath and swallow a glassful. Fortunately, the water worked through the gassy period and cleared after a time, as all ships' water improved over a period of three to four weeks. He found transferring water to his canteen helped the process along.

Privacy was another issue. With his own set-up in the deckhouse, Murphy was better off than the men in the forecastle, stacked on top of one another, but no one could go off by himself any longer than five minutes. He found himself in good company with this frustration, however. Darwin, too, had written about his "want of room and seclusion" while sailing aboard the *Beagle*.

On July 22nd, the ship lay halfway between Martinique and Dominica. In the middle of a docile afternoon, a large flock of noddies and terns followed a shoal of blackfish and porpoises. A few boatswain birds kept to themselves, apart from the mixed flock.

Mr. Vincent's harpooner is already on board the larboard boat. To the right of the pulley is the boat's loggerhead, the thick post around which the whale line will be snubbed. Once lowered, the remaining members of the boat's crew will slither down slide boards

The shoal lay to the windward, about a mile off, calm and with backs afloat. The captain ordered two boats lowered, but as the boats closed in, the blackfish spooked (or gallied, as a whaleman might have said) and the chase was on. Watching through his binoculars, Murphy saw one boat make fast with a harpoon then be pulled rapidly ahead. The straining animal jerked characteristically from port to starboard then back to port and then to spin. A lance was driven home and Murphy saw red water, even at his distance. A man-o'-war, or frigate bird, glided into the scene, spiraling above with apparent interest in the opportunity of death.

The man-o'-war bird's name stems from its piracy of others' catches. Graceful and swift, it is built for motionless soaring and can remain airborne for hours. Its wingspread, at seven and a half feet, is larger in relation to its body, at only three or four pounds, than any other bird. Murphy might have enjoyed monitoring its progress if the blackfish gam—or group—had not been coming directly toward the *Daisy*.

Seventy-five or a hundred animals swam leisurely along the surface in groups of threes and fours clustered close enough to touch sides. The captain ordered a third boat lowered. By this time, Murphy had scrambled up to the main masthead where he could look directly down on dorsal fins, which were exposed much of the time. The blackfish alternately idled, with their flukes and heads submerged, and thrust their heads up to breathe. When they lifted their snouts, the slits of their blowholes opened like pairs of lips, and a slight shower of spray accompanied each gentle puff.

The huge, old bull in the van of the herd was the first to see the ship. He, like the others that followed, changed course immediately, some turning sharply right, others to the left. The gam divided itself around bow and stern, and as the *Daisy* advanced, the wary blackfish let go. Murphy watched them sink straight down without giving the slightest appearance of having altered or inclined their bodies in any way. With their descent, they went from black to green and then from green to indistinct shadows. In a few minutes, they surfaced some distance off and lured the whaleboat in a new direction.

Blackfish swam in such great numbers their sides nearly touched. The round melons of their heads yielded the finest watch oil.

This tease continued for an hour or more. By the time the boat was signaled to return empty, the gam was once again around the ship. By afternoon's end, three blackfish had been killed. A fourth was killed the following day.

The noddy terns and other web-footed birds that flocked around the ship and whales were no surprise to Murphy. Noddies are sea birds, and he was at sea. What he did not expect were hummingbirds several miles off the coast.

Bouncing back and forth between the islands, Murphy observed no fewer than seven of those tiny birds. He identified them as *Sericotes holosericeus*, or Green-throated Caribs. They skimmed as close as a few inches above the water and as high as forty feet and they appeared as far as nine miles from shore. A hummingbird has no facility for resting at sea; it has no choice but to get where it is going on its blur of rapid wing beats, but instead of progressing in a beeline, they dipped and swooped as they crossed the wide water. They appeared in all conditions, rain and shine. One of these diminutive migrators even passed the *Daisy* when the ship was tacking under reefed sails, but the bird flew vigorously into the teeth of the wind.

Murphy also noted the pleasure of seeing men in dugout canoes crossing the dangerous straits. They carried enormous sails and were ballasted with big cobblestones, leaving only a few inches of freeboard to keep the three or four people inside dry and safe. Murphy wrote, "I have been amazed to see such craft racing past us in a rugged sea, the occupants stopping their bailing, if not their balancing, long enough to give us a hail."

Conversation at the officers' table covered a wide range. One evening the topic turned to injuries, and Murphy spoke of cases in which the ancient Hawaiians had reputedly patched fractured skulls with surgical implants of coconut shells, whereupon Mr. Alves, the first mate, showed a scar just above his forehead. He told how the frontal bone had been repaired with a piece of calabash shell. He had fallen off a high wall as an eight-year-old, and a Portuguese surgeon had operated.

At fifty-three this mate came across as elderly, perhaps in part because of the lame foot he dragged around. He was a passive man from Brava in the Cape Verde Islands but, unlike most men native to that part of the world, was three-quarters white. According to Johnny the cabin boy, also from Brava, Mr. Alves had two families. His first—and legitimate—wife lived with their children, while another woman and mother of several more Alves children occupied a house across the road. When Mr. Alves was home between voyages, according to Johnny, he divided his attention impartially between the two households.

The formality of addressing the mates with "mister" ahead of their names was not in observance of their age. The other officers, Mr. Vincent and Mr. Lunda, were in their twenties, as were many of the greenhands. Nevertheless, officers were identified by last name while greenhands were not. Although not actually signed on as a mate at the outset of the voyage, John da Lomba would be addressed as an officer, too.

But waiting for this mystery seaman approached tedium. Murphy anticipated sending Grace the last of his Portsmouth letters. He wrote, "More blackfish taken today, so time is passing not too slowly. However, we can never come back until after we start, and I am eager to cross the real threshold of this separation. When we leave the West Indies for the cold south, I shall feel, in a way, homeward bound. My courage will grow and strengthen as the days and weeks pass, if only your last letter to me assures me that your heart is high."

To pass the time after supper one day, Murphy suspended a tomato can on a long boathook over the *Daisy*'s stern and brought up his little rifle for the officers' amusement. Everyone took a shot or two, but no one hit the mark until Captain Cleveland's turn. His bullet made a loud *ping*, spun the can around, and threaded daylight through a pair of holes. Others shot again, but only the captain hit the bobbing can. Finally, he, too, missed. By then Murphy was disgusted with his own bad aim. He loaded up fifteen balls then stood amidships and fired, bang, bang, bang—about twice a second and lacing the can with holes at every shot. After that the men thought Murphy had been fooling at first, too polite to outshoot the others. He wrote in his notes that night that his reputation was intact.

The blackfish and porpoise shoals continued to come around. In the midst of a rough afternoon, the captain ordered two of the three larboard boats to be lowered. Murphy volunteered himself to pull second oar in Mr. Vincent's boat. It was Murphy's first time at water level, giving him a new perspective among the cetaceans. Waves crested above the boat, shutting out sight of the other boat, save for times they rose on neighboring waves simultaneously. The boats pulled back and forth in pursuit of dark fins cutting the water, now here, now there, but always traveling rapidly. Mr. Vincent stood at the long steering oar, urging the men on.

Porpoises are said to be most easily approached and struck in rough water. Not so that day. The animals were wary. They came along with nearly every roller, half a dozen abreast in brigades, which Murphy likened to the chariot horses he had seen in Egyptian art. But the porpoises turned away at critical moments and eluded. Some turned parallel to the waves to glide lengthwise embedded in the glassy green crests.

If the wind was in their favor, rather than pulling the oars, the crew hoisted the whaleboat's sail and shipped the rudder for steering.

By then the brig was approximately two miles to leeward, so Mr. Vincent ordered the mast set up to save the men's arms on their return. They hoisted the lug-sail, a trapezoidal canvas, and soon were cutting merrily along. Murphy wrote, "Every few seconds the whaleboat would be caught on the downward slope of an overtaking wave, and we would be carried forward at breathless speed for fifty or seventy-five feet, just as Hawaiian swimmers are borne on their surf-boards."

As they drew alongside the *Daisy*, their boat's tiller snapped with the force of a wave, putting them at the mercy of the wind and not necessarily going toward the brig, which was also under sail. Almost as quickly as the boat could luff into the wind, however, their helmsman had unlashed the spare tiller and clapped it into the rudder post. *Semper paratus.* Always prepared.

July 29th was squally. At four o'clock in the afternoon, Murphy noted the appearance of the most brilliant rainbow he had ever seen, low-arched, complete, and strangely close. He felt he could stretch out over the gunwale and touch the arc of it. The ends of the bow had the curious

appearance of angling horizontally on the surface of the sea. He
monitored it for two hours and
four minutes until it disappeared,
having climbed the vault of sky to
complete its semi-circle by the
end.

At five minutes after eight
that evening, a full moon rose to
twenty degrees off the horizon,
and a lunar rainbow appeared, opposite. Its right limb connected to
the sea through Ursa Major. The
Big Dipper was "pouring its

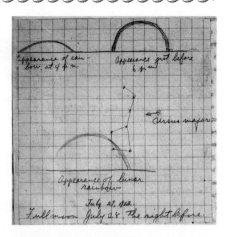

MA sketch from Murphy's journal of the
lunar rainbow.

water," and the arc looped around Merak. The left limb trailed off,
incomplete. No matter. Lunar rainbows of any kind are rare, and
Murphy was thrilled to see a silvery wraith of the afternoon's prismatic
arc. Its color was no more than an argentine glow. And then it was gone as
quickly as it had appeared, lasting a total of only six minutes, but leaving
Murphy in awe and writing to Grace, "Would to God I were sharing
such visions with you."

On the eve of da Lomba's arrival, Murphy continued his letter, "The
time for hearing from you, and then for a long severance, is at hand.
Tomorrow we go ashore. It is hard to be writing the last few lines that
may come to you for many a month. I'll leave a bottle note at any uninhabited island we touch, and drop others overboard at the Equator and
the Tropic of Capricorn. Perhaps some day one of them will come to our
grandchildren!"

Chapter Ten

IN ANTICIPATION of the last chance to modify his crew, the Old Man had been watching everyone with the acumen of a judge at a horse show. Two of the Dominican jailbirds were marked for return, something only the skipper and Murphy were aware of. One of these rejects was bright enough—maybe the smartest of anyone in the forecastle—but intelligence may have been his undoing. Cleveland had noted his influence over others and sized him up as a potential ringleader or focus of trouble between the forecastle and quarterdeck. Cleveland expected—and even tolerated—a certain amount of grumbling as normal. "It's when they're quiet you must watch out," he said.

The second man destined to be handed back to the Roseau police was a long-limbed twenty-year-old with an uncommonly small head. He was mean and he was a bully. Mr. Vincent had already confiscated a sharp-pointed knife, but the man had retained another weapon, the removal of which Murphy witnessed while reading in his canvas chair on the quarterdeck.

"Pinhead," as the cooper called him, strolled across the waist of the ship toward the scuttlebutt, the cask that contained the day's supply of drinking water. Just before Pinhead picked up the copper thief to lower through the bunghole, he looped a pair of iron knuckle-dusters over a belaying pin. These were nasty items with unfriendly-looking knobs on the business side.

Pinhead turned to his drink of water. Just then, Roderick, a small, bright and very British Dominican who had been a tailor's apprentice in Roseau, happened along. He spied the iron bruisers on the pin, grasped the situation, and without looking left or right or breaking the rhythm of his pace, deftly lifted them off the pin and dropped them overboard.

Pinhead gurgled over his draught of water then turned to gather up his "persuaders" only to be completely dumbfounded by their absence. He had not seen or sensed Roderick, who was long gone by then, and no one else was around. Two men sat on the carpenter's bench. They had obviously seen nothing. Murphy feigned absorption in his book while observing the scene. Toward the bow, Roderick mingled with a cluster of idlers. Pinhead continued in furtive scowls, glancing all around the belaying pins and water cask but finally had to shrug and give the whole thing up.

Also going ashore permanently would be Henry Spratt, the steward with a wooden leg. Captain Cleveland had discovered a box full of crusts and half loaves, and to the tune of sulfurous and prolonged expletives vulgar enough to singe a Cuban stevedore's ears, Spratt was discharged and told to pack his chest.

Spratt argued in vain that he had been saving the crusts for a bread pudding. Under most circumstances, one could not easily out-talk Henry Spratt; he was fluent in six languages, including Papiamento, a language used on only a few of the Caribbean islands, although not on Spratt's own St. Eustatius.

But Cleveland had his teeth in it. There would be no room on the *Daisy* for anyone who wasted provisions. Murphy overheard Cleveland's railing punctuated with the thump of Spratt's turned timber as he paced beneath the weight of the skipper's blasphemous oratory. Under a blue sky upon a bluer sea, Murphy imagined a still bluer haze emanating from the galley. João Rosa, the agreeable twenty-two-year-old "boy", nearly fell through the deck when Captain Cleveland asked whether he would like to try the steward's job henceforth.

On a whaleship the threat of attrition came from all directions, some more sobering than being put off the boat and shipped home at the expense of the vessel's owners. One night the cooper related the story of what had become of the ship's original second officer. It had happened on the first leg of the voyage, under Captain Reed's command—before Murphy and the Old Man had come aboard.

Murphy paid close attention to the cooper's account; he had, after all, witnessed the documents for Cleveland when the third and fourth mates had been advanced to fill the gap. Murphy, however, did not know the whole story until the cooper unwound it.

"About Mr. Eneas, it was like this," Correia began. "The morning of March 29th was clear and calm. We raised a school of sperm whales. Captain Reed ordered three boats lowered down. They were Mr. Alves' and Mr. Eneas' and Mr. Almeida's. Mr. Vincent stayed on board. Two boats pulled about a mile from the ship, but Mr. Eneas' boat stopped short of a quarter mile off."

The whales had surfaced and all three officers thrust their harpoons and made fast within minutes. Mr. Eneas' whale did not run, though. It stayed in its pod, and with the other whales crowded the boat. Mr. Eneas had no choice but to stand still at the bow, lance ready, and wait for them to separate.

Suddenly, the harpooned whale made straight for the boat, striking the bow and lifting it six feet in the air. Correia saw Mr. Eneas go head down. The flukes thrashed precisely where he had hit and the rest of the crew tumbled out the stern of the boat.

Correia had watched all this from the deck of the *Daisy*. Five men thrashed in the water—not six—grabbing at their broken boat. Captain Reed shouted an order for Mr. Vincent to lower his boat and crew to go after them. They rushed to haul everyone in, but no amount of searching the waves brought up Mr. Eneas. He never surfaced.

Mr. Lunda, the fourth officer, and his boat had been off at a distance. He lanced the whale on his own line. Then he came over and picked up the line from the smashed boat. He killed Mr. Eneas' whale, which never did swim away.

MURPHY HAD ALREADY seen the report filed by Captain Reed when the *Daisy* finally reached Barbados after the loss. It said only, "Antone Enos died at sea on the 29th of March, 1912, on the voyage from New Bedford to Barbados. Sworn to by Edwin J. Reed, Master. Attested by Chester W. Martin, American Consul." His names were misspelled and nothing was written about the life lived for forty-four years. Eneas' wife in Santo Antão would learn of her widowhood only if some sailor should think to send whaling gossip home.

With Mr. Eneas gone and with the three who were going to be put off in Roseau, that left the *Daisy* short one mate, two greenhands, and a steward. Captain Reed, who commanded the brig between the time she left New Bedford in October of 1911 and Cleveland's arrival, had been discharged and replaced as planned. Of his predecessor, Cleveland exhibited no admiration. "Pampers his crew," he said, "He's so soft-hearted he'd ship morphine to the sinners in hell."

Now, it was time to lower the whaleboat for Roseau one last time. The peg-legged steward had his sea chest ready and gave no indication of being the least downcast or bitter over his fate. The misfit jailbirds were not as snappy; they had to be rounded up and told to get their few belongings together while the rest of the men going ashore waited in the boat alongside.

Murphy had lost a small filling, so his first task on land was to make arrangements with a dentist. He joined the others for lunch at Miss Jolly's—"a regular stag party," in Murphy's words—ten in all, including da Lomba.

Born on Brava but a naturalized American citizen, John da Lomba was a scrawny, raw-boned, energetic, six-foot octoroon who electrified the group the instant he had greeted them at the waterfront. He struck Murphy as "a fellow of the right stuff" who would brighten things up conversationally. Da Lomba also carried magazines and letters from Grace, whom he had met before leaving New England and about whom he was decidedly enthusiastic. "My Gar," he said, "she swim like a feesh!"

Murphy bought a large envelope and got himself to the Dominica Library where he wound up his own packet of letters. "I am in a dull state of mind," he wrote back to Grace, "realizing that I am now going, and I have nothing more to write except that I love you."

The weather had been terrifically hot. The locals said it was one of the most insufferable spells ever known. A welcome breeze from the sea cooled Murphy as he sat at the table. He could make out the *Daisy*'s silhouette through a blur of rainstorm off the coast.

It was the beginning of hurricane season. Captain Cleveland was feverish to leave, and "the fret was on Mr. Almeida" to be hanging around bad waters as the crest of the storm season approached. He had lived through one hurricane—barely—off those same islands and kept mumbling that they should get the hell out of there.

And so they did. In the small hours of August 1st, with a light fair wind, the *Daisy* passed Guadeloupe. The sun rose and they cruised by Montserrat, the Rock of Redonda, Nevis, and St. Kitts' long, low sandy extremities. By evening St. Eustatius lay dead ahead, with the more distant Saba off the lee bow.

Night's black-shadow islands chased and tumbled through Murphy's keyed-up brain. Under a waning moon they passed St. Bartholomew, then Sint Maarten, Anguilla, and Seal Rocks in early morning. Sombrero, low and flat with a high lighthouse, slipped astern before noon. That would be the last land for a long, long time.

Not knowing when his next opportunity would be to send mail, he copied into his continuous letter to Grace—

> Weary with toil, I haste me to my bed,
> The dear repose for limbs with travel tired:
> But then begins a journey in my head
> To work my mind, when body's work's expir'd:
> For then my thoughts—from far where I abide—
> Intend a zealous pilgrimage to thee,
> And keep my drooping eyelids open wide,
> Looking on darkness which the blind do see;
> Save that my soul's imaginary sight
> Presents thy shadow to my sightless view,

Which, like a jewel hung in ghastly night
Makes black night beauteous and her old face new
  Lo! thus, by day my limbs, by night my mind,
  For thee, and for myself no quiet find.
WILLIAM SHAKESPEARE, *Sonnet XXVII*

Chapter Eleven

THE SARGASSO SEA is a lenticular veneer of exceptionally limpid blue water that circulates in the middle of the Atlantic Ocean. It is defined by the North Equatorial Current and the Gulf Stream, which power the sea's slow clockwise swirl. Weather and water are warm. Rainfall is rare; evaporation, humidity, and salinity are high. The surface is tranquil.

The *Daisy* would be making her way across this calm.

Sunlight penetrates the Sargasso's crystal clear waters, which, in turn, support an abundance of plant and animal life. In particular, clusters of *Sargassum* weed float over much of the sea's elliptical two-million-mile area. When Columbus encountered this expanse of vegetation, he assumed it indicated being close to shore. His sailors feared their ships would become entangled in the stuff, confusing the calm of the air with a drag on their hulls. In reality, the algae does nothing to impede navigation.

It seems strange that Murphy would be crossing this rich broth of biology before he could reach the icy waters of the south. For a windjammer, however, "a shortcut is the long way 'round." The *Daisy* had to sail far enough north into the trade winds of the summer season to get far enough east to clear Cape São Roque, South America's easternmost prominence and closest point to Africa.

An intricate web of life has adapted to the floating weed. Its name is from the Portuguese word for grape, *sargaço*, after the weed's bulbous air sacs, which are large enough and tough enough to support communities of tiny crabs, shrimp, anemones, flatworms, hydroids, pipefish, and octopus, many of which, if they lost their grip, would sink and perish. Most of these animals are similar in color to the golden green plants, and many of their bodies have evolved into forms that resemble their host. It is also the breeding ground for European eels; they migrate, mate, spawn, and die in these tropical waters, leaving their larvae to make the long journey back. Spadefish and small sea turtles swim by, looking for an easy meal.

For seven days the *Daisy* sailed on the same northern tack, heading ironically in the direction of home. In uncomfortably warm conditions on a smooth sea, Murphy puttered with decomposing blackfish heads, scraping flesh from bone and cleaning the jaws. He cemented teeth in place and coated them in shellac.

A shark took Murphy's buckskin bait on a line off the stern. This caused a hullabaloo on deck—not only that the shark was a five-footer, but by then the crew was well focused on coming up with specimens for Murphy to work on. He cut up the animal and saved the jaws. Mr. da Lomba took out the spine and drove a wire through, so he could make a walking stick at his leisure. He also excised the soft, limy otoliths from the inner ears, explaining in a roundabout way that, if the otoliths were crushed in salt water, they would act as a diuretic.

There was no doctor on board, and since "the personal plumbing systems of many of the lads" were not in ideal condition, the captain and first mate would have to function as the best available—if not *the* best—doctors. The ship supply firm in Barbados summed it up this way:

> Our Jolly salts have sorry faults
> Concealed beneath their breeches.
> They bring disease from overseas,
> The scurvy sons-of-bitches!

AFTER CONSIDERABLE PERSUASION on Murphy's part, the cook agreed to fry a large portion of the shark's back, which, despite the initial resistance turned out to be delicious prepared more or less in the style of New England creamed codfish but without fresh cream. Some of the officers requested a second serving, but the men forward would not even look at the stuff. Also served were boiled salt beef (known as "salt horse"), boiled yams, cabbage, clam chowder, and fresh biscuits with "ladies'" butter—Captain Cleveland's term for the Danish butter out of a tin that had been purchased especially for Grace and Mrs. Cleveland's brief occupancy. The *Daisy*'s other butter came in amorphous globs fished from a barrel of brine. To finish off the meal with a flourish, Murphy cut up half a fruitcake from what Grace had provided him and shared it around with the officers. He described the supper as "altogether in the nature of an orgy."

Most meals were not that elaborate, but the captain's mess was often one small notch beyond being absolutely plain. The Old Man, one or two officers, the cooper, and Murphy were first to be served, together with one or two of the boatsteerers or harpooners (pronounced *har*-pen-ers), who took the place of whichever officers were on duty. As soon as the first group finished, places were set for half a dozen more. Finally, the steward, the cook, and the cabin boy sat at the same table. That took care of all the occupants of the after-cabin, the main cabin, and steerage. All other members of the crew ate on deck or between decks, carrying their own plates and cups from and to the galley.

Murphy believed Grace's ladylike presence on the *Daisy,* when they had sailed from Barbados to Dominica, had had a positive influence on the men's table manners. Mr. Vincent, for example, discontinued his habit of eating directly from his knife and became rather dainty with a fork instead. The skipper's habits matched Murphy's, which were refined. Still, finger bowls were not exactly included in the table settings.

Chapter Twelve

THE CAPTAIN "broke out the slops," meaning he opened the ship's casks of clothing to supply the crew with blankets, coats, overalls, oilskins, caps, underclothes, knives (with tips broken off in case of disagreements), sheaths, needles and thread, and so forth. The cost of what the men chose became debts against their lay. Murphy, who made out the accounts for the Old Man, felt the crew looked more convincingly like a crew after having been outfitted in uniform sailors' garb.

At three o'clock in the afternoon on August 7th, Captain Cleveland gave a command to come about; it was the first change in course since leaving Roseau. Pointed southeast, the ship sailed into another brilliant rainbow. As the afternoon wore down, the arch gave way to glorious clouds, and the setting sun ignited streaks and splashes of carmine, flame, lavender, blue, green, and yellow across the western sky.

In the night it rained; they woke to a flat gray broken by sperm whale spouts. The crew went crazy at the sight. Blackfish suddenly seemed a trifle in the midst of serious prey. Finally, the real thing.

Blo-o-o-o-o-o-o-o-ws! wavered a strange falsetto solo. The note held for several seconds, pouring and climbing from a boatsteerer's throat. Then all four mastheads screeched in unison, *Blo-o-o-o-o-o-o-ws! White water! Ah, blo-o-o-o-o-o-ws!* The men on deck issued a sympathetic response to the cry, and the watch below came scrambling from the forecastle, pulling on breeches and carrying footgear like firemen responding to an alarm. Softer *Blo-o-o-ws* echoed the songs from above until the whole crew sounded and acted like a chorus gone mad.

Murphy did not have to ask in which direction the whales lay. All

Only when the skipper gave the command to "lower away" did the boats go down. Each whaleboat had room for its six-man crew, equipment necessary for the hunt, and nothing more. There could be no passengers.

heads and binoculars pointed to leeward. The Old Man took in vain two of the three names in the trinity. He snapped a few well-punctuated orders to the man at the wheel, picked up his own binoculars, and clambered aloft. Murphy followed. All but a single masthead scampered down to join their boats' crews. A scramble commenced to uncover line tubs, lift them in, to cast off the gripes—or lashings. Harpoons and lances were unsheathed. Everything was made ready.

The ship drew up slowly toward what proved to be a school of young sperm whales blowing and splashing at the surface. The shape and angle of their spouts distinguished them from other kinds of whales: a single plume, slow and forward-slanted. Then the whales went down. For ten minutes all was silent except for the Old Man's softly echoed orders. Then a subdued *Blo-o-o-ws!* rang out again as the whales reappeared about a mile and a half ahead.

The ropes were cast off from their tackle blocks, the cranes swung in, and, at the word of command, four boats were lowered almost silently to the water with a boatsteerer at the bow and a boatheader at the stern of each. The four crew for each boat descended to water level by way of slide boards and tackle. Each took his own thwart—or seat—with the boat-steerer at the bow oar. A few strokes moved the little craft safely away from the brig, which, by this time, was idling with square sails aback. Then the whaleboats' masts were stepped in, sails were hoisted, and the fleet of four was off in full pursuit.

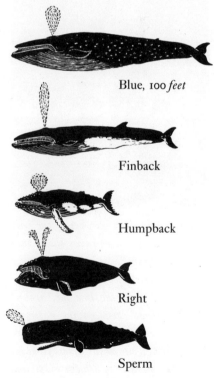

Blue, 100 *feet*

Finback

Humpback

Right

Sperm

Twenty-four men were down; ten were on board, and three of these were aloft—still enough shiptenders, since the *Daisy*'s entire crew had not been much bigger than that when she had worked as a merchant vessel.

They steered the ship into the wind and slowly trailed the boats. But the Old Man exhibited a growing disgust, first with the small size of the whales, which all appeared to be calves, and second because several killer whales, the dorsal fins of which stood distinc-tively high, followed, pestered, and even jumped over the backs of some of the sperm whales. Sev-eral times over, Mr. da Lomba's

By their spouts so shall you know them.

boat sailed up on a pod of calves only to have them sound just out of darting range. Mr. Alves' boat finally sank a harpoon and made fast. Its sail and mast came down; the harpooner and mate changed ends, as would be expected at that point; the crew "hauled up," and with scarcely a struggle, a young bull was lanced. With the relaxation of death, it turned "fin out," meaning it rolled to its side, staring blindly heavenward with one eye, in which a yellow waif on a staff was thrust. Without ceremony, the harpoon line was cut, and the boat rejoined the chase. By then, the pod was thoroughly spooked—or gallied—in part, no doubt, by the killer whales. Murphy overheard the Old Man mutter profanely that a signal flag should be hoisted to recall all boats to the ship.

It takes only a few strokes of the oars to clear the ship. Two razor-sharp harpoons, or "irons", project from the bow near the clumsy cleat. The harpoon line is threaded from the line tub, around the loggerhead, between the oarsmen, and out through the chocks in the bow. Each oarman sits as far across from his oarlock as possible to achieve maximum leverage.

The waif, the original meaning of which meant "something flapping," marked their lone catch, a six-barrel animal less than twenty-five feet long. They brought the carcass to the ship, hauled it on board, and began the cutting-in before dinner. Its total value figured to benefit Murphy by forty-eight cents.

"This minnow of a whale didn't seem to rate a shantey, and the windlass that hoisted the blubber was worked in silence, save for its own creaking." Murphy wrote. A shark and its pilot fish companion swam around the vessel during the cutting-in. Occasionally, the small, banded fish would dart aside to take a morsel of food, but

The whale has turned "fin out" Mr. Almeida prepares for the hard tow of its dead weight to the ship.

it would then hasten back like a child afraid of losing his nurse. It stayed close to the shark's dorsal fin, occasionally swimming beneath its protector. Just as a large piece of blubber was being cut away, the shark rushed up, pushed its head above water and buried its teeth in the luscious fat. The men on the cutting stage paid no attention. The whale's recent meal of many large squid drifted from its gullet and floated away. Blood colored everything.

Murphy photographed various stages of the process, although he did not enter in his notes any description of how the work was carried out. For that, he chose to wait for a "man's-size" whale. Nevertheless, in warm seawater, he developed his glass-plate negatives "well into the night"—or at least until ten-thirty, two hours after his usual bedtime of half past eight.

The cook served sperm whale cakes for breakfast. The flesh was lean and red, which Murphy welcomed, not having had much meat for six weeks except for a little duck at Miss Jolly's and a dab of tinned beef a few days before.

The boats were lowered again, this time in pursuit of a lone whale and under oar power on a glassy sea. Even at long range, Murphy could hear the boatheaders' voices across the calm. They urged on their oarsmen in a quaint mixture of flattery and imprecations (the Old Man tolerated profanity in the whaleboats). The officers wielded their twenty-three-foot steering oars, and the men on their thwarts doubled themselves to a long, whippy stroke in a regatta of four craft that never came closer than half a mile from their quarry.

Captain Cleveland said such single whales were usually old bulls. Cows and smaller whales usually swam in shoals of fifty or sixty members, traveling at about seven or eight knots—a snail's pace compared to porpoises. On a previous voyage, Cleveland had taken such a lone bull in the Sea of Japan. He alleged that it had yielded 130 barrels of oil, but Murphy had his doubts. Even a hundred-barrel sperm would have been something of a legend.

The skipper liked to find his whales in mixed groups of fifty or sixty. Unless they became gallied, they rarely swam any faster than four or five knots, and the boats could cut out the larger animals from among the lesser.

They boiled blubber most of that day, being short-handed during the hours the boats were down. The *Daisy* appeared not to move an inch in the broiling calm. Ocean insects skated alongside, and triggerfish emerged from the depths and pirouetted along the brig's bilge, or lower part of her hull. Some of them were accompanied by tiny, clinging remoras—suckerfish. Murphy tried to catch one or two of the triggerfish to have a look at their leech-like passengers, but he had no luck.

Murphy had taken to the sperm whale meat at breakfast. This was fortunate because there it was again for supper. Although Mrs. Cleveland's jar of guava jelly was a welcome treat at the table, the whale meat put Murphy in mind of chops, which put him in mind of baked potatoes (with *fresh* butter), then he fantasized onions, carrots, and all kinds of other things unavailable on board, including a bucket of cool spring water, for which he thirsted intensely in the Sargasso's concentrated heat.

August 10th he wrote, "Sunrises, sunsets, rainbows both matutinal and vesperal, and nights crystal and starry enough to make one gasp, leave nothing to be desired in the way of a spectacular setting here where I am. But the ship does not move. As a change from reading, I have just opened a bottle of figs. Still calm and hot. Here we lie, after the moil of the cutting-in, with limp and slatting sails, approximately where we were two days ago."

At loose ends, Murphy disassembled and reassembled his typewriter, having cleaned, oiled, and thoroughly fiddled with it. He caught up on his notes. He tried returning to reading. Evening finally came, bringing a soaking rain pattering on the deck above his berth. He lay listening in his berth long enough for the mainsail to be adequately washed then slipped above in the wet and caught a basinful dribbling off the canvas. That water quenched a nine-days' thirst.

Chapter Thirteen

STILL NO CHANGE. The *Daisy* lay like Coleridge's painted ship upon a painted ocean. Murphy lowered the *Grace Emeline* and scooped bits of gulf weed with a dipnet. He sorted and pickled, bottled and catalogued the crabs, mollusks, shrimp, and tiny fish he found tucked in the drifting gardens. Other biologists had already collected and studied everything there, but to Murphy it was all new. Until then the varieties had been mere names and pictures in a book.

He gathered a concentration of the *Sargassum* and its inhabitants in a big enamel tray and counted fifteen kinds of animals living in the floating orange forests, including a nudibranch (sea slug), a worm, a hydroid, a fish, and four kinds of crustaceans—two were crabs; two others were prawns. He had to poke around a fair bit to find these animals; they all looked much like the vegetation. He was astonished, for example, when a seemingly empty sprig of weed that he had handled several times and for several minutes gave up a fish the size of his thumb.

The sargasso fish—or, mousefish, as it was also called—fascinated Murphy with its strange composite of not much more than mouth, belly, and excrescences. Two tasseled poles protruded from the head, presumably to lure prey toward the gulping mouth. Arm fins (pectorals) worked like hands, bending at the wrist and folding ten long finger rays that grasped at whatever could be laid hold of. Foot fins (the pelvics) stuck forward under the belly like spread feet perpetually ready to hit bottom. The fish clambered around the weed like lizards in a thicket. And no wonder they were difficult to see at first; in patterns of brown, gold, orange, and white, they were fringed and dotted in precisely the colors of the *Sargassum* and its other animal inhabitants. Moreover, the fish could alter their hue, depending on the background colors, much as chameleons will adapt to their settings.

With whale meat as bait, the crew caught a shark's pilot fish and several tough-skinned triggerfish, which they called leatherjackets. These were about a foot long and meaty. Their bones were happily sucked clean at the captain's mess. Murphy wrote of the delicacies, "Man has to live on ship's fare for only a few weeks really to learn what a predatory animal he is and how deeply he craves the flesh of freshly killed fellow creatures." As the officers sat back from their meal, Mr. da Lomba told of a time he had driven a harpoon through a shark, left the iron in place and tied the line short. This held the shark struggling at the surface while its eight pilot fish flocked around their big companion and, one after another, allowed themselves to be hooked.

During the calm Murphy had plenty of time to acquaint himself with the crew. In all, thirteen men had been picked up in Barbados and Dominica to replace the deserters. Eleven were British subjects, one a French citizen from Martinique, and one a Cape Verdean. With the exception of two, none had been to sea before. The two were Edward Evelyn and José Gaspar. Evelyn signed on as a greenhand but struck for a lay of $1/180$, since he had been to sea on a schooner. Gaspar had papers proving whaling experience, so he was shipped with the rank and lay of a new boatsteerer, at $1/100$. The eleven others signed on with a lay of $1/185$ each—slightly more than Murphy's token share of $1/200$.

The crew's names seemed almost as liquid to Murphy as the sea on which the *Daisy* floated. A total of forty men had shipped on one or both parts of the two-part voyage. Of these, eleven were called by John or some variant—João or José. Four went by Antão. If that were not confounding enough, many of the surnames, such as Paul, Peter, Stephen, and Charles, sounded more like given names. Two men were named Almeida; two were Correia. There was a da Cruz and a da Luz.

And almost no Yankee captain spelled a Portuguese name the same way twice. Names might be entered as one thing in the ship's log but show up in other papers in a bewildering variety. William Stephens, one of the new greenhands, for example, was also listed as William Elwin. Names were Anglicized. João Pires (or, elsewhere, Pirez) was known as Johnny Perry. Antãeo Dias was, for some reason, never called anything but Ferleão. Vitor Ribeiro was known as Victor Robinson. Mr. Vincent, the fourth officer who had been promoted to third as a result of Mr. Eneas' death, was actually named Vincente Lunda.

Most of the men were in their early twenties when they shipped. Three were still teenagers; three had reached their thirties. Mr. Eneas had been forty-three when he signed on; Mr. Alves was fifty-three and junior only to Captain Cleveland, who was sixty-seven. Murphy had passed his twenty-fifth birthday.

The cooper, José Gonçalves Correia, was old-stock Portuguese from the island of Fayal in the Azores. He and the skipper and Murphy were the only Caucasians. Mr. Vincent was Filipino. The rest were all or part African. Mr. Alves, Mr. da Lomba, a boatsteerer, and a few of the greenhands were fair enough in their complexions that they were listed in the shipping papers as "light." There were only three categories: white, light, and black.

Finally, on August 13th, a breeze arose and began to move the ship in the direction of Bermuda, but it was short lived. Murphy found it difficult to occupy himself. He took naps; he slept "late" in the morning (six-thirty). He finished reading *Voyage of the Beagle* and began Moseley's account of the *Challenger* voyage. Both these books helped prepare him for sea travel and visiting the southern lands, but he worried about reading too much. In 1912 it was commonly believed that one could damage one's eyes through overuse. As far as the entertainment value went, he wrote, "There is even an end to reading."

He tried vainly to capture one of the dolphins whose blue and silvery bodies leapt and whose yellow tails flashed in the shadows beneath the ship's stern. The dolphins proved too deft for Murphy, however. They nibbled his bait but never took his hook.

He tried to be philosophical about the lull in the ship's progress. By

August 15th they had gained four miles. While traveling those four miles north, however, the ship had drifted twelve miles westward.

Meanwhile, he chatted with the officers, but apparently did not think much of the exchanges. He wrote to Grace, "A little stimulating conversation with someone who knows something would help me now. I miss human intelligence. Also, a little plot of ground where I might run a hundred yards, perchance to a spring of fresh water, would help. But best of all would be a room where I could shut the door, if only for an hour. You haven't any idea, until you go to sea, how strange it is to be imprisoned in a space 30 by 125 feet with 34 other men, mostly black, and to have to share even your cabin with the presence of one man and the sight of several others. But I don't care a rap, really; I live to do my duty on this trip and get through with it. The captain is certainly considerate and obliging, and he is living up to the letter and spirit of what he agreed to do. All the disadvantages are shared by him, and most of them are necessary. In fact, it is I who am in *his* cabin.

"Dante tells how the souls in Purgatory, though in the midst of suffering, are supremely happy. In a sense I feel that we are in Purgatory—developing ourselves through the power of love by our voluntary separation. We pray, and our prayer shall be answered, that selfishness, impatience, misunderstanding, may be burned out of our hearts by the long deprivation."

In addition to being becalmed, Johnny, the newly appointed steward, announced that the ship was both running out of tea and that the saluratus supply (baking soda) was entirely depleted. Not telling that those supplies were short turned out to have been Henry Spratt's revenge against Captain Cleveland for being sacked. To Murphy it was good news. The ship would be stopping for more provisions—probably at the Brazilian island of Fernando de Noronha, where Murphy hoped to get permission to collect specimens. So, in his view, it was worth going without tea. As for the leavening agent, "The cake the boy makes with it is no good anyhow."

Despite having made some progress and having lowered the boats a time or two when whales had been sighted, a fight broke out among the men on the forward deck. Murphy's heart skipped a beat when he saw Jean-Baptiste, the Martinican greenhand, holding another man by the throat and reaching for his sheath knife, then holding it close to his adversary's jugular vein. Mr. Almeida separated the two, but other men continued to maul and slug indiscriminately, even after the Old Man himself bawled at them to desist. Mr. Vincent and Mr. Almeida, each of whom was brawnier than any man in the forecastle, together pulled the knot of brawlers apart. One man knocked himself out by falling and hitting his head against the carpenter's bench.

"The Old Man, in vile dudgeon, then held court in the rain and dressed the bedraggled culprits down, ending with dire threats about the penalty if this sort of thing should ever happen again. Then he had the knife-puller handcuffed and put down in the stuffy lazaret on the afterdeck, with the hatch clamped down on him. Orders are that he is to be left strictly alone, to think matters over, until sunrise tomorrow."

Murphy faulted the captain and officers for not finding constructive methods for maintaining morale, but he recognized it as a more fundamental problem than providing an immediate task or focus. The *Daisy* and everything on it had already been "scrubbed, scoured, painted, slushed, polished, served, thrapped, tautened, or replaced, as the case may be; oakum had been picked, seams tarred, and countless unnecessary or trumped-up tasks performed." But the general living conditions in terms of quarters, food, recognition of service, and hope of a reasonable reward were as poor as anything Murphy cared to consider. He had already calculated what the eventual, likely payoff would mean to most of the men when the voyage concluded. If they took $40,000 worth of sperm and sea elephant oil, which would have been reasonable, Mr. Lunda's lay would figure out to be about $1,300 and a greenhand's something around $250. In each case, however, advances, slops, tobacco, and other supplies would be deducted. Not enough promise of money to keep a sailor in line.

The brawl was doubtless the result of not enough to do. Murphy's methods of dealing with boredom were more polished. He read *King Lear*; he noted the presence of a tired, semipalmated sandpiper and later, four barn swallows visiting the ship; he commented privately on Mr. Vincent's uncouth manner; he photographed one of the swallows; he developed his negatives. At one point the brig came within sight of a big schooner, which Murphy hoped the Old Man would hail, but the schooner never came within range.

They were at 31° 31' N, and 58° 40' W, roughly 360 miles east of Bermuda and more than a thousand miles south of Cape Cod. Despite this distance, land birds continued to show up in small numbers, bound for their winter range. A bird on a normal course of its direct migration from Nova Scotia to the Lesser Antilles would have made it half the distance. Murphy noted that the birds were capable of resting on a calm ocean surface before taking off again. Some spent the night in the *Daisy*'s rigging, but Murphy wished them on their way since there were no flying insects around the brig for them to eat, and the ever-present cockroaches were too big for the little swallows to surround.

In addition to the letter bag in which Grace supplied her husband with near-daily communications from friends and family, she had also packed a generous supply of delectables. Murphy turned to them when looking for a lift. On August 19th, however, he wrote to her, "I found it necessary to overhaul my Christmas Trunk, and take all the perishables up to the cabin. The cockroaches and cockroachesses are the most conspicuous element in the 'navifauna.' They are more numerous than pine needles in the Arcade Woods, and they eat anything of leather, paper, etc." Fortunately they had not injured the books, although the wrappers

A barn swallow lit on one of the whaleboats' oars, giving Murphy a stab of nostalgia. All oars were striped like this one for quick identification of position.

were nibbled. A package labeled, "Extra Choice Raizins" was little more than pits and stems, and a bottle which had contained molasses was now filled with dead cockroaches. They had eaten through the cork and their drowned bodies had continually raised the level of the molasses for succeeding invasions. "I thought I should have to throw the raisins over, but I'm very fond of them, so I picked them over one by one, shook out the young cockroaches, and threw away all the bitten raisins! So I managed to save about three-fourths of them, which I sunned and put in a tin box. Rats are somewhat less numerous but even more destructive than the cockroaches. We catch five or six every day.

"I had counted on enjoying your little can of cheese. It said 'sterilized' on the outside, but when I opened it I was obliged to contradict the label, and consign it to the deep. I like strong Camembert but not as strong as that was."

Chapter Fourteen

AFTER NEARLY SEVEN WEEKS at sea, Murphy's patience was finally rewarded and his curiosity satisfied. A full-scale blubber hunt was about to develop.

It was a Sunday. The men had been washing their clothes. Shortly after dinner the lookouts announced a school of whales. At first, the skipper and Mr. da Lomba thought they were only "killers" (orcas) and took no particular notice. But when the aggregation approached the brig, leaping and blowing furiously, it turned out to be sperm whales and killers mingled. All four boats were lowered right away. Murphy climbed to the main masthead to watch.

The first boat made fast to a whale. The killers disappeared. Fifteen minutes later Murphy saw a second boat make fast to a second whale and go shooting ahead, towed by the struggling animal on its line. Six minutes later the third boat planted its iron and took off on its own Nantucket sleigh ride. Mr. Almeida's boat was unlucky; it never succeeded in making fast.

Considerable intimacy between the hunters and the hunted was necessary for a whale to be successfully overpowered. Anyone who assumes a whaleboat's crew captured their prey by getting themselves somewhere in close proximity to their target so they could then throw their harpoon would be wrong. And it was not the harpoon that did the killing; it was merely an attachment to the whale until the creature tired itself out—either by diving or running at surface level. The boatsteerer/harpooner stood poised, weapon in hand, while the boatheader/officer kept eagerness in check with the firm order to wait for "wood to blackskin." The bottom of the boat—whether by wind or oar power—would actually pull up onto the whale's back. Then and only then would the harpoon be *planted*, rarely leaving the boatsteerer's hands until decisively sunk into the animal's warm flesh.

The harpoon included a wooden shaft and a forged iron head, altogether about six feet long. The shaft, by which the iron was handled, was usually slightly curved and with the bark left on. The head, barbed and honed to a fine edge, was attached by a slender shank. Two hundred fathoms of manila line had already been scrupulously freed of kinks by paying it out and towing it astern the ship before carefully coiling it in a line tub, which was lifted into the boat the moment before being lowered. As soon as the boat left the ship, the line was bent (fastened) onto the iron (harpoon).

If the iron was well planted—preferably in the flank, forward of the hump—the boat was fast to the whale, at which point the injured animal took off, sometimes diving at such a speed that the line, which had been wrapped around the loggerhead, might smoke as it ran out, necessitating that the stout post be doused with water to keep it from igniting. Even if the whale remained at the surface, there were still dangers. A singing line might take a turn around a man's arm or leg and either surgically remove it or yank the man from the boat and under the sea forever.

The boatsteerer and the officer went through the ritual of changing places in the boat, because it was the mate who had the honor of lancing. Considering the conditions in a crowded boat, possibly being pulled at top speed on water rough enough to shake the nails loose from their planks, this was no small maneuver.

Eventually the whale had to breathe. Inch by inch the men hauled the rough line until they were within stabbing distance of the beast, since it was not the harpoon but the petal-shaped lance that did the killing. Described by Murphy, its "wooden haft is machined straight and slender. Its blade is whetted razor sharp and, of course, has no barb. It can be yanked out of the whale by its lanyard as easily as it enters, and then jabbed in again. The kill is commonly finished broadside, with knifelike wrenchings and churnings of the keen steel."

If the iron were sunk into lung tissue, the whale immediately exhaled bloody vapor from its single-nostril blowhole, indicating the end. An excited cry might go up from the crew, "Fire in the chimney!" at which point the boat would back off to avoid being splattered by the gore.

The *Daisy*'s first boat lanced and waifed its catch. As soon as the ship-tenders saw that the whale had gone "fin out," they began hauling up gear from between decks—readying heavy fluke chains, cutting tackle, and other equipment for flensing, or stripping, the skin and blubber from the animal in a continuous spiral twist.

It took immeasurable courage for six men to approach a fifty-foot whale on its own territory. The victim was not always the whale. A thirty-foot boat was no match for a sixty-ton animal—especially once it was injured and enraged. If the creature rose up under the boat, the men would have been tossed into the sea. Both ends of a whale are lethal. The flukes can be twenty feet across, and a whale is built for slapping them down in hard, repeated blows. Fifty feet forward, an enormous jaw could grab a boat and splinter its cedar planks—delicate matchsticks in comparison to the row of teeth. Any men left flailing in the waves at that point would not necessarily know how to swim. They would be far from their ship, and their boat was not equipped with life preservers.

Mr. da Lomba's boat was about a mile downwind from the ship, so his crew had the added labor of towing their carcass rather than hoisting their sail and relying on wind to do the work. They looped a bowline from the flukes around the loggerhead for the long pull.

Murphy watched through the binoculars given him by Grace. At his distance it looked as if each stroke of the long oars dropped back into the same hole in the water left by the previous stroke. It took two hours for the crew to bring in their prize. That they towed the animal tail-first baffled Murphy, who expected to see the whale point the other way, but he accepted that there might be some basis for a difference of opinion.

Conrad, the timid and religious greenhand who had been incapable of climbing the ratlines at the start of the voyage, contributed to the afternoon's excitement. He was in Mr. da Lomba's boat. After the iron had been successfully darted, and the oarsmen turned to face the bow and haul toward their harpooned whale, Conrad, it seems, had collapsed in a dead faint. Emiliano, the twenty-two year old boatsteerer, splashed him with a piggen of seawater but to no effect. Seeing this, Mr. da Lomba put down his lance, "strode aft over the thwarts of the boat already whizzing along on its Nantucket sleigh ride, picked up a paddle and began to belabor the lump that was Conrad. Happily, the treatment revived him before it killed him. Conrad yelped, popped up, seized the line, and began to haul like a veteran."

Mr. da Lomba reported all this matter-of-factly to Captain Cleveland. Murphy pieced it together with details gleaned from other members of the boat's crew. Apparently, Conrad's reaction wasn't rare for someone's first experience, and no stigma was attached. The Old Man made it clear to Murphy, however, that "paddling a sailor whose behavior endangered the lives of his fellows was no infringement of the modern laws that forbid flogging."

Capturing a whale bore its own drama, but its death was only the beginning of hard work. The men in Mr. da Lomba's boat might have been exhausted from their two-hour haul of what had once been free-swimming and was now dead weight. Nevertheless, the cutting-in process was next.

"The operations of bringing a dead whale alongside the ship, and of attaching it, are called sweeping and fluking. After the line from the carcass has been passed on board, a heavy chain, made fast around a bitt on the forward deck, is paid out through the starboard hawse pipe. A light rope is then dipped under the whale's "small" (the tail end, just in front of the flukes), and is used in turn to pull the chain around. As soon as the slack has been drawn in, the whale floats on the starboard side of the ship, with its flukes toward the bow and its head stretching along past the waist. The process is simple enough in quiet weather, but today there has been a small choppy sea and the fluking was accomplished only with a good deal of hard labor by the crew and of still harder language by the Old Man."

As soon as the three whales had been brought alongside, the fall blocks

The Old Man oversees "sweeping and fluking", making a whale fast along the star-board flank of the ship. The boat on davits is Murphy's dory, the Grace Emeline.

were dropped, and all four boats were raised, saltwater streaming from plug holes in their bottoms. Then the order came to "supper the watch," and nobody needed urging to eat a meal long overdue.

Darkness closed in. The nearest whale lay on its side, yielding to each ocean swell. Its great blunt head and its closed eye and its tiny ear opening occasionally broke above the surface. Murphy could not easily count the number of sharks filing silently along, rubbing tail fins affectionately against the gray hulk as if anticipating the feast that would be the cutting-in.

They shortened sail with canvas aback to slow the ship through an increasingly calm night. At half past four and in the dim light of early dawn, every man was on deck and on duty. Murphy's only assignment was to watch the proceedings.

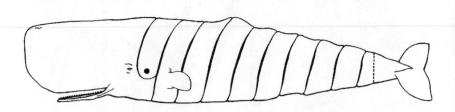

Starting behnd the eye, a long spiral was cut so blubber could be wound off and hoisted aboard as blanket pieces.

The cutting stage—a scaffold—was lowered from the ship's waist to suspend directly above the first whale. The officers stood on this unsteady platform. The cutting tackle—a cluster of enormous blocks— was suspended by hawsers as thick as a man's leg from the head of the mainmast, the strongest structure above deck.

A gash was made in the blubber, right behind the sperm whale's eye, to accept a massive iron hook suspended from the cutting tackle. The hook weighed about a hundred pounds just by itself. Tension on the line began to lift the carcass above the water. Then the officers, working with blubber spades whose handles were fifteen or twenty feet long, leaned against the rail of the cutting stage to steady themselves and began to slice a flap of blubber around the inserted hook.

The morning brightened while the officers jabbed and stabbed, sometimes seeing where their blades struck and sometimes not for the waves and blood and foam. Their blades dulled rapidly. Their shouts of "Sharp spade, Cooper!" kept Correia busy on the quarterdeck renewing edges while another man turned the grindstone. All the while Correia cursed under his breath at the recklessness with which the officers chipped their spades against bone or the embedded harpoon. Finally, the last cut was made.

At the other end of the cutting tackle, double hawsers ran through the great blocks to the windlass on the topgallant forecastle. Under the watchful eyes of the Old Man himself, the greater part of the crew

The flensing process begins by lowering the cutting stage. There, the officers stand and hack the spiral cut that will be peeled from the whale's carcass by means of a block and tackle suspended from the mainmast.

The fourth officer, Victor Robinson, rigs the cutting tackle, suspended from the main-mast.

The gangway board has been removed from the bulwarks for the cutting-in and the hundred-pound hook begins to lift the blubber strip.

rocked the windlass and hoisted the blubber as it peeled off the whale in a continuous strip. This hard work was accompanied by song. To the percussion of squeaky bearings and clicking pawls hitting the teeth of the windlass's ratchet wheel, a husky chorus rang out

> Come all ye brave sailors who're cruising for sparm,
> Come all ye bold seamen who sail round the Horn—
> Our Captain has told us, and we hope it proves true,
> There's plenty more whales 'long the coast of Peru.

As the first strip of blubber began to rip from the whale's body, sharks scrambled to bury their teeth in exposed fat. Now and then a shark would end up on top of the slowly spinning carcass until the thrust of a blubber spade would "put an end to the shark's ambitions."

An acre of water around the brig was stained with blood. When the blanket of blubber could be hoisted no higher, Mr. Vincent used a long-handled, doubled-edged sword called a boarding knife to cut a pair of

Men at the windlass take a much needed break winding blubber off the carcass with a block and tackle. The blubber is so tough the heavy chain would fail or the block would crack before the skin would begin to tear at the insertion point.

holes through the suspended blubber at deck level. A chain was looped in and out of these holes and connected with the "port falls," a second hawser of the cutting blocks. With the new attachment secure and drawn taut on the windlass, the boarding knife slashed across the blubber just above, and the upper piece swung free across the deck (to the peril of any in its path). This first blanket piece was slithered down the main hatch and into the blubber parlor where men with short-handled spades minced it into pieces small enough to stow.

The second strip was still draped in the gory sea. The chain that held it ground against the gunwale of the waist until that strip, too, was raised dripping onto the deck and eventually cut when yet another strip was begun. And so on, down to the small of the whale, which was cut through and hoisted aboard, flukes and all.

An unusual—and much hoped for—byproduct of the operation was ambergris, a gray, waxy substance formed in the lower bowel of a small percentage of sperm whales and nowhere else. Whether it is the result of

disease or part of the normal digestive process has never been determined. Intestinal secretions seem an unlikely component of luxury perfumes, yet for centuries it was fabulously valued for its strangely pleasant aroma and ability to "mother" other fragrances. The Marine Mammal Protection Act of 1972 made trade in ambergris illegal. Today's perfume shoppers know a synthetic's warm fragrance

Mr. Almeida uses a boarding knife to cut a hole in the blubber where a heavy toggle will be passed. He will slice the upper blanket piece free so the next one can be lifted.

simply as "amber." In Murphy's time the real stuff was sold by the ounce, like gold.

The officers plunged their

spades into the mutilated carcass one last time, now aiming at the viscera. They punched and drew out their blades, each time smelling the tips in the hope of detecting the sweet, earthy fragrance that could make them wealthy men. They had heard stories of whales impacted with hundreds of pounds of the stuff.

But there was no ambergris, neither in the first whale nor the two after. Their peeled bodies floated high, bloated by eighteen hours' decomposition. Sharks massed like squirming maggots.

Murphy's fascination with the details of what had happened up to that point consumed him to the extent he spent the remainder of his afternoon and then the entire evening writing up his notes and developing photographic plates of the hunt. The first stages of boiling the blubber escaped him. It would be the morning of the third day before he recorded the steps the men took and the tools they used to reduce their mountain of fat into clear, odorless oil.

Chapter Fifteen

By the time the cutting-in had ended, the *Daisy* was littered, aslop, and glistening from one end to the other with chopped-up squares of blubber. Working with gaffs and pikes, Feddy Lundy and Jean Paul, barefoot, shirtless, and with pants rolled up to the knees, dragged and pushed their cargo to the main hatch, where it tumbled to Elise St. Rose, who guided it into the blubber parlor, where wooden pens prevented it from slithering around dangerously.

The huge strips of fat and skin peeled from the whales had ended up in sections that weighed about a ton each. These "blanket pieces" were necessarily cut to manageable bits, reduced first to "horse pieces" which were subsequently sliced into "Bible leaves," which, when splayed out, resembled thick, white pages of an open book bound with tough, black skin. Mincing the fat facilitated the release of oil. Bible leaves were forked back up through the hatch to men on the deck, who tossed them into the trypots, just abaft of the mainmast.

The tryworks fire was kindled with wood but became self-supporting as soon as brown, crisp scraps floated to the surface in the two bubbling pots. Men scooped out the blubber clinkers and used them to feed the flames.

The process was a hot one. The furnace raged under already-tropical heat. Smoke and soot belched from the chimney. Steam wafted dense and stinking above the pots. Oil ladled from the trypots cooled in a tank. More bible leaves were added. And so it would continue into the night and the next day with sails aback and goosewinged until all the fat had been rendered and the cooled oil run through a canvas hose to fill casks in the hull.

The cutting-in is complete, and the deck glistens with grease. The boiling will take place in the tryworks, to the right and covered with canvas.

Feddy Lundy and Jean Paul use gaffs to push large pieces of blubber to the main hatch.

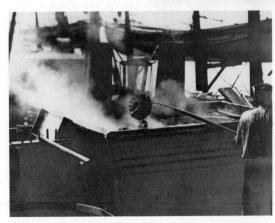

With a fork, the bibles are tossed into the try-pots. The oil is ladled into the iron pot at the left, where it will cool before it is run through a canvas hose to the casks in the hull.

Blubber oil was all very fine, but it was the animals' heads that were most valued, and because the natural state of the "head matter" was already in liquid form as it came out of the still-warm whale, the heads were handled separately.

About one-third the length of a sperm whale is forward of the skull. In that great, blunt snout was a pot of gold, as far as a whaleman was concerned. Whatever the purpose is to the whale, the material called spermaceti was considered far superior to any oil rendered from the blubber. This white wax, which hardens when cooled below body temperature, gets its name from its resemblance to semen. Spermaceti can be baled directly from the head, once an opening is cut and—in the instance of a big whale—a sailor lowered in. If the whale were small, like the first one taken by the *Daisy* and the three that day, the head could be hoisted on deck. The heads of old bulls, however, could not be lifted from the sea lest their weight break the blocks, part the hawsers, or even force the foot of the mast through the keel and scuttle the ship. The biggest heads had to be emptied while supported by water. It was worth it. A large bull could give up almost a thousand gallons of the peculiar liquid that would eventually burn in railroad signal lanterns and in parlor lamps of the New England wealthy.

The front part of the massive head is called the case. The idea was to cut the case free so it could be up-ended and opened. The top was then gingerly slit with a spade, after which a round-nosed oak bucket, was lowered inside the great, warm, sloshing well. Over and over this was repeated until the last few gallons were bailed out, and the empty purse was cast adrift to sink. Someone assigned as slick-skimmer scooped up whatever spermaceti had leaked onto the planking. Oil from the "junk" (head) was three times the value of blubber oil.

Murphy was fascinated, positioning his camera and tripod here and then there to document the moments. He was not the only creature to register the process, however. Cockroaches scuttled from the heat, moving "aft into quarters of a rising social order" not pausing at the steerage, where boatsteerers and the cooper were quartered. Neither were they

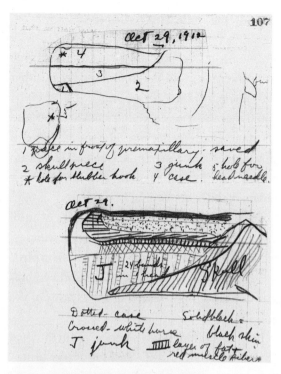

LEFT: *Murphy's cross-section diagram of the tissues lying ahead of a sperm whale's skull, including the location of the case.*

BELOW: *On a head too heavy to hoist onto the deck, a round-nosed bucket is suspended on a whip and pole from a block on the foreyard. When the last few gallons have been bailed, the case resembles an empty purse, which is then cut loose to sink.*

content with the officers' domain. They kept on their sternward trek until, in the end, there was nowhere to avoid the smoke and the heat but the Old Man's and Murphy's territory in the after-cabin.

Murphy had already noted that the ship's breed of cockroaches (and "henroaches" as he joked) was unfamiliar to him. He wrote, "One of them is not to be feared alone, at least by a man in fit physical condition and armed with a belaying pin, but three of them together could easily best and drag off a he-Airedale in the prime of life."

The insects had already made themselves at home with advances on all perishables, including "anything not soldered or welded inside seamless metal plates." They considered the leather and paper of Murphy's library a delicacy, leaving a dainty twist of "hieroglyphics and symbols pertaining to the language of the exceedingly ancient insect family of the *Blattidae*."

The insects also made intimate advances on sleepers. Murphy had already awakened several times with a gesture of "dashing a large brute" off his lips, which, in turn, escaped to his bookshelves and, from that safe distance, jeered him—or at least seemed to.

A few got what they deserved by being cooked alive. Any that wound up in the flour, for example, ran the risk of being steamed into a pudding. Murphy saw the cooper flick one off the surface of a lobscouse—salt beef hash known primarily to sailors. From the catapult of Correia's knife-point, the offender sailed across the cabin like its own ghost, through an open port and into the sea.

But Murphy was well aware of the insects' place in the natural order of things, or, at best, as the least of possible evils. As a species, its predation knew no bounds, gobbling up other vermin. Conveniently, they also ate their own eggs and young. And they would go anywhere to get at them.

By Wednesday the boiling was finished. The golden oil had been run into casks; the gear was stowed; the *Daisy* was scrubbed and tidied. A strong breeze pushed them eastward and rolled the scuppers under. Murphy occupied himself with *Hamlet*.

The Skipper pored over his Bible. A man full of pious instincts, he was rather religious but not in the least bit "churchly," griping for one reason or another about most of the sects known in the New Bedford area. Quakers led the list, probably because of their historic and famous success as whalemen, having almost monopolized the industry on the island of Nantucket. Chances are Captain Cleveland had fallen afoul of one or two astute Friendly rivals in his long career at sea.

However, he in no way limited his bitter words to one religious body. He made known his displeasure with the Episcopalians, Congregationalists, Baptists, and so on down the list.

Eventually, the dreaded question came, "Mr. Murphy, what's your religion?"

"Well, Captain," he responded. "I'm a member of the Unitarian Church, and—"

"Oh, I have *great* respect for the Unitarians," the Old Man said. "They don't believe in a goddam thing and they live up to it every day of the week, Sundays included." And with that, Captain Cleveland returned to his Bible.

They were sailing 1,800 miles east of Savannah, Georgia, in the heart of the Sargasso. Murphy landed a large barracuda and went below to load camera magazines. While he was in the dark of the ship, an order came to lower the boats. By the time he had finished with his camera, two boats had harpooned, lowered sail, and lanced a bull so large it made all previous whales—even the ones just flensed and boiled—seem insignificant.

Chapter Sixteen

IN EARLIER WHALING DAYS, when horsewhips and corset stays were still end products of an industry based partly upon bone, the returns of a voyage had been greater. By 1912, the value of oils had dropped. Spermaceti and sperm oil sold for one half or even one third of what they once had. Petroleum and electricity were taking over.

Even in the heyday, however, it was the men behind the mast who made the money. The rewards for those ahead of the mast were chiefly in the wealth of experience. A greenhand who exhibited sufficient character became—successively—boatsteerer, officer, and master—perhaps ending up as Captain Cleveland had as principal owner of two whaleships, lord of a tight little mansion on Pleasant Street in New Bedford, and likely amassing more wealth than any museum biologist ever would.

The net profits of a voyage included everything of value that could be taken. They were divided strictly in accordance with every man's share. Nothing was reserved for the skipper, owner, or anyone else. Whether a stick of timber salvaged from the sea by a greenhand or a haul of ambergris discovered by an officer, each member of the crew had a monetary interest in every addition to the cargo. Even the proceeds of the galley's soap grease were divided *pro rata*.

However, each man's lay was figured by a method that took no account of the whales actually captured during his term of service. Instead, he would be paid by the ratio of his service to the entire voyage. A man who had been a member of the crew for only six months out of a two-year trip, for example, would be entitled to one-fourth of his lay regardless of

whether whales had been captured—or even sighted—during his particular half-year aboard.

Ships were stocked and equipped by the owners, who took roughly
two-thirds off the top of the profits upon the ship's return. The remaining one-third went to labor. If there were no profits, and nothing was due
a sailor at the final accounting, a "generous" owner would give him a five-
dollar gold piece in compensation for a year or two of hard work. In the
case of the *Daisy*, Captain Cleveland would be entitled to a cut from each
side. Usually, a captain's lay was between a fifteenth and an eighth,
depending on his whaling record.

Some voyages failed so miserably they did not recover their fitting out
costs. Others, such as the *Onward* out of New Bedford, came home with
a catch of bone and oil worth nearly $400,000, which returned to her
master a lay of $40,000 and to the least member of her crew, about
$2,000. As a point of comparison, Murphy's museum salary was
increased to $125 per month toward the end of his year at sea.

By the time of the fifth whale's capture, Murphy had gotten the hang
of the process, although this bull measured close to fifty-six feet long, the
biggest so far, and therefore commanded attention for its sheer size. It
would yield more oil than that of the first four put together.

But a biologist can be as much interested in sharks as whales. While
the leviathan was being fluked, two blue sharks, accompanied by three
pilot fish each, played the part of tugboats ushering an ocean liner to the
pier. A third shark appeared, this one with six pilot fish, then more
sharks, more fish, numbering in the scores and hundreds by the time the
cutting-in had begun.

Most of the sharks seemed patient, cruising along the whale and
around the brig in a macabre procession. They were slender and sleek,
blue-gray on the upper surface of their bodies with small but conspicuous teeth, and averaging eight feet long. The species was common to the
tropical and subtropical Atlantic but one not seen as often near continen-
tal coasts.

Supper was late. In an unusual move the captain ordered a halt to the cutting-in until morning. A sixty-ton carcass could be a hazard lashed to the ship in rough seas, but the Old Man trusted the calm of the Sargasso.

The men were at it again in full force by daybreak, and the sharks had lost their apparent patience. During the dark hours they had helped themselves to innumerable neat mouthfuls of blubber, leaving white gouges in black skin. With the blubber spades working up and down again, the water became once more reddened. The sharks went berserk, jumping and wriggling around and onto the whale, where they were methodically chopped to bits by the officers on the cutting stage.

Murphy wrote, "Some were washed back into the water badly mutilated but still able to swim, and these, even though their entrails were hanging out of the side of a body that had been cut away, would turn over again toward the whale, bury their teeth, twist, yank, and swallow. I believe, though I am not quite certain, that one or more of these insensate fish were taking food in at the mouth and immediately losing it through a stomach that had been severed by a blubber spade."

Using whale meat as bait, Johnny hooked three sharks but he and Murphy succeeded in wrestling only one of them on deck. The brilliant wet back—steel blue in the sunshine—was a thing of beauty to Murphy, who excised the jaw and a piece of skin for later identification. During the process he sank a razor-sharp tooth deep into his finger—one in a long series of minor lacerations that he chalked up to getting the full experience of the adventure. Bone, spine, scale, rough rigging, and now sharks' teeth were part of the package. A little skin seemed a small price to pay.

Johnny also caught some dolphins. Their flesh, along with sperm whale meatballs and some baked beans, became everyone's supper that night. The biggest dolphin was thirty-nine inches. Murphy watched its color change as it died. Rainbow tints passed in rhythmic waves along mother-of-pearl flanks. The living fish, as it lurched helplessly on deck, had been burnished silver overall, blotched with old gold on the upper sides and back and with ultramarine spots along the flanks and belly. The dorsal fin was mixed dark blue and green, speckled with the same ultramarine as the belly. The mouth was edged in Antwerp blue. Murphy expressly noted that these colors were not figments of his imagination but were rather "pigments of precision," because he had made direct reference to the plates in his copy of Ridgeway's *Nomenclature of Colors.*

Processing the whale continued. The Old Man estimated it at eighty barrels and that it would be worth $1,300, thus elevating Murphy's wealth by $6.50.

The first four whales had been small. Each head had been hoisted on deck to get at the case, open it, and bail out the fragrant spermaceti and stringy masses of snow-white fat through the use of copper scoops. The head of the big bull alongside weighed many tons and had to be handled much differently.

The blubber had all been stripped. For the first time the Old Man himself appeared on the cutting stage. He and Mr. da Lomba worked together to cut transversely into the enormous mass of tissue, exposing the condyles of the vast skull and decapitating the whale. The head was then attached to the ship's lash rail, where it floated until the bloated, grisly carcass could be cut adrift.

Next, the entire front and upper part of the head—including not only the case but also a huge mass of fat called the junk—was severed from the skull. Case and junk were then separated from each other by cutting through a fibrous mat known as the "whitehorse," which formed a sort of floor for the case. The junk was hoisted on deck where it was chopped up for the trypots.

The great cistern of the case—with its hundreds of gallons of precious spermaceti inside—was left floating in the sea.

José Gaspar, a boatsteerer, "volunteered" to be lowered into the gory, seething waves for the purpose of preparing the fastenings on the case. He was secured with nothing more than a monkey belt, a braided rope knotted around his waist. Well-timed yanks on the rope kept the huge case from crushing him against the ship as they rolled together in the swells. Officers stood on the cutting stage, sending one shark after another to the impenetrable depths below the *Daisy's* keel.

Gaspar, between being thrown high against the slippery case to which he instinctively clung, and nearly drowning in foam and froth, completed his task of lacing a sort of web around the aft end so the heavy line from the cutting tackle could be attached. This "delicate bit of tailoring" was accomplished with a head needle—two feet long!

With the case securely stitched, Gaspar was hauled back on deck. Next time, a different boatsteerer would "volunteer," until each had had a turn in the waves.

The back end of the case was then lifted part way out of the water to be level with the ship's planksheer near the gunwale while most of the weight remained supported by the sea. Using a short-handled spade, Mr. da Lomba gently tapped his way into the store of spermaceti, exercising care not to spill. The few cupfuls that splashed on the deck were quickly scooped up by slick-skimmers, meaning anybody in the vicinity who was not already occupied.

Through a light tackle hung from the tip of the foreyard, a long, narrow, round-bottomed bucket suspended at the end of a thin pole was

Officers on the cutting stage watched for sharks while José Gaspar sewed the cut end of the head.

lowered through Mr. da Lomba's carefully made slit. The pole was used to push the bucket in and then to haul it out, full and dripping. This was repeated many times until the bucket, descending fifteen or twenty feet to the bottom, had drained the last few gallons. The luscious and valuable spermaceti was poured into butts and tubs to be boiled separately from body blubber. At the end, the great sack, emptied of its treasure, was cut adrift. Cutting-in was over. Boiling continued.

August 25th was calm, hot, and wet, with rain clearing by

noon. Blubber work was completed until the next hunt would fire up the process once more. It was Sunday. Men washed their greasy clothes. A few occupied themselves with fishing.

Precisely a quarter-year had passed since Murphy and his new wife had boarded the *Guayana* in New York, bound for Barbados. Murphy looked at the date and grew nostalgic. "Up home, it is getting near the end of summer," he wrote, "but here there are no seasonal divisions. One day is like another; save that I know this is a Sunday. In Mt. Sinai at this season they have an annual high tide, which, goaded by the same southeast wind that blows us here, floods the meadows even to my brother Ed's beehives. . . . City people pack their belongings and are gone, leaving the still warm waters of the harbor to be enjoyed exclusively by the amphibious Murphys. Then the autumn flowers appear, the first leaves begin to turn, and the woods along the Sound become full of migrant warblers, with always a rare one to be found. The brakes are peopled by woodcocks, flocking after summer; the salt meadows harbor little northern finches for several weeks, and bats fly earlier in the afternoon. . . . Oh, this is when Pan pipes in the Long Island woods and I'm not there to hear! On such mornings I used to be up with the blue jays and off to the beach and the red-cedar woods. . . . It seems as if I'd now give all the penguins of Antarctica for one glimpse of an Ipswich sparrow on the old Nonowantuc beach—with my wife beside me."

Chapter Seventeen

FOR THE REMAINDER OF AUGUST and into September, Murphy made the most of a trying situation. He was on a ship that was not getting him where he wanted to go. There was little wind to move them forward, and what slight distance they did cover took them more toward the bulge of West Africa than in the direction of the Polar South. He had not seen an albatross; he was nowhere near a penguin. And there were no more whale sightings to break the monotony.

Alternating between patience and frustration, Murphy resorted to whatever amusements and occupations he could find. He mended his clothes, writing to Grace, "Did you know I can sew the buttonhole stitch?" As practice, he painstakingly prepared a rat's skeleton, cleaning and wiring tiny bones. He studied spiders' behavior in his cabin and made notes on his observations (later published as a paper entitled "Reactions of the Spider, *Pholcus phalangioides*"). He sharpened and oiled his instruments, took naps, studied his biology books, read *National Geographic* and other magazines sent down by Grace with Mr. da Lomba, but finally entered in his notes, "I have written all I know about whaling and spiders. There are no specimens to work on. There is no one to talk to. I don't want to sleep. There is no use in staying awake."

Despite this entry, he did chat with the crew and officers. His most cerebral and satisfying exchanges were with José Correia, the cooper. Correia spoke Portuguese to Murphy's English, but they were able to come up with enough of each other's vocabulary to discuss the Papacy, the Hague Tribunal, Jules Verne's writing, Victor Hugo, Garibaldi, Francisco Ferrer, and others. These exchanges became the foundation for a mutual respect and association that would last for decades. Correia was a voracious reader—and a generous one. Mr. Vincent, for example, although he was an officer, could not decipher a single word and depended on the cooper to explain captions under the pictures in Murphy's magazines.

In addition to illiteracy, superstition permeated conversations. Johnny, the cabin boy, wide-eyed and earnest, singled out Murphy as the most scholarly of the ship's population and informed him one morning that he had seen a *sereia*, the Portuguese word for mermaid. Murphy milked the claim for all the entertainment value he could wring from it—probably at the innocent cabin boy's expense. He kept the amusement to himself, however. Correia, who was distinctly unsuperstitious, would have disapproved of Johnny making such wild claims.

On September 2nd a piece of wreckage floated along and, as was usual with flotsam, it was accompanied by many large fish. Murphy caught the first; fourteen more were successfully hooked. Murphy also collected crabs, worms, etc., before the men salvaged the nails from the sea-softened boards of what had once been part of a vessel's cabin.

Although Murphy had made good on his sham title of Assistant Navigator by assisting with navigation, it was Mr. da Lomba whose official task it was to take the longitude. But he was a man who had never attended school. He sat on deck with a slate, all arms and legs, knees crossed, twisting strands of curly hair around his finger in bewilderment and looking quite backward while trying to get the hang of adding degrees, minutes, and seconds. The mystery of logarithms was another matter altogether. Mr. da Lomba was as capable a seaman and whaleman as any that could be found, but performing a

Murphy scoffed at Johnny's claim but sketched how the sereia *might have appeared.*

task without instruction would put any man in misery. Captain Cleveland was too impatient to teach, periodically threatening to find a club to let some daylight into the man's thick skull.

Perhaps the Old Man's ill temper was brought on by a painful back. He had wrenched it while going aloft. Murphy rubbed "some sort of horse liniment from the medicine chest" along the painful area, and either that or the simple passage of time led to improvement.

The thought of the captain being even vaguely incapacitated gave Murphy the shivers. At odd moments such as drifting off to sleep, his mind opened itself to the terror of their vulnerability. If any among them were stricken with appendicitis, for example, he would die. Compound fractures did not seem out of the question, given the necessary risks taken, yet how could they be dealt with? Already, the men had begun to turn to Murphy with their minor injuries. What if something major happened? Murphy imagined, "When a troglodyte with a swollen jaw climbs out of the dark forecastle, respectfully approaches me on the afterdeck, and asks me to wrest out of his jaw the half-buried stump of a molar— with the ghastly rocker, or turnkey, which is the *Daisy*'s whole dental equipment—then, I assure you, I have to put up a hypocritical brave front to hide the quailing of a cowardly heart." With no more than a biologist's training, he feared becoming the brig's loblolly boy—or ship's surgical attendant—yet he, more than any other on board, bore the closest resemblance to anything approaching a physician.

The *Daisy*'s medical equipment became something of a morbid fascination to Murphy. The bulk of supplies consisted of Epsom salts. One potion was labeled simply as "Pain killer." Various bottles contained—or had once contained—fluids for internal and external use—or what had once been fluids and had desiccated to indeterminate powders. Bandage wrappers had yellowed, appearing to have been on board for years. There was one scalpel, an assortment of surgical needles, and a pair of forceps but no sutures. The "doctor book," which included chapters on infected wounds, fevers, scurvy, and other serious maladies fairly chilled Murphy's blood. It had been published in 1872, forty years before, when

The medicine chest, like this one, contained numbered vials, the contents of which were administered by the Old Man.

Benjamin Cleveland had been Murphy's age and was still working his way up the ranks.

At one time whaleships had carried medical chests in which vials of drugs were identified by numbers that corresponded to recommendations outlined in an accompanying list of symptoms. Murphy had heard the story of a skipper called upon to minister to a sailor with fever and stomach cramps. The skipper consulted the label inside the top of the kit only to find that vial No. 14 was empty. No matter. He pulled vials No. 6, for ague, from its compartment and No. 8, for stricture, and since the two numbers added to 14, mixed the white powder with the green liquid and headed toward the forecastle where his sorry patient lay.

As if health threats and boredom on a calm ocean as far from anywhere as everywhere were not enough bleakness to bear, meals were nothing to look forward to. Despite the cook's discovery of another tin of

Danish butter, Murphy began to wish "for the festive board of prison inmates." The Old Man had grown stingy with the sugar, making certain that others at the table would notice each time he stirred only a quarter teaspoon of the brown crystals into his coffee, after which he would grunt disgustedly, "Too sweet!" His example was not effective, however. Mr. Almeida made a habit of shoveling three or four heaping spoonfuls into his cup, while Mr. da Lomba grew impatient waiting his turn, asking to have the sugar bowl shoved within darting distance if it was not too much trouble. The Skipper grumbled and threatened that anyone with undissolved granules left at the bottom of his cup would be drinking his coffee plain for the remainder of the voyage.

Murphy, himself, had given up coffee, and the tea had long since given out. On the advice of a friend at home, he simply chose hot water. According to his notes, it "satisfies the eye, for [our water] is the color of strong tea, and when I put in a liberal supply of condensed milk and two spoonfuls of brown sugar, it satisfies the inner Bobbie as well." By calling this drink *eau sucré*, he convinced himself it was a treat.

The supply of vegetables—including potatoes and yams—had also long since given out. Meals consisted of salt meat, salt meat hash (made with hard bread and dried potatoes), baked beans, bean soup, pea soup, corn soup, canned tomatoes, and coffee. Three times a week, dessert was served at dinner: apple pie made from dried apples, mince pie, or bread pudding. Occasionally, they had rice, but the cook did a bad job with it. A couple of times a month a can of beans or peas would be opened.

Fresh fish, when they were caught, were a welcome treat, although they were invariably fried in pork fat like everything else out of the galley and like the foul-smelling salt cod the men were intermittently subjected to. The disadvantage of fresh fish was that the bones and skin would be boiled as the foundation of an alleged chowder that would show up the following day. At least there had been canned milk. The officers and the cooper, who had sailed with Captain Cleveland before, said the grub had never been so poor on his ship.

On September 4th Murphy wrote to Grace. "Something whispers to my mind that we are going to touch at the Cape Verde Islands." This would mean a restocking of provisions. But more importantly, it would mean Murphy would be able to send letters. The Old Man saw no need to inform anyone of his plans or immediate destination, however, so Murphy continued to scan the horizon for the possibility of any vessel passing close enough to hail. That would be the next best way to get letters out. A big, full-rigged ship bore toward them at one point, but the weather was too rough for a gam, or visit, and she passed about half a mile astern of the *Daisy*. Although the day was exceedingly dark with storm, Murphy photographed the ship: " a beautiful sight. Imagine an all square-sailed vessel of 2500 tons tearing along before a squall, the great spread of wings carrying her faster than a steamer. The Captain thinks she is a Spanish vessel bound for the Canary Islands."

Wind and rain came in tremendous puffs that day. Black clouds scudded across a white-gray sky. After dinner Murphy put on his long leather boots, his sou'wester, and an old rubber coat. He walked the deck in the rain, hoping with all his heart that his suspicion of touching the Cape Verde Islands was well founded. He was too proud to ask. That might seem like schoolboy hounding. What he did know was that the provisions were down to two cans of condensed milk and enough hard bread and flour to last only until mid-winter.

Chapter Eighteen

THE BRIG'S PROGRESS FORWARD had been consistently erratic. Glassy, motionless calms alternated with squally days and nights whose winds either did not last long enough or were not organized enough to get the vessel anywhere. After three months at sea, Murphy calculated they could have returned the *Daisy* to her homeport of New Bedford with a sail of no more than three weeks' duration.

September 9th brought the smoothest sea he had ever seen. The ocean lay like a polished silver plate, mirroring the sun's blinding glare, which had Murphy putting on blue-lensed glasses for protection. The air was insufferably hot. Yellowish globs of tiny marine organisms known to whalemen as *tallow drops* or *whale feed* drifted slowly past. The brig's sails were furled, as were those of the big Spanish ship that lay a few miles off, as stationary on the surface as the *Daisy*.

With Conrad as his oarsman Murphy lowered the *Grace Emeline*. Using pieces of grease from the galley, he chummed unsuccessfully for birds, fish, or anything that might be enticed to investigate a nibble on a hook. The water was dotted with an armada of jellyfish known as sallee-men, cousins of Portuguese men-of-war. Their translucent, gas-filled sails of an inch or so glinted lavender, pink, and yellow in the sun's rays, with tentacles dangling beneath. Insects left creased wakes in the flat, impressionable sea. Murphy had wanted to take advantage of the calm with a swim, but Captain Cleveland put a stop to the urge by warning, "There be wanton and scurvy sharks beneath our keel."

But even without a swim the long row in the dory was a pleasure. They ventured a mile from the *Daisy* and were 800 miles from Africa.

Presently, a petrel came along, which, when dropped from the sky with a rifle shot, proved not to be *Oceanites oceanicus* (Wilson's petrel), as Murphy expected, but *Oceanodroma furcata* (fork-tailed Storm-Petrel), like some he had shot on Long Island in 1905. The bird, a male, was in molt, but Murphy prepared the skin, enthusiastic over its value as a specimen.

As for the continuing supply of mammalian specimens for taxidermy practice, he resorted to setting spring-loaded traps below decks, since the rats had become wary of the cage variety.

The *Daisy*'s steady eastward course made it appear that the skipper was heading for the Cape Verdes. Murphy hardly dared to hope for this, but the clues were in place, including the fact that supplies were growing short. A stop for replenishing them would make sense and probably lift morale. More than fresh fruit, potatoes, and greens, however, Murphy had been monitoring the diminishing supply of tinned milk. Not that the Old Man would care much of a hoot if his men had to go without, but it so happened the Captain was especially fond of milk in his coffee. Fond enough to induce a stop? Murphy did not ask. But he watched for signs.

The vessel cut through a rippled dark-gray sea. At long last a spanking breeze came up, and she keeled over for the first time in a long while. Murphy positioned his canvas chair on the starboard, since the wind was from the east and that put him in the shade of the mainsail. He had patched the chair just recently and wrote to Grace what a blessing he felt in its comfort, adding his Brown sweater and a monocular as his second and third comforts, each of which she had been responsible for.

They were 350 miles from land. If the wind kept up, they could make the Cape Verdes in two more days. Murphy had counted on sailing the *length* of the Atlantic but not its *breadth*. The possibility of visiting new territories excited him, along with the prospect of mailing letters.

Mutton birds flew all around with an occasional petrel among them. A sperm whale was sighted but Captain Cleveland did not order the boats lowered. A gam of blackfish—mostly cows and calves—followed in the *Daisy*'s wake, but still no boats were lowered.

September 15th came up dark and blustery. A strong wind and a stronger adverse current caught the *Daisy* in an invigorating battle—a marked contrast to the sleepy stretches of the mid-Atlantic doldrums. Murphy wrote, "Mutton birds flew singly or in pairs. They did not fly near the vessel, but we passed very close to one that was feeding on what appeared to be a carcass—perhaps of a squid. The bird stood with raised wings and pecked rapidly. It did not fly until we came abreast of it. Those who have seen a marsh harrier foraging over vast windy salt meadows, alternately soaring and beating its wings, now rising, now just skimming the pulsing waves of the thatch grass, wandering capriciously, and suddenly darting downward, have a good mental counterpart of the flight of the mutton bird over the waves of the sea. Of course, the latter is longer winged and shorter tailed than the hawk."

Shortly after two o'clock in the afternoon, the loud cry, "Land ho!" rang out from the masthead. The southern point of Santo Antão—a prominence of some 7,400 feet—rose abruptly into the clouds, about twenty miles off. At four o'clock, a tired-looking European barn swallow welcomed the *Daisy* and flew on board. Murphy, in turn, thrilled to see his first wild bird of the Eastern hemisphere, greeted the swallow first by photographing it and second by gathering it in—much as he hated to— and recording it in his specimen log as #1244.

As soon as it became apparent to all that Captain Cleveland did, indeed, intend to touch land, he ended his oyster-like silence and brought out a chart of the Cape Verde islands, a tiny, drought-stricken archipelago that lies about 275 miles west of Senegal. The islands were first settled by Portuguese sailors, later joined by Africans. The volcanic land—about equal to Rhode Island in total area—is steep and dry. A connection to New England whaling began when ships, desperate for crews, regularly sailed through to pick up men eager to leave hardship behind and who would work for low pay. A trickle of immigration to Massachusetts grew to a flood through the 1800s. Most of the *Daisy*'s crew originally hailed from Brava, one of the ten islands that lie astride the mid-Atlantic trade routes.

The brig's approach was from the east. She stood offshore through the early hours of September 16th. Murphy was up on deck at the first peep of dawn. A line of stratus clouds lay low on the horizon, and only the high southern point of Santo Antão was visible. Eventually, clusters of stone buildings and red roofs emerged. They stood out against backgrounds of green terraces and steep garden plots. A white lighthouse stood partway up a hill, below which a furious surf crashed against a beachless shore. Thin streaks of sunlight leaked through slits in the still-dark clouds and illuminated the shiny sides of flying fish that leapt before a school of albacores.

According to Captain Cleveland, the natives there were among the best swimmers of the world, ranking with Hawaiians. But he also grumbled that they were a belligerent lot, often with wholesale killings of each other in monthly—or even weekly—revolutions.

The *Daisy* anchored in the harbor of Porto Grande before dark, under a clear sky. The moon rose, illuminating a jagged, crumpled horizon. "Dante might have taken his infernal inspiration here," Murphy wrote Grace. "You are a great traveler, familiar with the Alps and Rockies, eight or ten thousand feet is not much to you. But to your little Bobbie who is very provincial, these precipices and bare rocks rising straight from the Atlantic are quite awe-inspiring." Rock strata lay at all angles piled indiscriminately over the entire island, each upturned into a terminating peak. "It is the most hellish place I ever saw," he wrote of its red, desolate disarray, "and yet some of the men in the forecastle danced with patriotic joy and said, '*My country!* I not see him for years.'"

The next day a contingent of skinny, uniformed men came out in a launch. In Murphy's view they were a sad and funny-looking lot who did not treat the Old Man with the same respect that the British colonial officials had displayed. In fact, the Portuguese officials refused to board the *Daisy*. Instead, they ordered Captain Cleveland down to their launch and fairly bossed him around. He said the Portuguese were always that way. No surprise he had spoken ill of them! Murphy was amused to see the Old Man on the receiving end for a change by a "little shrimp of a uniformed puppet."

Rain fell on São Vicente that day, seven miles across a strait. Murphy asked one of the officials how long it had been since there had been rain on his own island of Santo Antão. The man replied, "Oh, it rained last year," which underscored the fact that it sometimes goes three or more years without any precipitation on the northernmost of the islands. Beyond the cultivated areas, brick-colored hills lacked much of anything green, save for an occasional clump of lavender—and even that was more gray than green.

Chapter Nineteen

FIRST AND FOREMOST was for Murphy to get himself to the post office. He had been accumulating letters written to Grace since August 5th, beginning with, "I don't know whether this letter will ever be mailed. I'm not going to put it in a bottle, but shall save it for a sure chance, which may come at any time or no time. But I saw Captain Cleveland writing a letter yesterday, so I thought it best to have one ready for an emergency . . . if I have to break off hurriedly you will understand. . . . I am well, comfortable, and happy. . . . The news and all my thoughts, I shall jot down concisely in the little red book. . . . We are going to stop at the Brazilian island of Fernando Noronha. . . . I shall send a letter from there. . . . [at Sea, September 14th] It looks now as though I were really going to be able to send a letter to cheer your heart. . . . I know how you will jump for joy when the hoped-for but hardly expected envelope comes. . . . We are bearing straight toward the Cape Verdes. The Captain hasn't volunteered any information; perhaps he expects me to ask, but if so he is not to be gratified.

"We've had calm after calm and one adverse wind after another . . . [but the] trials are nothing; they don't even ruffle my equanimity. Just bear that in mind all year, my beloved wife . . . everybody treats me with respect and kindness. The Captain has made things as comfortable as possible. . . . The members of the crew are all glad to help me when they can, because I have given them old shirts and socks from time to time, and pieces of plug tobacco when they couldn't get it from the Captain. (I don't use tobacco, but keep it for that purpose.) . . . but in general I live unto myself. Very little is said at mealtimes; the Captain bullies and insults the first mate and fires oaths at the steward. . . . I occasionally talk a little there, but spend most of my time chewing, and in consequence I'm putting on flesh.

"My daily life is something like this: —I get up at 6:30 and take a walk on deck before breakfast. Then I work at something in my outfit, or label and pack away specimens, or photographs, or get out my lines or nets and try a haul, or fish up gulf weed for crustacea. . . . When the sun gets behind the sail I open my blessed chair on the top of the cabin, and read. Fortunately I brought along enough material on the mammals to keep me busy for several years. . . . I shall be much better fitted for my work when I return . . . mastering fields I never even entered before. After dinner I work out the longitude as a rule, and then read again. I alternate the scientific reading, of course, with Dante, the Oxford book, the New Testament, etc., and have read or reread fourteen plays of Shakespeare. So you see, I'm not neglecting my mind! . . . In the evening I take a long walk on deck, if it may be called a "long" walk, standing just as straight as I can, and breathing way down to my toes. . . . I go to bed before nine.

"I hope you may use our canoe this fall. And please do your exercises every night except when you are tired. I do trapeze stunts under the main boom sometimes, and pull myself up ropes."

Thinking this might be his last chance to send letters, Murphy wanted to write some sort of prediction about when Grace might anticipate his return the following spring. In explanation of not having inquired about when the voyage might end, he told Grace "You can't depend on anything Captain Cleveland says. I have seen enough of his dealings with the crew, and heard enough of his reputation to know that he is a chronic prevaricator. Last voyage the Cooper says he lied the entire trip about when they were going in, and I could give several instances on this trip. Even when he says a thing positively and emphatically he is apt to crawl or change his mind. He doesn't get a chance to lie to me, because I avoid asking him questions. . . . If you don't hear from me from St. Helena [on the way home from South Georgia] it is no sure sign that we will go into Barbados or Dominica. As near as I can learn, there are five ports, any one of which we may touch without previous warning. . . . You can't *demand* anything of the Captain because he always falls back on the poor excuse that he doesn't know any more about it than I do."

Then Murphy asked Grace to rise above all the uncertainty of when she might next see her husband. "I am on this trip for you and me, and our success is quite independent of the meanness of Captain Cleveland. The fact that we'll be late in reaching South Georgia won't interfere particularly with my work. The weather, indeed, will be much better; it is very bad during September and part of October. The egg season doesn't commence until November either. I don't think it will make us later next spring, because the elephant season lasts only so long anyway, and besides we are not provisioned for a longer trip.

"Give my love to all the people who are helping to keep you happy during the separation, especially to your mother. And when you write my mother be sure to tell her that I'm getting stouter; that will please her most of anything."

THE TOWN OF PORTO GRANDE on Santo Antão was a busy place of 9,000 inhabitants. At the pier to greet those of the *Daisy* lucky enough to go ashore, were "business men" who had "nice gals" to let out by the hour or day. Murphy brushed past; he was focused on getting to the post office. He sent a registered letter and three picture postcards to Grace, along with other cards to his brothers and associates.

Although he dismissed the "nice gals," Murphy did note with enthu-
siasm the beauty of the native women. Most were slender— even the coal carriers around the pier and the ones pounding corn in huge mortars and the young girls who fixed their wavy hair with "Spanish elegance." Women wore bright blue and pink silk dresses with shawls, earrings, and

Murphy's first order of business at Porto Grande was to mail letters home.

bracelets. Mothers carried their babies astride their hips or strapped on their backs. The fact that the women smoked briar pipes and went barefoot around town was a discordance in femininity for which Murphy was unprepared. Similarly, he was startled to see three-quarters of the children below age ten going about dressed in nothing more than a single coral bead tied at the neck.

Murphy found the buildings of Porto Grande substantial and appealing, with shade trees gracing the streets. The chief business was that of supplying ships with coal and provisions, although most of the meat and fruit had been transported from neighboring islands. After the post office, Murphy went immediately to the office of the American Consul, where the diligence of Mr. J. B. Guimaraes, the Vice-Consul, resulted in a beautifully scripted permit to collect birds and other specimens, granted on the spot by the governor. After a pleasant breakfast with Mr. Guimaraes, Murphy set out for the country, taking Conrad with him to carry whatever they might be lucky enough to find — with the exception of any quails, which he had been asked not to shoot, since they were at the advent of their breeding season.

Which delighted Murphy more — collecting specimens or simply being off the ship for a few hours? The first wildlife he spied were white "pharaoh's chickens" (Egyptian vultures) feeding at garbage deposits on the outskirts of town. Mixed with them were ravens. Both species were

Mercado. S. Vicente C. V.

Murphy bought postcards in Porto Grande, this one of an open-air market.

tame, and it was reported that boys often caught vultures with their bare hands.

They crossed a stony, dusty plain on which almost nothing grew except lavender — three stalks to an acre, more or less. They climbed the hill above town. Nothing moved except a gecko, a variety of beetles, and a few grasshoppers. Murphy turned toward the sea, passed the white-walled cemetery, and entered a tract of tamarind where grasshoppers were so large he mistook them for birds more than once.

With Conrad as his "boy" Murphy looked every bit the part of *naturalisto americano,* as he was described in his permit letter. He wore a white helmet, a soft shirt with a tie, brown jacket, white trousers, and pigskin puttees, or leggings. He hung field glasses from his left side and his shotgun lay across his right arm. A geologist's hammer dangling from his belt completed his outfit. At a respectful distance in the rear, Conrad, as Murphy's *factotum,* carried additional impedimenta in a botanical can and a haversack.

They returned to town dusty but successful, with Conrad laden down with truck and carrying a great white vulture over one shoulder. Using words from *Hamlet,* Murphy ordered him to "lug the guts" to a waiting whaleboat while Murphy sipped a whiskey and soda with Mr. Guimaraes and the Governor.

Murphy turned in early that night. He was stiff from walking and climbing hills after months at sea. At the last minute the next morning he sent one more letter and several postcards ashore with one of the Portuguese sword-bearing guards who had been assigned to the *Daisy* while at anchor. "I hope the guard was not villainous enough to keep the stamp money and not mail the letter. I gave him 200 somethings, which were equal to half a dollar."

Captain Cleveland had loaded on potatoes, tea, fruit, salt, canned meat, onions, rice, flour, and other assorted provisions. Since he had had to pay $30 a barrel for salt meat (double the usual price) he would be cutting the crew's meat rations down to once a day. Everything else would be the same as it had been. Although the Old Man had been known to declare he could not enjoy coffee without condensed milk, Murphy's predictions were wrong. Captain Cleveland's penny pinching overcame his appetite. He had bought no milk.

Their time ashore had been short, but Murphy was pleased with his first experience in the "Old World." He had shot and collected finches

(*Passer jagoensis*) known to that island group and nowhere else, so they seemed a very good part of his haul. He packed away all his small birds and had three big ones drying.

A terrific squall sent the *Daisy* on her way, heeled over almost to the rail. They passed the island of Brava and its active volcano, Fogo, second in elevation only to Tenerife in all the Atlantic. During the night the trade wind resumed business and the brig ran well, heading south by west, which had been the point of beating north and east all along.

Chapter Twenty

MR. ALVES, THE FIRST MATE whose foot had been injured by a cart in Barbados, resigned as soon as he touched the shore of his home country. Mr. da Lomba, never having officially signed on at Dominica, took his place. His lay was recorded as one-eighteenth, second only to Captain Cleveland's. As first mate, Mr. da Lomba would be officer of the starboard whaleboat with Emiliano Ramos as his harpooner. Mr. Vincent, second mate, commanded the larboard boat with Francisco Nicolau wielding the iron. Mr. Almeida, third mate, commanded the waist boat with Antão Neves at the harpoon, which left Victor Robinson commanding the bow boat with José Gaspar as his harpooner.

Although he was the fourth officer, Victor was not addressed as Mr. Robinson, since he still resided in steerage (for want of room aft) and because he often served as harpooner when only three boats were lowered. Francisco Nicolau, called simply Frank, was not in good health and sometimes remained on board as shipkeeper when a hunt was on.

Otherwise, the formality of rank and title was strictly followed. The captain was never addressed as anything but Captain Cleveland, although he could be referred to indirectly as the Old Man—while at sea but not on land. In the privacy of his cabin, Captain Cleveland probably addressed the first mate as John, since his relationship came close to that of a foster father, but on deck or at table, it was always Mr. da Lomba.

In addition to the slight adjustment to the crew, a mongrel fox terrier had been taken on at Santo Antão. The animal was guaranteed to kill rats.

Murphy was delighted to have it aboard. "Many times a dog is better company than a man. A good dog never has moods."

The four harpooners harbored the fox terrier in steerage for three days for fear the Old Man would disapprove. However, once she was turned loose on deck, the skipper, who looked only momentarily startled, announced grimly, "Fine! We'll keep her on the v'yage to kill the rats. Her name'll be Lizzie."

But her name was not Lizzie. The Portuguese had already been calling her—and continued to call her—Cadela. With its soft, liquid "l," Murphy thought this was a beautiful and euphonious name. "Who was Cadela? Someone in history?" he asked the cooper, Murphy's best resource for such information. "Was she a queen of the Old Kingdom or is it just a girl's name?"

Correia replied simply, "Cadela ees justa *portuguesa* for bitch."

Murphy was taken aback by the casual vulgarity. Nevertheless her musical name rang out from topgallant forecastle to quarterdeck as officers and crew alike played with the pup. Of less importance was a kitten that had been brought on board. She and the dog tumbled and cavorted on the main deck. "Like other members of the crew, they are not supposed to come abaft the mainmast except on official duty. So far they have had none. In temperament they both resemble their human compatriots of the Cape Verdes, being chummy and merry."

Four days out, September 23rd, was Grace's twenty-fourth birthday. First thing in the morning Murphy opened a five-page letter that she had dated for that day but had written the previous April. Not having the slightest idea of when he would be able to post it, Murphy began his reply immediately after breakfast. Just then, however, he saw petrels astern, so he set his letter-writing aside, took Conrad as his oarsman, and lowered the *Grace Emeline*.

The birds turned out to be *Oceanites oceanicus*, Wilson's petrel, a species that migrates to the North Atlantic for the northern summer but nests in the far south during the austral summer. Murphy surmised these were headed home to lay their eggs. He anticipated seeing their chicks once he reached South Georgia—except for those of the three he shot, of course. He also collected an arctic jaeger, or robber gull, small and with a long tail.

The remainder of the day, under a hellishly hot sun, was devoted to skinning and preparing his specimens. The brig lay twelve degrees north of the equator and under a dead calm that had the *Daisy* stuck to the ocean as if at anchor.

The day before a sixty-pound albacore had been hooked from the bowsprit—so massive it took two harpoons to secure it and bring it on deck. The entire fish was fully consumed within three hours. But a bigger, private "feast" for Grace's birthday would be augmented by what her brother and sister-in-law had packed for Murphy's trunk: a bottle of Mouton-Rothschild Bordeaux.

In late afternoon, he wrapped the bottle in a wet towel and brought it on deck to expose it to whatever breeze might move across the top of the cabin. He knew from experience that evaporation would cool it. And, indeed it did, lowering the temperature of its contents from eighty degrees to sixty-six. Murphy's jaeger was prepared for dinner; the taste was fine, but the meat was tough, softened, no doubt, by the effect of the wine and the camaraderie of sharing the bottle with the captain.

It was a full-moon night on a flat sea. Murphy grew nostalgic. "If you were here," he wrote to Grace, "I'd take you for a row in the dory," and as he longed for her companionship, he envisioned the contrast of her refinement to the *Daisy*'s rough crew. In a rare moment of indulgence, he wanted to be far from their ignorant ways.

The days that followed were a mixture of heat and rain and calm. Sharks, albacores, and blackfish nosed around but none was caught. Conditions below decks were intolerable, and life on board turned dull. Cadela provided a degree of entertainment, although she was not a rat-catcher by any stretch. Most of her waking hours were devoted to ambushing cockroaches. Like a cat she would lie in wait then pounce at the first sight of a brown, varnished body.

In an effort to train her to bigger prey, some of the men took a rat from a cage trap, tied a string to its tail and turned it out on deck to see how the dog would respond. When the rat ran away from the dog, the dog followed, but when the rat turned toward the dog, Cadela curved her tail between her legs and fled. Murphy had never heard of a dog that would not shake the life out of a rat in a matter of seconds. The Old Man tried to make the point that Cadela's cowering proved she was pure "Portugee dog" through and through, an insult to the crew, which irritated Murphy no end. He could make a distinction between lack of education and the assumption of racial shortcomings.

For want of other focus Murphy logged all wildlife sightings. A butterfly hit the mainsail, then a dragonfly. Both likely had been carried on board from Porto Grande. Lice emerged from a raven's skin in large enough numbers to warrant an entry in the notes, the raven having been collected on Santo Antão. A couple more dragonflies—or darning needles—flew around. Murphy shot more petrels, another jaeger, tried to get a mutton bird and a couple of terns. A shark approached the hull, took a hook, and came on board, accompanied by three remoras. A swallow visited but did not stop. Another butterfly. A flock of white terns passed close.

They were near the equator and barely moving a ship's length. Daylight had shifted. Darkness settled abruptly after sunset, the evenings not dawdling through dusk. Breakfast was now eaten by lamplight.

On September 27th Murphy requested permission from the captain to lower his dory, as was the routine when he wanted to go birding. He took the cooper with him, and they set off in calm air on a rolling sea with swells so high that at one point, while the dory wallowed in a trough, the *Daisy* was completely obscured save for her topmasts. All else was ocean. Then, when they were lifted to the height of a crest, a big shark appeared. It circled the *Grace Emeline* and looked menacing enough to induce Murphy and Correia to pull for the brig. But the shark clung and followed, rubbing along the dory's planking and thrusting its back fin alongside. While it did not make any identifiably aggressive moves,

Murphy and the cooper had the distinct sense that the shark wanted to eat them.

As far as Murphy was concerned, the encounter came out even, because it was they who ate the shark. They lured it all the way back to the *Daisy*, where the harpooners fed it from the deck until one of them could get a hook sunk. They also hooked its hapless pilot fish.

Later that day Murphy had an upset gut, his first of the voyage. It could not have been the shark, since six others had eaten it with no ill effect. Whatever the cause, the Old Man chose not to go to the medicine chest for a remedy. Instead, in a surprisingly maternal gesture, he poured some blackberry cordial and had two pieces of toast prepared for Murphy's supper. That and a cup of tea did the trick.

With recovery came a fair wind. As Murphy lay in his berth, grateful to be feeling better, he perceived the indefinable sensations that indicated the brig was sliding forward. He hoped it would be with purpose.

But his hopes were not met. By morning, calm alternated with rain again. It was too dim to read below deck and too wet to sit above. Murphy donned his oilskins and walked the deck, discouraged and homesick. Drops hitting his sou'wester sounded the same to him as on the old shingled roof under which he used to sleep. Mt. Sinai and Long Island were a world away.

Chapter Twenty-One

MURPHY BEGAN HIS FIFTH MONTH away from home October 1st. Cadela had advanced to killing an occasional rat or two, possibly out of sheer boredom, and the kitten, only seven inches long herself, had pounced on a small victim as well. The brig was still nearly eight degrees north of the equator. Of his own boredom, Murphy wrote, "I am lonesome. I do hope it will be more exciting in the southern hemisphere, and that we will reach South Georgia before Christmas. Sometimes when I think of the calm, tedious weeks coming south I rather fear that it may be equally bad coming home. The last time they took nearly seven months from South Georgia, but then they wasted a lot of time attempting to take sperm whales all the way home. We must hope and pray for the best."

But moods could turn quickly. At nine in the morning the mastheads called out *Bl-o-o-o-ws!* in response to a sperm whale exhaling big, regular spouts to windward. While the boats were being lowered, Murphy scampered halfway up the rigging in time to be rewarded with a terrific view of the big bull as he swam across the bow. Murphy saw the whale rocking and pitching; he saw its blunt junk and hump alternately rising and falling.

Then the spout broke the surface a split second before the snout burst through. The spray of water and vapor angled forward and lasted only a couple of seconds. When the snout reached its high point—about eighteen inches above the water—the opened lips of the single-nostril blowhole sucked inward with the lungs' huge gasp. Then the head angled down; the long back rose, leveled, and gleamed. The skin looked surprisingly crinkled and rubbery. The angular hump pitched above water, briefly exposing the lesser knobs and notches along the back's crest between the hump and the flukes. When the hump reached its highest, the junk was submerged to its lowest and vice versa, all in rhythm of apparent ease despite the beast's impressive mass.

And then the whale was out of sight. Murphy was ecstatic over his close-up view. A Melville quatrain from *Moby Dick* came to him, which he spontaneously set to his own melody.

> Oh the rare old Whale, mid storm and gale
> In his ocean home will be
> A giant in might, where might is right,
> And King of the boundless sea.

Despite the excitement, an hour later the boats returned empty-handed, the whale long-gone and no others on the horizon. Murphy watched the whaleboats skimming over calm water toward the brig and marveled again at their design, efficiency, and the leverage of their long oars. Each rower sat far opposite—or athwart—his oarlock. Second in length to the twenty-three-foot steering oar was the midship oar, eighteen feet. Its oarlock was fixed to the starboard gunwale. Bow and tub oars, respectively fore and aft of the midship oar, were shorter and identical in length, both resting on the port gunwale. Harpooner and after oars (the stroke oars) were shortest of all and were likewise identical in length; those were nearest bow and stern. Their oarlocks were mounted on the starboard; so, the distribution of power was one long and two shorts to starboard working against two mediums to port.

Sometimes the whaleboats became widely scattered during a hunt, such as the following morning when an entire pod of whales was sighted. One of the three lowered boats went so far toward the horizon it could no longer be seen from the brig. By half-past three, the trio of boats returned, each towing a small whale. Mincing, boiling, hacking, and stripping commenced right away, and the brig was at a standstill once again. Murphy saw the cutting-in as an impediment to achieving his own goals, especially since the whales did not amount to much. "We are cut-ting whales again—3 miserable little sperms, the biggest not more than 30 feet long. It means about 24 hours more of tiresome lying-to. . . . Lunch was served [late] and was such a poor one I had to resort to my trunk."

Others might have succumbed to a permanent state of sulking, but Murphy's incessant curiosity got the better of him again—that and a supper of whale meat, corn hoecakes, and hash made with onions. The opportunity to extract a four-inch round worm from a whale's blubber and plop it into a specimen bottle was more than enough to rekindle Murphy's glee. Also, the three captured whales gave him more measure-ments to take. He had already noted considerable proportional variation in the length of the head forward of the mouth and of the maxillary pro-jections (jaw). He also noted how limber and flexible their bodies were, the length of them undulating with the motion of the waves.

The men hoisted mountains of blubber aboard. When the blubber parlor overflowed, they heaped the stuff on the main deck. Continuing in a state of observation, Murphy wrote, "I stayed up until all hours, watching every process, . . . sitting atop the cabin, in a whaleboat on the davits, or anywhere else that offered a good view. If there is any modern counterpart of an uncouth revel around a witches brew, it is the scene of the trypots at night.

"It was eight bells (midnight) when we had cut-in the final fish. The Daisy, with topsails aback, rolled gently in the quiet swell, while the officers on the cutting stage punched with their spades as best they could in the dismal light of lanterns and oil-soaked torches. The flickering glare showed the hulk of the whale alongside and the flash of bloody wavelets beyond. On deck a cresset, or bug light, of burning blubber scrap, and the fiery chimneys of the tryworks in full blast, cast enough illumination to reveal the great blankets of blubber and the greasy, toil-ing figures scurrying about amid the shouting of orders, the creak of tackles and the clank of chains. At six bells the last strip came over the plank-sheer. The severed head of the whale floated at the starboard quarter, lashed securely and ready to be handled at daybreak. Only the rite of the whaleman's ultimate hope remained to be carried out before the flensed carcass should be cut adrift."

The rite Murphy wrote of was the exploration of the whale's intestines for ambergris. "The Old Man joined his officers on the cutting stage. Then, with methodical movements, he and the three mates thrust freshly sharpened cutting spades deeply into the guts of the whale, twisted them, cautiously withdrew them, smelled the bright steel blades, and scrutinized them painstakingly in the glow of a lantern, while the crew looked on in fevered anticipation. Back and forth along the stage the four men trod and jabbed, until the vitals had been intimately explored. But nary a whiff of the longed-for odor. . . . 'And so to bed.'"

In the morning there was a mess of blubber to process. By the time the carcasses were cut adrift and the spermaceti was bailed from the cases, every member of the crew had reached the point of near collapse from "hustling, hauling, chopping, lashing, stowing, rocking the windlass, and slipping galley-west on the greasy planks." They were ready to begin the boiling.

Some skippers used to allow a pleasant interlude between cutting-in and cooking — a break known as "splicing the main brace," when each sweaty man would file to the quarter deck and gulp down a tot of rum. No such custom prevailed on the *Daisy*. Captain Cleveland felt there was already too much drinking (and profanity) in the world. He was not about to indulge his men in more.

The blanket strips were cut into slabs about two feet

Jean-Baptiste, on the left, works with Ferleão to cut horse pieces, which will then be minced for rendering.

long and as wide as the blubber was thick. These were slung by long-handled two-pronged forks into heaps along the port rail to be minced with huge, double-handled drawknives. One man held a meat hook and pushed the horse pieces along a table while another slashed across and back with the drawknife, cutting the strip into thin slices—not fully severed but left clinging to the skin to create the bibles. The purpose of all this slicing was to maximize the surface so heat could penetrate the fat and extract all the oil.

The primary component of the tryworks was a pair of enormous iron pots on the forward deck. They were supported by a brick firebox, which was insulated from the wooden deck by a water bath. The minced strips were cooked until they released their oil and rose to the bubbling surface, crisp and golden brown. These clinkers then became the fuel for the fire beneath in the self-supporting process. The boiled-out blubber scraps of one victim were used to cook the next. Although they were drained before being fed to the already-roaring flames, the clinkers burned blistering hot, leaving almost no ash.

The boiled oil, clear and amber, was ladled from the pots into a rectangular iron tank called the cooler, before entering the canvas hoses for storage below. At that point the *Daisy* could get underway, and the mastheads could remount their perches. The deck was scoured, the rigging was cleaned of grease and soot, and the watch—under the cooper's supervision—ran the oil through the bungholes of the great casks in the hold. All this was going on when the Old Man cast a weather eye aloft and ordered the mastheads to look sharp and raise the next whale. He was in no mood to waste time

In truth, everyone longed for the next crack at hard labor because each barrel of oil was one step closer to having a full ship. As soon as the barrels were full the brig would be homeward bound.

A school of blackfish lay close the next afternoon. The boats had been lowered to go after sperms again, but porpoises cavorted about the whales thick as fleas, as Mr. da Lomba put it. They scurried around the whales, "sprang over them by the dozens and galleyed them so that the

Viewed from the shrouds, crisp scraps of cooked bibles rise to the surface of the bubbling fat. These, in turn, are fed to the flames under the pots. On a good day the cook would fry doughnuts.

whales were exceedingly wary." Whenever the boats approached, the whales would let go and sink into green depths. One small porpoise was harpooned. A shark immediately sensed the carcass and began following. "It is uncanny the way they appear on the scene whenever there is anything dead in a boat, be it a porpoise, fish, or petrel."

Three other vessels were in sight on the horizon that day, one of which—a big bark—ran abreast of the *Daisy*. Murphy was suddenly up to his ears in things to watch. In addition to monitoring the far-off vessels, he had a porpoise to skeletonize, new species of fish to identify, birds to photograph, and parasites to pickle. While the crew slithered around on greasy decks again, toiling at night by the flaring light of oil-soaked rope ends, Murphy got back to work recording the details of anything that moved or breathed.

Petrels were all about. One was attracted to the glare of the nighttime tryworks operation. In his excitement to catch the bird, Murphy lunged and slipped on the oily deck, striking his head on the iron corner of the main hatch. It did not knock him cold, but the impact made his head spin and ache for a good part of that night. While he lay in his berth nursing the lump behind his ear, the crew caught two of the birds, which Murphy then photographed in the morning. After taking their pictures he fitted one with a numbered aluminum band from the American Bird Banding Association and gave him his freedom. The other was dispatched for its skeleton.

Porpoise meat was served for lunch, which, in Murphy's view was only so-so, but porpoise liver was a hit. They also ate a blue-lined runner, a kind of fish streamlined for apparent speed, forty inches long and thin as a spindle. It had contained a double skein of eggs that Murphy thought were as toothsome as shad roe. The captain opened another tin of Danish "ladies' butter." This pleased Murphy to no end. "Nothing ever seemed better. I ate several biscuits and spread them thickly with the golden luxury."

With all the activity on deck, Murphy had been taking lots of pictures. At night he developed them by the oil-burning, ruby-colored safe light in his cabin. He was thrilled with the results: leaping porpoises, flying petrels, their crew of whalemen cutting in. But Sunday, October 6th, the shutter on his Graflex jammed.

Murphy's Graflex was a large-format bellows camera. Much of the success of his expedition depended on the photographs he would be bringing back home. If the camera gave out, a large part of the year would be wasted.

Captain Cleveland was sympathetic. He offered his assistance as Murphy cautiously disassembled the camera's mechanism. Hours later, after tense scrutiny of how the parts fit together and after meticulous reassembly, the shutter was still jammed. Murphy was almost undone, frustrated that the manufacturer published no directions for getting at the problem the way gun manufacturers routinely did. Discouraged, he set the camera aside.

The following day with renewed patience and determination and with the continued assistance (or at least moral support) of Captain Cleveland, Murphy worked all morning at doing what he could with the camera, figuring, probably, he had not much to lose, since the mechanism was useless as it was. He took the instrument all to pieces and had a terrible time getting everything back where it belonged. "I learned its anatomy readily enough," he wrote, "but its *physiology* troubles me." But finally, the problem was identified and solved: a clogged shutter mechanism, which was cleaned, oiled, and put back into service.

With the confidence of success, Murphy was ready to tackle any kind of troublesome gizmo. "Before my siege with the Graflex, I would never have had the nerve to examine the 'innards' of so delicate an instrument as a reflecting camera. But now nothing is too complicated for my mechanical genius. I could mix up the works of six watches, a chronometer, a gun, and a sewing machine—shake them in a bag, and then assemble them without hybridizing!" So, he took on another camera, an old Reflex, moldy and rusted to start with but clean, oiled, and operational by the time he finished.

The *Daisy* was running west by south before the monsoon wind that had been blowing for several days. The big bark on the horizon, estimated at more than 2,000 tons and with her nineteen swelling sails, continued parallel.

October 7th was stormy and dark all day. Just before nightfall the crew caught an albacore. Murphy examined its stomach contents to find two species of small fish, a small crab, and a snail looking fresh enough that it might not have even been dead. The snail confused him, since that would indicate proximity to land. But the nearest islands, St. Paul's Rocks, were 440 miles away. With a little research he identified the delicate creature as a member of the *Janthina* family, a snail that lives by building itself a raft of bubbles. It was related to the Mediterranean species once used to prepare a dye called Tyrian purple. The one in his hand was the first such example Murphy had seen, and he was grateful to the albacore for its delivery to him.

The next morning a man fell sick, too sick to report for duty. The Old Man examined him and fetched some medicine. The sailor refused to take it. The skipper then gave him ten minutes in which to make one of three choices—join his watch on the job, take the medicine, or be put in irons. Not choosing either of the first two options, he was assisted aft by two of his fellows to be confined to the lazaret. This was a grim reminder of the Old Man's authority. At midday and evening, the hatch was lifted, one handcuff unlocked, and hard bread and water were passed down. At nightfall the man received a blanket. "What a prospect!" Murphy wrote. "Sick, manacled, lying on a coil of rope, in a sort of maritime dungeon that stinks of bilge and paint . . . but as the skipper says, he remains there only at his will."

After a day and a half of incarceration the man agreed to swallow the dose of medicine. The captain went to the lazaret with a spoon and a bottle of God knows what, and, after a gulp of the stuff, the sailor was free to walk to the bow on his own, appearing in better shape than on the previous day. Murphy surmised that thirty-six hours of essentially going hungry might have been the cure his insides had needed all along.

With a thin new moon rising, Captain Cleveland called Murphy to notice the evening star. A big bank of cottony clouds had hung in the west since mid-afternoon, making for a glorious sunset. Blazing above the edge of the clouds was Venus, "shining as she does only in equatorial climes . . . brighter and larger than I knew a planet could be. To the north of her was Mars, as ruby as wine, but the great radiating light of the goddess will be fixed in my mind forever."

Chapter Twenty-Two

THE MORNING OF OCTOBER 10TH BROKE gray with a strong wind whipping the ocean. The mastheads stood watch, as they did in almost all conditions. At eight o'clock a squall brought a torrent of rain, which was just at its height when a school of sperm whales rose only a few hundred feet to windward. The boats were cleared on the davits at once and all hands stood by. The rain slackened and the weather brightened enough to see two pods of whales spouting. Captain Cleveland shouted, "Lower away!" and the order was echoed in confirmation.

Up until then, Murphy's observations of the actual hunts had been from the deck or the rigging of the *Daisy*, and often the whaleboats were at a great distance from the brig. Murphy wanted a first-hand view. With the combination of courage and Captain Cleveland's permission, Murphy chose that morning to slip down a slide board into Mr. da Lomba's boat. There was no place for a passenger; so substituting for a Dominican greenhand, Murphy took stroke oar like a veteran. The greenhand remained with the shiptenders in Murphy's place.

The whales' spouts were moving quickly to leeward, so Mr. da Lomba ordered his crew to step the mast of their boat and raise the sail, but because the wind was brisk and the sea choppy, the sail was immediately reefed. The whales sounded, indicating that they were foraging and not the least alarmed by the boat's presence, its zigzagging, or its jibing.

Men hastened to put all gear at the ready. They lashed the line tubs to the thwarts, poured sea water over the rope, and watched the *Daisy* for signals, since it was the mastheads who had the advantage of standing above the waves. As soon as Mr. da Lomba saw the blue waif that signaled "whales up" he pulled sharp on the tiller to jibe in the direction the mast-heads indicated with their flags. The boat made off before the wind, flanked by the two other whaleboats running abreast.

By this time the rain had returned, and the deluge soaked everyone to the skin.

The boats bore down toward the school, now steaming and puffing at the surface in preparation for the next big dive. Just then two bulls popped up unexpectedly ahead. The nearer of the pair came for the boat's bow. Mr. da Lomba's harpooner, Emiliano, ready and cocked in position, held steady until boat met beast.

Emiliano drove the iron hard into the whale's right side, just ahead of the hump. The whale leaped forward, his whole massive head breaching above the surface, his flukes grazing the keel as he dashed past. The wet harpoon line tautened and groaned as it ran out around the loggerhead, pulling the boat behind.

Sail was dropped, mast lowered, and rudder unshipped as they skimmed the waves under whale power. The harpooner and mate changed ends to set up the mate for the ticklish business of lancing the whale once they drew up to the prey. But a surprise lay ahead.

"Our whale's run was for only a short distance. Coming up with others of the school, he joined them, and we could see him lying calmly at the surface. We four oarsmen now hauled line, the boatsteerer holding the turn around the loggerhead and coiling slack in the stern sheets as it was paid in. We pulled as hard and as fast as we could and, when we neared the whale, a strange sight was presented through the curtain of rain. Our whale lay wallowing, the harpoon shaft projecting from his blubbery back; beyond him were three or four half-grown calves. On the near side lay a second bull, belly up, his jaw and most of his head out of water, and our harpoon line caught between two of his teeth.

"Mr. da Lomba gesticulated frantically for the other boats to come up, and we waited silently but in a shiver of impatience. Before Mr. Vincent's boat could arrive, the bull which had fouled our line and which had probably been puzzled by the obstacle, allowed it to slip from his jaw. We then hauled up on the whale to which we were fast and, when the keel pressed his side, the mate drove in the long keen lance to the socket. Within the same instant the hump hove up, the great flukes reared into the air, our bow went down with a jerk, and we shipped a couple of barrels of waters as the whale sounded."

"Forty-barrel bull!" Mr. da Lomba shouted.

Galvanized by the announced estimate, Murphy's thoughts leaped to what the Old Man had said weeks ago, that a forty-barrel bull is at his prime, probably experiencing the most vigorous period of his watery life. Others may be bigger or might yield more oil, but none is likely to make as much excitement for a boat's crew as one that size. This might have been more than Murphy had bargained for on his first venture into a whaleboat.

It was not yet nine o'clock in the morning. They bobbed about on the sea for fifteen minutes, waiting to see where their prey would emerge from his dive. The line was snubbed well around the loggerhead, slackened by Emiliano as little as necessary while still keeping a safe distance from the injured—but submerged—animal. Finally, an eruption of vapor appeared to windward; the wounded head—lopsided now—burst up and began to oscillate with the hump in a vigorous run. The whaleboat began what would become a nine-hour Nantucket sleigh ride.

Mercifully, the sun had broken through the clouds, thawing out the drenched and chilly men as they strained at the line and hauled it in, gradually gaining on their harnessed beast. But the beast was aroused, fully alert, and nowhere near surrender. The lance puncture had not done enough damage to slow him down. He sounded again, jerking the boat, pulling it swiftly across two miles of ocean.

The whaleboat carried two line tubs, the large one containing 200 fathoms neatly coiled. But 1,200 feet was not enough. The whale plunged deeper, drawing more and more line smoking with friction around the loggerhead. The men added the length of the small tub—100 fathoms more—but it quickly became evident that their 600-foot extension would be exhausted. Eighteen hundred feet in all, and the men were about to reach the end of their rope. Just in time one of the other two boats sailed alongside, and they bent on borrowed line.

Murphy was putting all he had into the effort but he later wrote, "In the middle of this fight . . . I confess to a certain sympathy with the enemy. It seemed reasonable at least that after being pricked with the harpoon that still galled him, and pierced through with the horrible lance, the whale should wish to steer clear of us. This, however, was not at all the mate's idea of good form and fair play. Standing like an armed crusader in the bow of the boat, Long John da Lomba would scratch his head after the whale had sounded, and mutter, 'I cain't understan' what make that animile so goddam shy!'

"Our status, I thought from time to time, was that of the tin can on a dog's tail. We annoyed the whale, but were otherwise pretty helpless.

"Time flies with a fighting whale on one's hands. The sun climbed to the zenith and its pleasant beams alternated with cold showers while we sped over the rugged, white-capped Atlantic, wearing the skin off our palms in this yet undecided tug-of-war."

The whale battled valiantly for his life, sounding, spinning, running. At one point he swam against the resistance of three whaleboats and two drogue tubs, one of which was said to equal the drag of four boats. It is a wonder the harpoon was not ripped from its purchase on the animal's blubber.

John da Lomba, Mate.

But the harpoon held fast. Midday brought the roughest phase of the struggle when the whale pulled the boat cross-sea over troughs and crests. Combers slopped over the gunwales, and the situation looked sufficiently grave for the men to kick off their oilskin pants, the better to swim unencumbered, should swimming become necessary. Murphy was the only man wearing shoes. Those came off, too. Over and over the bow was pulled completely under. Three times they half swamped. The whale stole line while all hands bailed. The piggins and even the men's sou'westers were put to almost continuous use trying to slosh water out of the boat faster than it came in.

Murphy wrote, "I have a dreamlike mental background for the day's play—the choppy, spumy water and the varying sky, the heliotrope Portuguese men-o'-war that seemed to bob past us, the bright flying fish scared up, the inquisitive Mother Carey's chickens that fluttered astern; and focus of it all, straight ahead, the rocking, shiny back of our forty-barrel bull, with an impertinent little harpoon sticking there."

All this time the brig shunted and hovered about, now abeam, now off the bow, now astern. Fortunately, the whale was generally moving in wide circular tracks. If his path had been a straight line he would have pulled the boat dangerously far from the brig and the men would have had to give up and cut themselves free.

More than once the men slackened the line, trying to give one of the other boats an opportunity to approach the whale and plant a second harpoon, but the brute was too wary. "When the boats came ever so softly within three or four lengths, he would kick up his big flukes and be gone. Mr. da Lomba eventually shot a bomb lance into the whale's back, but the rubber-feathered end of it broke off and went whizzing over the sea, while the cylinder failed to explode. Three more bombs from a shoulder gun were likewise vainly spent, and the mate concluded that the charges were water soaked.

"The turning point of the struggle came when the frantic whale once more fell in with a gam of his fellows. The calming influence of neighbors was soon apparent, for he allowed us to draw right toward him. We pulled ourselves through an acre of sperm whales, big bulls that we might have touched with oars, cows at arms' length, and tiny calves, ten or twelve feet long, with huge remoras clinging to their flanks. Such company lay unconcernedly awash all about us, but we paid it scant attention because it is quite sufficient to be fast to one sperm whale at a time."

"Shush, easy, easy boys," whispered Mr. da Lomba; "trim the boat." He reminded them not even to shift their quids—slang for plugs of tobacco—from one cheek to the other.

They hauled up and came softly along another whale. When their line was "as short as a dog leash," the mate braced himself in the *clumsy cleat*, a plank at the bow of a whaleboat that was notched for the exact purpose of an officer fitting his left thigh into a steadying position while thrusting the lance. Mr. da Lomba raised his long powerful arms and buried the five-foot shank into fat and flesh. The whale quivered and sank.

All eyes peered tensely over the side of the boat. They knew the sounding would be brief and that the whale could surface anywhere—including underneath their boat.

"Stern all!" The whale rose under the keel, nearly capsizing the boat but not quite. The mate thrust his lance two—maybe three—times more through froth and fury, and the whale got under way once more for another lap of the race.

Once again the men were drenched. Again, they bailed and hauled. They slackened and hauled, bailed, hauled and slackened and bailed.

In the meantime Mr. Vincent's boat had returned to the *Daisy* to pick up a case of dry bombs. These were transferred to Mr. da Lomba's boat. The sun had slipped into late afternoon. Again, they entered a group of whales—including the one they had been fixed on for so many hours—and Mr. da Lomba succeeded in shooting a bomb into the animal's lungs, where it exploded with a muffled crack.

The whale leaped one last time, half filling the boat with water, but he no longer had breath enough to sound. His spout, which had been thin, white, and delicate while making rainbow prisms with the slant of the setting sun, became pink, then crimson, then thick with blobs of blood.

"His chimney's afire!" said Mr. da Lomba with a heartless chuckle.

It was six o'clock. Mr. Almeida's boat came up and thrust more lances between the whale's ribs. Sharpened steel sank deep and churned flesh in a gruesome flurry. All the while squid poured in belches from the creature's gullet until the boats floated on a slimy pool of their remains.

Nine long hours after sinking the harpoon, the whale died and turned fin out. The men chopped a hole in one of his flukes, attached a line, and rested. Murphy was weary but content. There was hard bread to eat from the lantern keg, and fresh drinking water. They waited the arrival of the brig, which was luckily windward and therefore able to sail toward them. The sun set on a calm sky. Mars hung "like a lamp on the waters when the *Daisy* bore down and gathered us in."

Murphy was exhausted. His hands, cut a thousand times by the rope, were stiff and swollen. He stumbled to his cabin, found his pen, and, under the dim flicker of his lamp, wrote, "This has been the most exciting day of my life."

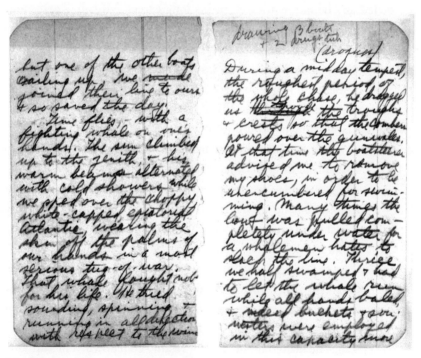

Murphy's journal entry describes going after the forty-barrel bull.

Chapter Twenty-Three

THE MEN WERE IN A FINE STATE of mind during the cutting-in, belting out verses—bawdy and otherwise—of *Whiskey Johnny* and *Sally Brown* and *Blow the Man Down*, singing at top volume as they worked. Mr. Da Lomba's estimate had been close. "Murphy's" whale tried out forty-seven barrels of oil. The long struggle in capturing the bull was the talk of the ship. The Old Man admitted the effort exceeded any he had witnessed in his long career. Murphy's arms and back ached for days.

The *Daisy* was decidedly in whale territory. No sooner had the cutting-in begun on one carcass than spouts were seen in the distance. Some got away. Others did not.

On one unsuccessful hunt Mr. Almeida made the mistake of harpooning a large, unusual dolphin for Murphy's sake. Captain Cleveland took this to mean that Mr. Almeida had been more fixed on appealing to Murphy's scientific interests than the primary business of the voyage. There had been a similar, recent episode in which Mr. da Lomba brought back a specimen but no whale, but the Old Man apparently had more faith in his first mate's judgment than his third mate's—possibly because Ben Cleveland and John da Lomba had a personal relationship.

In any case the skipper flew into a rage as soon as he saw the carcass in Mr. Almeida's boat. Murphy wanted the dolphin. He had a hard time intercepting and reversing the captain's order to pitch it overboard but eventually succeeded. This did not turn the Old Man's mood around, however. Once he heated up he did not readily cool down. The captain's anger seemed to spin itself in higher and higher spirals, and while continuing to direct the cutting-in and trying-out, he started in on a whole-sale assessment of the third officer's "ancestry, complexion, character, courage, and ability." Captain Cleveland spun himself to a level of vulgarity that he would not have tolerated from others. His hairy-chested name-calling rang out across the deck and fell upon the waves. The browbeating reached a painful degree of cruelty to which Mr. Almeida made no reply and that others met with disapproving silence.

The tone remained icy. The next morning was Columbus Day. Murphy started to thaw out an exceedingly frigid breakfast atmosphere by singing to the skipper, two officers, and the cooper a silly song about the historic landing in the New World 420 years before.

At least he had his dolphin. The fateful specimen proved to be *Lagenorhynchus electra*, reportedly rare and never before captured in the Atlantic. Scientifically significant or not, it was the first of Murphy's specimens in which the Old Man took no interest whatsoever.

The crew was boiling blubber while under sail. Their operation belched a black trail over the waves. Suspended above the tryworks was a smoke sail, but it kept only a small portion of the soot out of the after cabin, and it kept none of the men's faces clean. Their already-dark skin was darkened more, as if rubbed to gleaming with stove polish. Murphy thought they looked like a minstrel show on Noah's Ark.

Work continued through the night with the fires under the trypots blazing and the bug light burning bright. By morning the *Daisy* was scudding along to the best breeze she had had since leaving the West Indies, running southwestward and pitching among the whitecaps.

Grateful for forward motion at last, the crew hoisted an additional sail, the fore-royal—the fourth and highest up the mast, small, and used in light winds. But they quickly thought better of it and furled the square canvas. Not long afterward the main boom cracked. The crew scurried next to take down the mainsail immediately, and they set to work fitting iron hoops to "fish the spar," which meant splinting the mast with a long, auxiliary timber.

With their steady progress—even with the excitement going on in the

José Gaspar stands at the tryworks under the smoke sail as the chimneys belch soot. On the right, men scramble with bible pieces.

rigging—Murphy was keenly aware of the ship's latitude. He was excited about crossing the equator. In anticipation he had prepared something to mark his entry into the southern hemisphere. Also anticipating one last opportunity to mail letters home, he wrote to Grace, "By now the motion of the ship seems perfectly natural. This morning I shaved without the slightest difficulty, although everything was sliding around on the floor." Murphy used a straight razor all his life; no doubt it took some getting used to, angling that blade against his throat as the

Murphy illustrated their rough conditions in his letter to Grace.

ship rolled and pitched unpredictably. He continued, "I was thinking how pleased you'd be if you could see me, because my cheeks are so plump and I have good color. I do hope I may continue to gain in health and come home to you with all my accumulated improvements. . . . One of my best is my beautiful moustache. . . . We are one degree from the Equator and there is a bottle downstairs all sealed and flagged and containing a little note, to you, my Grace, which I shall drop over as soon as we cross the Line."

The weather had been prevailingly cool. Bundled up, Murphy continued to occupy his chair on deck and write, "You ought to see me eat of late! Never have I had such an appetite. It may be due to cool weather, because for a week or more it has been necessary for me to wear a sweater most of the time, even at midday. My dear old watch, which I'd been thinking of giving to my brother Dan on my return, has been ruined beyond repair. While chasing friend whale, the old timepiece filled with water and is a mass of rust inside and out. Moreover, it broke both crystal and mainspring, so that it is a hopeless wreck. I shall miss it for practical reasons, and also because it was my first gift from my wife-to-be and her mother.

"I feel happy as I write this in thinking that my two letters from St. Vincent must have reached you by this time, or at any rate, the registered one.

"We are running WSW at a terrific rate, lying over on our beam ends, before the S. monsoon. It picked us up a week ago and has carried us . . . across the Atlantic in racing style. It is the first respectable wind of the whole cruise. Last evening the Captain told me that he was going to Fernando de Noronha. The mails from there are just as they happen, but I'll leave this letter and trust to Fortune that it will be delivered when you least expect it. A line or two coming some morning just before breakfast must make quite a commotion in the Barstow household, and subsequently among a little circle of relatives. I hope too that it will help to keep the sunshine in your heart for a long time. Let this letter assure you at the outset that I am happy, busy, and well fed—in splendid condition save for a cut 2.8 millimeters long on the post-axial surface of my right index finger (covered by a piece of your adhesive plaster).

"Since leaving the Cape Verdes I have gathered many specimens, in the way of birds and porpoises mostly. One of the latter doesn't seem to conform to any known species. For a couple of weeks we had continuous calms, and I was frequently down in the dory on the great Atlantic, collecting petrels and jaegers (parasitic gulls that steal other birds' food). I never returned to the brig empty handed. The Captain and crew don't like calms, of course, but I'm hoping for one or two when we get well into the South Atlantic, where there is such an abundance of birds.

"The notes and photographs are still coming along rapidly. Photography is getting to be second nature to me, and I'll surely have something worthwhile to show from this trip.

"It is funny to be absolutely cut off from the world for so long. The Consul at St. Vincent gave me several fairly recent N.Y. 'World's', but they didn't contain much intelligible information. In a couple of weeks we'll be having a new president—I suppose he'll be a new one. It is queerest of all to have to wait months and months, for such news as that.

"It has been cool down here lately. Yesterday we passed from autumn to spring in as much time as it takes the ship's length to pass a given point . . . and I suppose it will grow warmer for a while as we catch up with the sun.

"I am still doing a fair amount of reading, mostly on the mammals, though not so much as formerly, because my porpoise skeletons take a good deal of time. From now on I shall probably become more and more busy as the bird life increases, and at South Georgia, of course, I shan't be able to look at a book except for an occasional reference to help me in my work. I am very thankful for all the time I've had for reading and study. It has been a great help to me.

"The letter bag is the best of all my outfit. It is a continual encouragement. Your uncle's letter, in which he said again that I ought to write a book, redoubled my energy in taking notes. Dr. Lucas's letter I am holding unopened for the day of the first albatross. But your own sweet notes are best of all, and I'm always happiest when I find one of them.

"We've been rushing like a steamer all day. The old Daisy can surely fly when she has a breeze. Only think—a few days ago we were off the African coast; now we are less than two days' sail from Brazil.

"I judge more than ever from my talks with the Captain, that we shall be home fairly early next year, because we are provisioned for a limited time only. Since leaving the Cape Verdes we have had a fine variety of food, including delicious beans, peas, white potatoes, and onions. We also have various Portuguese mixtures of corn, peas, and sweet little red beans. One called curchupe is delicious. The bread, baking powder biscuits, and cakes have been specially good lately, and apple pie desserts have been increased to three times a week. So you see, life is quite worth living. I eat like a bear. Next to eating, sleeping is my strong point. The Captain says he never saw anyone slumber so like a log.

"The 19th of this month is the Captain's birthday. Without saying anything I'm going to find something special in my trunk and have it brought on at dinner. Yesterday was my brother Tom's birthday if I'm not mistaken. I'll be glad when mine comes.

"It is getting late for me—8:30, so I must close. I want to be up betimes for we may sight land early. I'll write more tomorrow, and get a few lines ashore, so as to tell you my experiences up to the last minute—Land ho! They have just sighted the lighthouse. We shall have to lie off until morning. It is quite thrilling. I'm going on deck a while before turning in, so as to see the light. Goodnight—"

At some point late that night, or early the next morning, the *Daisy* slipped unceremoniously over the equator. This geographic achievement brought out the boy in Murphy. He noted that even in the bottom half of the world, east still seemed to the east, and west to the west, and that he appreciated no sense of standing on his head. "In fact, it looks, sounds, and feels just like plain Long Island Sound, except that it is very rough and there is no land in sight."

A white booby flying across the deck indicated that the ship was bearing rapidly past St. Paul's Rocks, which lay northward and leeward. These uninhabited outcroppings are 540 miles off the coast of Brazil. They lie directly between the Cape Verde Islands and Fernando de Noronha, the *Daisy*'s immediate destination. Darwin had visited both these island clusters on the *Beagle*, so Murphy's interest was keen.

As the brig continued at a fast clip through the blue headwaters of the Gulf Stream, three boatsteerers on deck hulled corn for *samp*, a Narragansett word for a kind of porridge similar to hominy grits. Unlike the New England method of soaking the kernels in lye, the boatsteerers used five-foot pestles in a mortar carved from a section of tree trunk. They struck a beautiful rhythm. Each blow seemed to keep time with the rocking and leaping of the brig, and wind whisked the loosened hulls out of the mortar without requiring a winnowing process. Normally, such work would have fallen to deck hands, but the three strong boatsteerers, Antão, Emiliano, and Victor, pounded for the sheer fun of teamwork and the singing blows—one, two, three, one, two, three, which Murphy fantasized as an ancestral memory of tribal dance among their forebears.

For two days the *Daisy* ran freely, canting well over to starboard. A gathering presence of passing sea birds told the men, as they once told Columbus, of the nearness of land. At nine in the evening, the revolving light of Fernando de Noronha twinkled under a bright quarter moon. The crew hauled back their square sails and laid to for the night. They were two-hundred miles from South America's easternmost bulge.

In the middle of the night Murphy awoke in his berth to hear the Old Man, standing by the wheel, grumbling for the benefit of all on the quarterdeck. Murphy listened sleepily to the familiar sound, and then sat up with a start when he realized this time the subject was him.

"Good God!" Murphy thought, with the recent memory of Mr. Almeida's drubbing in mind. "If this gets started, there'll be no holding him for the rest of the voyage."

Murphy had no idea what the matter was, but he climbed on deck and faced the captain. For a few moments both were silent. Then, in a voice of the same volume the skipper had been using, Murphy said, "Captain Cleveland, if you have any complaint of me, I'd like to be the first to hear about it."

The Old Man's head of steam fortunately lost its pressure. It turned out that his water closet, which only he and Murphy used, had jolly well flooded him, and he chose to assume that Murphy had tossed in something that plugged it. Murphy had done nothing of the sort, which he quickly made known—while keeping to himself that Johnny, the cabin boy, frequently took that shortcut in the disposal of small lots of garbage.

Murphy remained on deck long enough for the conversation to simmer down to a casual level and then turned in again. When he next opened his eyes, it was in the short, pervasive twilight that heralded an equatorial dawn. He found the Old Man seated in a whaleboat on the davits and joined him there. Fernando de Noronha lay to the southwest at an estimated distance of nine miles. It doubtless looked much as it had to Darwin in 1832 except the lighthouse and several tall wireless towers had been erected since.

As they drove rapidly toward the island before a fair wind, the rim of the sun peeped up on the port quarter, lighting like a candle the summit of the famous Pyramid, said by some to be the most arresting landmark in the whole South Atlantic and described by Darwin as "the most remarkable feature, a conical hill, about one thousand feet high, the upper part of which is exceedingly steep, and on one side overhangs its base." The rock is phonolite, a fine-grained volcanic that rings when struck, and is divided into irregular columns. Darwin continued, "One is inclined to believe that it has been suddenly pushed up in a semi fluid state . . . however, [it was] formed by the injection of melted rock into yielding strata, which thus had formed the moulds for these gigantic obelisks."

A strip of rough hills, which had at first seemed continuous to Murphy's intense scrutiny, gradually broke up to show the straits that separated several islets off the northeastern end. The climbing sun revealed a green lowland, well clothed with shrubs and small trees and a higher zone of bare, weathered peaks, among which the Pyramid stood nearly twice as high as any other.

The length of the whole chain is about seven miles. According to whalemen's reports,

The island's phonolite crags were visible for miles.

the leeward side of Fernando de Noronha had once been heavily forested, but the larger trees were all felled to prevent the exiled convicts—practically the only human beings to share the sea-beaten spot with countless ocean birds—from building *jangadas,* or Brazilian catamarans, sufficiently seaworthy to carry them to the mainland. Every now and then a rascal had been known to disappear, never to be heard of more, and the republic was saved the cost and trouble of his keep. Much more rarely, someone actually succeeded in crossing the distance to the continent on a frail raft. Then, as the Old Man told it, the authorities concluded that the enterprising fellow had earned his freedom, and they no longer bothered him so long as he remained inconspicuous. The skipper went on to say that, while Brazil had neither capital punishment nor life imprisonment, there was no law to prevent a culprit from being sentenced to Fernando de Noronha for a hundred years.

Murphy made time to put an addendum on his letter, "—Good morning. I was up before sunrise in the beautiful morning twilight, if such it may be called. The island lay ahead. To the south of us lies a steamer. Many sight the island every day, for it is on the main route between Europe and South American ports. I made a sketch of it in my notebook."

Landing was predicted to be very treacherous, necessitating a scramble through surf. But the skipper needed a full boatload of supplies. He sent ashore only Mr. da Lomba and a bare crew to bring off provisions. Accordingly, those with letters to post turned them over to the departing da Lomba and expected to remain all day on board, waiting his return.

Murphy closed his words to Grace, "I am very sorry not to see the place, and to miss collecting. I shall have to send this ashore with Mr. da Lomba, along with the Captain's letter.

"Goodbye, my wife. It always tears my heart to end a letter, just as it does to really part from you. If this letter ever reaches you, half our days apart will be past; that is the comforting thought." Having no assurance that mail could be registered, Murphy did not send his notebooks.

As it happened, after Mr. da Lomba and his crew set off in their whaleboat, the weather turned docile, and Mr. Almeida's crew and boat prepared to set forth on a fishing expedition. Murphy took down his gun and went along. On the way toward land they were surrounded by noddies, stout web-footed terns that display an easy familiarity with humans. The enormous flock stretched away into the distance until the birds looked like swarming insects.

Passing several conical islets on which man-o'-war birds nested, Mr. Almeida's whaleboat entered a cove of grottoed rock with a crescent of sand at its head. Behind this beach the fissured, yellow wall of a cliff, conforming with the semicircular outline of the cove, rose sheer to a height of three or four hundred feet. Thousands of black noddies clustered on their scaffold nests along its upper surface, and pairs of snow-white fairy terns—the first Murphy had ever seen alive—sat side by side on twisted boughs at the foot. There was no sign there of surf as had been predicted by the skipper. The singularly peaceful water had no more than a slumbering swell, and the satiny white breasts of tropic-birds flying overhead reflected the pale green of the cove below.

The allure of this emerald pool was not wasted on Murphy. He soon peeled off his clothing and plunged into water for the first time in the four months since he and Grace swam together at Dominica. The blurred image of a green turtle glided away, and a shoal of porpoises undulated across the inlet. When he came out on the pristine sand, it seemed appropriate to wander about ungarbed "like wild autochthonous man" while beginning to collect samples of the island birds.

The first report of his gun caused a horde of screaming sea fowl to pour down off the rocks. Other inhabitants may also have been disturbed by the roar and its bewildering echoes, for Murphy stood from picking up a specimen and found himself face to face with a tall, black, muscular fisherman, carrying a tattered net over one shoulder but otherwise wearing just what Murphy wore—nothing. Then, out of the shrubbery came a fellow of lighter skin, clad in short sailcloth breeches and a blue tam-o'-shanter, and having a wicker basket slung over his back. Murphy imagined the pair passing as Robinson Crusoe and his man Friday.

Not knowing Portuguese, Murphy called along the beach for the cooper to come out of the whaleboat, shake a leg, and join him, in order that they might enter into conversation. At Correia's first words in a familiar tongue, Crusoe's cap came off and both men extended the right hand of welcome. The subsequent exchanges were then carried on through interpreting.

The two men were murderers. The smaller one had been confined to the island slightly more than fourteen years; the other seemed uncertain about the length of his sentence to date. Neither had any particular complaint. They were free to wander until dark each day; the fishing was good. They had gardens, and many edible fruits grew wild. The clothing ration was insufficient, however, and there were altogether too few women on the island. Finally, they asked whether Murphy or the cooper might happen to have a little tobacco that could be spared? They did.

There was plenty of tobacco on the *Daisy*, Murphy volunteered. On no authority whatsoever, he even went so far as to invite one of the men to come off and ship with them. Their departure would leave no trace.

The convict shook his head. Any time up to two years before, he explained, he would have jumped at the chance. But his imprisonment was to terminate within eight months, after which he could return for the rest of his days to his native Pernambuco. He then informed them that around a small headland to the west there was a bigger beach, with access to the country behind, and he offered to meet Mr. Almeida's boat there. So, they presently pulled offshore, while the islander, after taking a pair of hide sandals from his basket and tying them on his feet, toiled up a stony, winding path across the ridge, leaving his comrade to cast the net alone.

The whaleboat rounded the point, and a curve of golden sand stretched to another promontory a mile away. Beach sloped gently under the sea, which for a long distance from shore was wondrously transparent. The upper beach was a riot of morning glories with leaves shaped like a goat's footprint. Mingled with them were many slender-stalked cacti. Beyond, a thicket, alive with small doves, concealed the base of the precipice, the lower face of which was covered with vines that clambered up the seams. The crest was bordered with the small, leafless, pinhão trees in full blossom of pink and orange. Sharp slabs of rock projected here and there from the wall, offering perfect nesting sites for the birds that appeared in hosts every which way the men turned.

For the sea fowl it was always springtime. The year breaks up into wet and dry periods. According to Murphy's guide, they were in the heart of the rainless season. But the birds, he said, had no fixed or limited time of breeding. Eggs and young could be gathered and eaten in every month of the twelve. He grumbled over the fact that these could often be seen but not taken, because of the inaccessibility of many nests. Murphy thought, "Now, there's something to be thankful for!"

Their convict guide then set about showing where more birds could be found—not only the salt water species but also a flycatcher and a vireo that lived nowhere on earth except this tiny island. He chattered glibly to the cooper, stopping only while snaring lizards with a loop of grass. They were joined by a handful of half-clad or nearly unclad fellow prisoners, as well as by several pitiful boys, the sons of convicts, all of whom seemed to be twisted by rheumatism or as a result of some dietary deficiency. Young and old followed along for the sake of empty cartridge shells, which Murphy at first had dropped on the ground but later passed to outstretched hands.

The cooper and the whole native party finally went off through a gap in the cliff to visit the convicts' village. The whaleboat's crew rowed to a reef for fishing, which left Murphy alone on the shore. He scrambled up an almost perpendicular footpath into the woods and then as far as possible up the bare, steep side of the Pyramid. He was surprised at the density of vegetation, including the disagreeable, stinging *Jatropha urens*, also known as bull-nettle or stinging spurge, a plant that can cause numbness on the skin and raise red welts for as long as twenty-four hours and which had caused another naturalist, Henry Moseley, no end of trouble in 1873. Luckier than Moseley, Murphy swam offshore to retrieve a bird he had shot and discovered that seawater instantly allayed the sharp pain.

Finally, from the summit of a hillock strewn with loose pebbles Murphy looked across a broad vista and down on the picturesque beach, where throngs of mixed ocean birds crossed and recrossed. Everything seemed as sharp as a diamond in the clear air, from the glittering dragonflies close in to a flock of migrant golden plovers far off on the sand, or even to crabs skittering over the wet rocks and to fishes in the clinkstone tide pools. To him it was Prospero's isle, fanned by tireless trade winds, with Ariel masked as a boatswain bird and the plovers playing the part of Shakespeare's sprites. "That on the sands with printless foot do chase the ebbing Neptune and do fly him when he comes back." And Caliban?—a black-skinned murderer who might appear at any moment.

It was an island where fruit trees flourished without cultivation, a tropical resort that the Brazilians could have promoted as a second Bermuda, yet it was given up to the most miserable of exiles.

By the time Correia and Murphy met up with their fishing party in late afternoon, they found the whaleboat laden with melons, colorful tropical fishes, and several sharks. The sharks had been a great nuisance all day, biting small fish from the hooks before they could be drawn to the surface, and nipping the larger ones clean in half.

Toward evening they sighted the *Daisy* bearing down the coast. Murphy had been on land precisely ten hours. Reluctantly, they sailed off to join the ship, leaving forever the pleasures of Fernando de Noronha. By dusk the brig was running swiftly athwart the trade wind once more, the Pyramid still showing faintly astern through a bluish haze.

Chapter Twenty-Four

AT FERNANDO DE NORONHA they loaded on bananas, plantains, beans, farina, squashes, and matches. "Twelve dollars worth of stuff for thirty-four," the Old Man grumbled. They also took on four pigs, which were given the run of the deck. The little porkers had not been to sea before. They were wobbly on their four legs and more than slightly seasick their first day but, like all hearty islanders (in Murphy's estimation), they took to the waves in no time.

In fact, not a single one of the beating hearts on the *Daisy* had originated on any of the seven continents. Every being aboard was an islander—including the pigs. The skipper hailed from Martha's Vineyard; the "Assistant Navigator," Long Island; Mr. Vincent, Mindanao; the cooper, Fayal; the others—including Cadela and the cat—were from the Cape Verdes or the West Indies. Even the stowaways—rats and cockroaches—had hopped aboard from islets.

The brig was headed southwest with strong winds blowing them along. The coast of Brazil lay fifty-five miles toward the setting sun. Murphy was busy for two days with the haul he had made while on land. He had lizards, fish, mollusks, and eighteen bird skins in various stages of preservation.

Cadela knew to stay out of the men's way, but the pigs often did not.

October 19th was the captain's sixty-eighth birthday. Murphy brought up a portion of the mincemeat Grace had supplied for his trunk. He asked the steward to make a pie. Later, Murphy and the skipper shared a split of Bordeaux.

After supper the boats were lowered for what had been reported as a pod of sperm whales. From their quick, puffy, irregular spouts, however, the Old Man identified them from the rigging as humpbacks. He had a bad history with humpbacks, so the boats were recalled. Very near that same position on the Atlantic on a previous voyage, Captain Cleveland had encountered hundreds of humpbacks. After a huge amount of effort, his crew finally succeeded in killing a twenty-barrel animal. But one boat had been staved and another had lost a new sail in the process when a whizzing whale line had looped around the canvas and ripped it out as it went. In Captain Cleveland's mind the crew had been lucky that a few arms and legs had not gone with it.

The next day a pair of finback whales passed close to the brig, blowing thin, quick spouts, but the captain had no interest in finbacks. They do not float when dead. He was happy to leave them to the modern steam whalers; they carried gear for inflating the carcasses.

Sperm whales almost always floated after being killed. Right whales usually floated, and those that did not, the skipper felt, sank from excessive lung puncturing. He had seen five go to the depths in a single voyage. Once, in the Japan Sea, where the ocean was only forty fathoms deep, he used the knowledge that dead whales will eventually rise after decomposition begins. He attached a large, empty cask to the harpoon line and continued cruising for a few days. "Then he returned to the position and found a floating whale as big as a capsized frigate! By sailing down the wind toward the swollen carcass, he kept his crew from committing suicide or staging a mutiny. They cut-in that whale, they did, and saved the whalebone, which was none the worse for the putrefaction of the carcass. They also tried out thirty-five barrels of oil which, the Old Man euphemistically admits, was 'rather dark.'"

Winds continued steady and strong. By October 22nd the brig was thirteen degrees south. More finbacks and humpbacks swam and leapt around. The pigs seemed to feel at home on deck. It was not unusual to have livestock on board ship—what better way to preserve the meat? The Old Man told of once taking *seventy* on his little bark, the *Bertha,* across the Gulf of Guinea off the curve of West Africa. Unlike the four pigs on the *Daisy,* which were a mismatch of two white, one red, and one brown, the *Bertha's* "navifauna" were all razor-backs, which, to Murphy, suggested they could not be seen end-on, but only broadside.

Weather was cooling; wind remained steady. In one day they made two degrees and were already a thousand miles below the equator. The waters were whaley, with an orca swimming swiftly by with its low, bushy spout. A humpback and her calf cavorted within range of Murphy's binoculars. A finback breached and blew. None of them interested Captain Cleveland.

Murphy began reading about animals of the cold latitudes. By October 25th the *Daisy* reached twenty degrees south. Wind had shifted to the north. They furled the mainsail, which was a fore-and-aft canvas, and the vessel ran freely under only the square sails of the foremast. These were the foresail, the lower topsail, upper topsail, and topgallant sail. The royal had been taken down. As a whaler, the *Daisy* was never in a hurry and therefore possessed no such clipper-ship accessories as a skysail, stargazer, or studdingsails. (None of these names was pronounced as people would read them now. Topgallant sail, for example, was reduced to "togansl" and studdingsails were called "stunsls.")

In late afternoon a greenhand bawled out "Grampus!" and Murphy rushed on deck. He was delighted to see a rare species of beaked whales called ziphioids. Captain Cleveland recognized them from a previous voyage; only he called them "algerines."

The grampuses were about twenty-five feet long, slender, and graceful. They put on quite a show, frolicking and turning their white bellies upward as they shot passed the bow. Some dove amidships to reappear on the other side. One turned a back flip. How many were there? Four? Five? More? Murphy could not count, they moved so fast. "After playing for some minutes before an audience in which I believe there were several other spellbound members," Murphy wrote, "they darted sharply away from us, turned astern, and disappeared. But this was only to tease us, because after a few moments they came puffing up our wake again from an astonishing distance. Their blowing made an extraordinary metallic sound, as though the bottom of a skillet were being banged with a mallet. Eventually, four of them turned off from us again, running absolutely abreast at high speed, with their round backs and little trigger fins all showing together. Then pouf! They were gone for good, like magic."

Murphy believed the grampus display to be the sort requiring mammalian brains. The animals' behavior was quite unfishlike. He felt the whales saw the brig and its crew and recognized the presence of another species. "What a pity," he continued, "that unwieldy circumstances prevent us from becoming well acquainted with the personalities of whales, as we have, for example, with those of the sea lions that learn to toss balls and ride horseback! I suspect that a whale's predilection for becoming chummy and companionable might astonish the world."

The next day came up dull after a stormy night. Headwinds made it necessary to tack. One photograph of the ziphioids would have come out well if it had not been for cockroaches walking across the glass plate while the gelatin was still soft. Little legs made a hundred punctures in the emulsion.

The first skuas—or sea hens—of the voyage flew close. Murphy quickly shot one and Mr. da Lomba ordered the dory lowered. The dead bird was half a mile astern, but Murphy was out and back before the Old Man emerged or knew that anything had happened without his orders. The skua was of the form that breeds in the Falkland Islands and had never been reported as far north as where they were; they were at the latitude of Rio de Janeiro. The specimen from that day was destined to be the first of its kind in the collection at the American Museum of Natural History.

Continuing south, Murphy dug out a sweater and an undershirt made of heavy linen mesh. He slept under a blanket for the first time since leaving Barbados. Meals improved. Tiny red beans called *feijães* from São Vicente were delicious when paired with bacon. Australian tinned beef was good and Johnny miraculously unearthed another can of Danish butter from some dark and moldy corner.

Temperatures dropped below seventy degrees. A heavy swell indicated stormy weather to the south. At six o'clock the morning of October 28th the steward came to announce that a "gony" was about. Murphy hurried on deck, and there it was: the long-anticipated sight, even more majestic, more supreme in its element, than his imagination had pictured.

"I now belong to a higher cult of favored mortals," he began his notes that day, "for I have seen the albatross! Long before I dared to hope, up here on the 23rd parallel, I have been watching the wonderful gliding of the grandest of birds during much of the day.

"It was mature, all white and black, doubtless an adult male, and as it turned and turned, now flashing the bright under side, now showing the black feathering that extended from wrist to tip on the upper surface of the wings, the narrow planes seemed to be neither beating nor scarcely quivering. Lying on the invisible currents of the breeze, the bird appeared merely to follow its pinkish bill at random."

Murphy, of course, was interested in its dimensions. From tip to feathered tip, *Diomedea exulans* is among the biggest flying birds. But he did not believe the reported expanse of seventeen feet that he had read in the *Encyclopedia Britannica*. The one before him, he estimated to be closer to ten feet—a big bird, however, from anyone's perspective.

The albatross stayed near the brig for only a few minutes, but it returned at noon, "covering tens of miles in the swift wide circles that it traversed astern. When banking, it sometimes tilted to an angle of 90° so that the point of the lower wing cut the water. Twice it dropped into the sea, where it looked as gigantic as the iron birds on the swan boats of my boyhood memories, and allowed the *Daisy* to draw away a great distance before it arose to overtake us. It was a curious sight when the albatross prepared to alight under our stern, and then, changing its purpose, ran heavily on the water for a hundred paces before its wings, beating ponderously, could lift the great body into the air."

In his letter bag, Murphy had a message that Dr. Lucas, the museum director, had marked for the occasion of that day—whatever the date. In the letter Lucas described his own first sighting of an albatross, nearly fifty years prior.

As if that were not enough wildlife excitement, a large flying fish found itself on deck in the night. The men on watch got it to Murphy first thing, and Murphy got the fish into formalin before the steward could get it into the galley and onto the table. Remembering Grace's gusto for flying fish in Barbados, he entered in his notes that "specimens come before the belly."

At eight o'clock, the *Daisy* ran among a widely spread shoal of sperm whales. Murphy ran up to the mainmasthead for an incomparable view. He saw a dozen whales leap almost—or maybe fully—out of the water, making great splashes as they reentered the ocean. Captain Cleveland believed these leaps to be for the purpose of shaking off the remoras—or suckerfish—that often clung to their sides.

The whales were traveling at high speed, and a high swell was on the sea, the combination of which made hunting difficult. One boatsteerer missed what looked like an easy dart with his harpoon. Mr. da Lomba's boat was the only one to make fast. "Long John" made a corpse of his victim within minutes of planting the harpoon. It was a small bull, maybe thirty barrels, but during its flurry it vomited fifty or more squids. Mr. da Lomba thought to take Murphy an example, a two-foot body with tentacles of an additional three or four feet. Murphy labeled it, wrapped it in cheesecloth, and stowed it beside that morning's flying fish.

Meanwhile, the Old Man was gloomy—not uncharacteristic by any stretch, but this time he was silent. Silence from him felt more ominous than his usual bellowing and vituperations. It seems the boatsteerer, Francisco—or Frank, as he was called—had committed an inexcusable sin in missing his dart with the harpoon, and the skipper had to "break" him by telling him to transfer his belongings out of steerage into the forecastle. Frank followed orders with the appearance of resignation, almost like someone approaching the headsman's block. Everyone was solemn. Men began whispering speculations as to who would be promoted to the vacancy created.

The air was cold enough for spermaceti sloppings from Mr. da Lomba's whale to solidify on deck. Only a single shark sniffed around the floating carcass, and this was a fish of a new species. The equatorial cuttings-in had been more frantically attended.

Frank worked as a common lumper at the windlass. Having dealt with him as necessary, the Old Man was content to sit with Murphy and string his pearls of whaling wisdom as they watched the blubber peel off. Cow sperm whales, the skipper related, rarely ran larger than twenty-five or thirty barrels. Twenty-barrel cows were common; the biggest he had taken was forty. Portuguese sailors ate the cows' nipples and mammary glands. The size of the bulls, the skipper continued, indicated their success in fighting for females. The bulls were polygamous and fought hard to win their place in a herd. Captain Cleveland had seen bulls with jaws locked on each other, vying for position. He had once killed a bull that was scarred from losing twelve inches from the tip of his jaw—probably to a rival whale. Lone bulls—often very large—were those that had passed their prime and had been driven out of the herd by a younger, stronger male.

On October 30th strong southeast winds whipped up a rough sea. The crew was boiling oil, the smell of which permeated every corner of the *Daisy*. By afternoon, they had re-hoisted the mainsail, reefed it, and were proceeding on course in the teeth of the wind, escorted by albatrosses.

Murphy estimated the air speed of those glorious birds at forty miles an hour. That rate, combined with the wind speed, meant their ground-speed calculated to ninety miles an hour, an observation that made the birds seem all the more majestic.

Meanwhile, both the first and second officers had approached the captain to plead Frank's case, but the Old Man would hear none of it. However, without consultation, during the post-boiling clean-up that day,

Captain Cleveland interrupted Frank from swabbing the deck and called him aft. He instructed the poor boatsteerer to fetch his things from the forecastle and take up his place once again in steerage.

Whale meat is lean and dark, like beef. It butchers into thick, boneless slabs. Supper that night was pot roast of the sperm variety. Murphy ate heartily. Little did he know that night would bring on the roughest weather they had had and would test his tendency toward *mal de mer*. The brig sailed at new angles with the sea bubbling and frothing through the scuppers on each roll and sloshing across the main deck on the next. But his concerns were alleviated; he felt no queasiness, even after the big meal. The motion felt natural enough to him by that stage of the voyage that he confidently and calmly developed photographs in his cabin. He even forewent the safety light of his ruby lamp.

As he worked his mind was on the albatrosses and how they had swung through the gale that day, "swaying from side to side and garnering their momentum from nobody knows where, into the wind or before it, up or down, is all one to them. They continually rock, and sometimes keep their gliders atremble, but an actual wing beat is rare and is usually confined to the hand or last segment. Four little strokes are the most I've seen one make consecutively. One wonders why they don't fall," he wrote to Grace, "When the secret of their perfect balance has been learned and applied to man-made planes, then we'll go a-flying."

SECTION III
Austral Summer

Chapter Twenty-Five

THIRTY-ONE YEARS AFTER his voyage on the *Daisy*, when Murphy wanted to verify that he had been correct in identifying Mars and Venus the evening of his forty-barrel whale, he consulted his museum colleague in New York, Clyde Fisher, chief curator of astronomy at the Hayden Planetarium. Dr. Fisher set the date of his artificial sky for October 10, 1912, and he set a latitude of four degrees north and a longitude of twenty-two degrees west, the brig's calculated position on that date. After waiting a few minutes for the sky to wind back in time, Mars appeared on the horizon just as Murphy had observed its bright red light above the Atlantic that night. It sank shortly after the planetarium's simulated sunset. Venus, too, was where he remembered it. This proved that Murphy had not mistaken a pair of bright stars as the two planets.

Since at least the time of the Phoenicians, sailors have known something about finding their way by observing the night sky. The word navigate stems from two Latin roots: *navis*, meaning ship and *agere*, meaning to move or direct. Until the last century, navigate usually referred specifically to ships and how they found their way at sea.

In celestial navigation, position is determined by observing the sun, moon, planets, and stars. It may seem like simple arithmetic and trigonometry to locate a ship relative to those heavenly bodies, but none of the relationships is stationary. The ship moves subject to wind and ocean current, and the heavenly bodies move—or appear to move—along their own paths and rise and set above and below the horizon. The earth rotates; things shift around.

Add to that complexity that the intended direction of a ship is often not the actual direction in which it is pointed. Like other sailing ships, the brig *Daisy* moved at the mercy of the elements and could only occasionally go precisely toward her destination. More often she zigzagged an approximation of her course.

Ideally, a ship's route would follow the arc of a great circle, since this is the shortest distance between two points on the earth's surface. But navigating a great circle would be tricky even if the wind were cooperative.

The meridians converge at the poles so are not parallel. The track of a ship sailing along a great circle intersects each meridian at a slightly different angle (unless the ship sails precisely due north, due south, or along the equator). To maintain a perfect great-circle course, a ship's compass direction would have to be continuously altered.

More realistically, a ship's direction would be corrected at regular intervals—every few hours, for example—making the vessel follow a sequence of rhumb lines, crossing all meridians at the same angle and then altering the course.

Captain Cleveland probably used a nautical chart on which all meridians were plotted as straight lines. With this he used a compass, a pair of dividers, parallel rulers, a chronometer, and a sextant to determine his

position. He recorded the brig's longitude and latitude each day at 3:00 P.M., unless otherwise noted. His calculations were made in degrees and minutes but not seconds.

To get a daytime reading required being able to see the sun's location. November 1st was rough and overcast. Captain Cleveland was not confident in his position. November 2nd cloud cover again obscured the sky, and the Old

Captain Cleveland used a sextant for navigation.

Man failed to get a reliable sight for longitude. He began muttering about making a stellar shot at twilight when both the horizon and navigational stars might be clearly discerned at once.

Even in 1912, it was commonplace for men at sea to shoot the stars at dawn or dusk. On the *Daisy*, however, the event was made out to be a last resort—a bold and esoteric rite. Captain Cleveland went about as if preparing himself for a great ordeal, studying a star chart and eliciting whispered rumors that "the Old Man's going to try a stellar!" He pored over the *Nautical Ephemeris*, an almanac for finding latitude and longitude; and Nathaniel Bowditch's book, *The New American Practical Navigator*.

Murphy had already noted four pairs of bright stars that could be used for way finding: Capella and Vega, Hamal and Deneb, Aldebaran and Altair, Fomalhaut and Nunki. Whether any of these would be visible depended on the clouds.

As it happened, Murphy became distracted with the first appearance of a Cape pigeon and lost interest in the navigational efforts. The bird was a checkered black and white petrel, the best-known sea bird of the southern hemisphere. Captain Cleveland called it a Cape Horn pigeon, but Murphy privately scoffed at that. Everyone knew the Cape of Good Hope simply as "the Cape." Cape Horn was "the Horn," but the tip of South America had not been rounded until long after the species had its name.

As for the stellar shot, the Old Man had not found a simultaneous star and horizon anyway. It was not until well after dark that the sky cleared. The Pleiades had been dropping to the north, lower each night as the *Daisy* traveled away from the equator. The small irregular galaxies known as Magellan's Clouds climbed overhead.

Weather had been rough. Murphy's back was sore from maintaining equilibrium when awake and from sliding back and forth when in bed. It was hard to move about the ship without a firm hold on doors, ropes, or other security. Temperatures cooled despite the fact that the southern hemisphere's November compares to the month of May above the equator. It was spring, but the *Daisy* had left the tropics behind. Daylight grew longer and the slant of the sun's rays more angular.

One of the four pigs had learned to edge the others out at the feeding trough and had grown to be the biggest. "Be a hog if you want to," said Mr. da Lomba. "You'll be the first one fat enough to knife." With the same approach to the world, the officers broke out a dozen or more lances especially designed for sea elephant slaughter. These were put to the grindstone in anticipation of arrival at South Georgia Island.

Winds were strong. The fore-and-aft mainsail was replaced with a small trysail. Then, at 2:00 A.M., as Murphy had his head poking above the after hatchway to view the riotous weather, the lower fore-topsail blew clean away, making a sound like something between a puff and a clap, which would have been pleasant except for its implications. It was gone, carried into the night and over the sea like gossamer. The event was like a warning from the wind, with the canvas tearing out of its bolt ropes.

The brig was forced to luff into the wind. Not until noon did the weather clear enough to restore the mainsail to its boom and gaff, re-hoist it, reef it, and bend on a new fore-topsail.

Loggerhead turtles were coming around—first two, then three, one of which was captured as it swam across the stern and Mr. da Lomba jerked a trailing fish line that hooked the turtle's neck. Its stomach was crammed with *Velella*, related to Portuguese men-of-war, and the flesh had a rank odor familiar and unpleasant to Murphy but welcomed by the Portuguese sailors as a choice item for their menu.

Perhaps in reflection on what the turtle ate, Murphy peeled the final banana of his Fernando de Noronha bunch. It would be the last fresh fruit he would see for several months.

During the middle of the day, the cooper set up a hand lathe on the carpenter's bench and went to work on thick pieces of West Indian firewood that had been brought up from the hold. Part of the anticipated sea elephant slaughter would involve clubbing the animals prior to lancing. "They have also been talking about the manufacture for each officer and boatsteerer of a *manduc*'—apparently a Cape Verde Island word for bludgeon. It seems that in this beastly sealing the smaller males and the cows have their skulls bashed with clubs, only the large bulls being dispatched with a bullet in the brain. All are then lanced and bled for the sake of blanching the blubber and the oil that is prepared from it. Something tells me that the 'elephanting' at South Georgia is going to shrivel the very marrow of my bones."

The men worked enthusiastically at their truncheons, fashioning them individually. Like miniature, ornamented baseball bats, each *manduc'* was a dark and deadly looking weapon. The waste turnings from the lathe littered the main deck.

But Mr. da Lomba wore a sardonic grin that hinted at an inside joke of some sort. Mr. Vincent and Mr. Correia were obviously in on it. These three and Captain Cleveland were the only ones on board who had ever seen a sea elephant or who had been to the Antarctic rim. Murphy did not know what was so funny about the industrious production of clubs, but he could tell the experienced ones were amused. With patience, he figured, and arrival at South Georgia, the joke would reveal itself to him.

Meanwhile there were turtle guts and they made good bait. For the first time Murphy succeeded in catching birds on a fishhook that he trolled astern. A giant fulmar took hold and offered so much resistance Murphy feared his codfish line would snap. As the name suggests, giant fulmars are the biggest of the petrels. Sailors called them variously Nellies, gluttons, or stinkers, and were not generally fond of them or their ungainly, uncouth appearance. They feasted on carrion and compared to other birds as sharks did to fishes.

Catching the stinker on a fishing rig elated Murphy. The sea became rougher, and other petrels and albatrosses gathered around the turtle innards. The Old Man and crew members joined in and were soon hauling aboard other seabirds, the birds first hooking themselves in the water then flying like animated kites before being hauled down onto the deck. With the captives on board other birds flocked to the hullabaloo, both human and avian. They bit eagerly. Even those that escaped one hook while being pulled in, returned for another chance to snap up more bait on a second hook. Murphy added five kinds to his collection, four of them new. He identified thirteen species. Four of them were albatrosses, six were petrels, and two were Mother Carey's chickens.

The wind shifted and howled. November 4th was the roughest day yet, and the next day rougher. Anything not lashed in place slid this way and that. Chairs fell over and banged. Murphy felt in constant danger of being thrown against something. Nevertheless, he worked at skinning birds. His utensils rolled all over the floor of the hold. All the big sails had been furled, and the brig "plyed to windward under only a dishrag and a napkin."

Chapter Twenty-Six

NOVEMBER 5TH, 1912 was Election Day in the United States. Despite Murphy's keen interest he did not expect to know the outcome until spring. As it happened, it would have been appropriate to celebrate aboard the *Daisy* that Wilson won in a landslide over Taft and Roosevelt. There was no way for news to reach the *Daisy* while at sea, and they did not expect to cross paths with anyone while embayed at South Georgia. Correia said that on the brig's earlier voyage to that island, they had seen two steam-powered whaleships but only in the far distance— too remote for any exchange. That was how isolated they had been for several months.

Not having the slightest knowledge of what the voters' mandate had been brought on a wave of nostalgia. Only a little more than one third of his twelve-month exile had elapsed, and the hard work still lay ahead. It was the time of year Murphy—if he had been home on Long Island— would have taken his shotgun down to Old Man's Harbor to hunt ducks under a crisp autumn sky. Everything familiar was a hemisphere away.

It felt like autumn below the equator, however. The *Daisy* had been progressing rapidly to the south. Murphy was bundled up. It was too cold to read on deck, and too dark below. Weather was rough, wet, and leaden. "*Tempo vai, tempo vem,*" said Mr. Almeida, meaning time comes as fast as it goes.

On November 7th, the captain ordered what seemed like a turn-around; they switched to a northwesterly tack under short sails. Suddenly the Old Man seemed in no rush to get to any destination. They had reached the River Whaling Grounds, where the Rio de la Plata that separates Uruguay from Argentina discharges its flow into the Atlantic. The Old Man was itching for some of the sperm whales that frequented those waters.

The delay irritated the officers, who feared they would miss out on the best part of the sea elephant season if they did not continue south as fast as they could. Discontent spread like a contagion. Grumbling about the quality of meals started up again. Some of the men claimed Captain Cleveland had not issued enough warm clothing. There were threats of desertion at the first port (wherever that would be).

The mastheads sighted blackfish, porpoises, a finback, and even an ocean sunfish, the world's largest bony fish, measuring up to eleven feet and weighing as much as two tons in its roundness. But even with their careful scanning, nowhere could the mastheads raise a sperm whale.

The Old Man stalked the crew like a predator. Then suddenly he noticed someone missing, "Where's Frank?" he blurted.

Mr. Almeida seemed uneasy but he finally answered, "Sick." The boatsteerer had not been on deck for two days, and none of the officers had said anything.

"Sick! Why hasn't he reported? What's the matter with him?" snapped the captain.

"Blue balls," meaning buboes, or swollen lymph nodes in the groin.

"Bring him up," the Old Man roared. "Blue balls, clap, pox, strangury—good God, what next? He'll die on deck, he will, not down in that steerage. What kind of officers have I got, to let a man cuddle his guts without reporting for medicine?" The captain strode aft and went below.

The Old Man was responsible for the crew's health.

Frank was unable to stand. He

was assisted up the ladder, wearing only underclothes and wrapped in a blanket. He immediately lay down on the hatch. Murphy could see the man was plenty sick.

Captain Cleveland grimly worked Frank over, testing his swellings and examining his gums, throat, eyelids, and the skin of his legs. He ordered the man back to his bunk, after which he sent a concoction to be administered four times daily by the first mate, Mr. da Lomba.

Murphy felt the captain did all that could have been done, given the circumstances, but he feared Francisco Nicolau would not be saved from an early death, concoction or not.

It would not have been appropriate for Murphy to monitor the sick man's progress. Furthermore, Murphy's society was largely limited to the elite of the ship: the officers and idlers whose doings were generally focused behind the mainmast. Wind continued to rough up the ocean. For lack of other interest, Murphy fished for birds then shaved his beard, leaving an enviable moustache intact—envied, at least, by Johnny the cabin boy.

Murphy longed for something from home, wishing for more of the milk chocolate he had finished in early October. Going through what remained in his trunk, he decided to treat himself by opening a jar of marmalade, which he spread generously on crackers.

Finally, the weather calmed. Late in the afternoon of the 9th, Murphy obtained permission to lower the *Grace Emeline*, and he took the cooper with him. Birds darted and soared above quiet gray swells, indifferent to the presence of the dory. The first petrel flew within range, but Murphy inexplicably missed his first eight shots. Then began a successful slaughter, however, one that Correia joined in. Each was determined to collect the biggest possible variety from the thousands of waterfowl flocking overhead. After a while they rowed back to the brig to offload their catch. They stayed on board long enough for supper then set out for more shooting. The birds did not seem the least fazed by the gun blasts.

They collected thirty-six specimens that day, all very fat. One was an Arctic tern on its winter migration to southern waters. The rest were

Tubinares, including a single specimen of the great wandering albatross, two smaller albatrosses called mollymauks, two black nighthawks, an ashy petrel, and many examples of two species called mutton birds. Ten species in all were taken and some were first captures of the voyage. Murphy worked at a big table the cooper had made for him, where he skinned twenty-one of the birds. He reserved six of them for skeltonizing; two, he preserved in alcohol; and seven others were badly shot and bloody. From those he reserved only the skulls before turning them over to the steward intact.

The Old Man put up a fuss about having shot an albatross. Murphy could not tell whether this was genuine or obligatory ritual in reference to the ancient taboo. Apparently it was acceptable to catch the big birds on fishhooks and lines, to hit their heads with belaying pins, to dedicate their stripped carcasses to the stew pot, to use their snowy feathers as swabs, to make pipestems and needle cases from the shafts of their wing feathers, to make tobacco pouches from the skin of their big webbed feet. Shooting one, however, apparently still came with a curse. To offset the possible charge of "diomedeicide," Murphy took all the credit he could for having provided an abundance of mutton bird meat for a delicious fricassee—enough for all hands to enjoy. They were back to using butter again, too, after depleting the oleomargarine supply. The St. Vincent product was "not the finest creamery print butter, but it tastes awfully good, nevertheless. Mustard has appeared on the table, too. It goes well on the meat. Everything is cheerful."

Fog and overcast continued to obscure sextant sightings. Longitude remained undetermined. Masses of kelp floated by. Finbacks passed close to the ship. The crew salvaged a floating timber on which skuas were resting. Lengthening light pushed dawn and dusk farther apart each day.

On November 13th, position was determined to be 41° 00' S, 44° 48' W, directly below Rio de Janeiro and as far south as Tasmania. A school of blackfish passed close enough that "the animals practically rubbed the weed off the *Daisy*'s waterline."

The cook stuck the biggest pig. Fresh pork and blueberry pie put Murphy into ecstasy. "I happened to be seated on the leeward side of the table," he wrote, "so my wedge of pie contained more blueberries and juice than the portions of the first officer and the cooper, both of whom sat up to windward!"

The next morning the steward served blood pudding. Murphy opened a letter from one of his brothers and reread several from Grace. He had finished reading the New Testament, which Grace's aunt had given him. In the afternoon, Johnny gave Murphy a haircut. It felt like Long Island Indian summer as Murphy's brown locks fell to the deck on that bright and dazzling afternoon. Sunny weather had a nip in the air, though, with mist on the horizon and a hint of mackerel scales in the sky.

When Murphy was a boy, his Great Uncle Herbert taught him how to cut a pen from a goose quill. His method could be applied to albatross feathers as well. Murphy set aside his fountain pen November 14th and made notes in his usual bold and angular hand, describing right whales and spouting finbacks, porpoises cutting the waves—all written with an albatross pen.

A dozen kinds of birds rioted over the quarterdeck at sunset the next day. Then Murphy heard an odd sort of braying that came not from the air but the waves. There it was: half the ship's length to windward, the first penguin. Soon there were others, all heading north. They dove like porpoises, swimming underwater, only occasionally lifting their sleek, reptilian heads and upright tails above the surface. They were gentoos, or "Johnny" penguins, a kind that Murphy expected to see in great numbers once he landed at South Georgia.

The *Daisy* progressed into cold. They were approaching the Antarctic Convergence, where south meets north. It is an invisible boundary but as clear a margin as any physical feature on earth. Antarctic glaciers were beginning their melt. Every spring frigid water flows northward until it collides with and slides beneath the warmer Atlantic seas. Year after year these deep, cold waters support a wealth of krill, which in turn foster an abundance of wildlife. Albatrosses and petrels feed on the bounty.

The first sign of the Convergence was a noticeable drop in temperature, accompanied by the fog and mist of cold water meeting warm at that biological frontier. Mittens and heavy coats began to appear on deck. Blankets were brought out. Temperatures were just below fifty degrees Fahrenheit, but the West Indians, who were used to a tropical climate, shivered and complained.

Wind came from the southwest, wintry and howling with penetrating squalls. The captain continued to man the mastheads, but it was unclear what the lookouts' purpose could have been if whales had been sighted, since it was too rough to lower boats.

The crew was miserable with cold. Captain Cleveland must have believed immersion would toughen the men, because he allowed wind to sweep through the cabin, and he would not let Johnny build a fire in the stove. Murphy added a blanket to his sleeping bag.

The time came for the Old Man to take down from his rack two high-latitude charts of the South Atlantic to follow the pencil track of his earlier approach to South Georgia. They were grimy old charts but gaily backed—one with light blue calico, the other on red-and-white checks.

A gale blew sleet from the southwest. Hailstones bounced on the deck. The sea was enormously high in mountainous waves "as high as from Market Square to the Atheneum." Murphy wore a suit of heavy underwear, a pair of heavy woolen socks that came up outside his trousers, a wool flannel shirt, and his college sweater from Brown.

Finally, the skipper ordered no lookouts sent up. Food and dishes at mealtimes showed "an aversion toward the table and an affinity for the deck underfoot." Murphy found it unsafe to sit, stand, or lie down without a solid grip on something. The sextant was useless.

But through all this Murphy was entranced by the birds. Mollymauks, or small albatrosses, followed in increasing numbers. Black-browed albatrosses sailed back and forth across the quarterdeck, "jerking up their heads like spirited steeds . . . they wiggle their feet with a running motion, even though high in air; sometimes they tip up and halt as abruptly as though they had struck an invisible barrier. They sweep

Dwight Franklin had the right idea on the lengths to which Murphy would reach when it came to collecting specimens.

across the stern so close that I can see the recognition in their brown eyes and hear the humming swish of their stiff quills. I can watch the action of elevators and depressors (in the form of tail and broad-webbed feet), and the perpetual adjustments of slender, quivering planes."

Murphy continued to "fish" for birds, trailing bait on a line. His victims dropped "like pillows, spreading wide their legs, throwing their bulging breasts forward and their heads far back, thus assuming awkward and ridiculous attitudes on their way toward the water. Before alighting, they stretch down the legs and turn the toes upward. Then the huge webs strike the surface obliquely and the birds glide forward several yards, like boys on an ice slide, before they slowly settle into the buoyant swimming position, with angels' wings held high above their backs. But then they are apt to waste time by quarreling in a laughable, solemn way, sidling around each other and croaking loudly while the bait is relentlessly towed out of their reach."

Chapter Twenty-Seven

By NOVEMBER 18TH, the *Daisy* had reached a latitude of 48° 39' S, more than halfway between the equator and the pole. An Antarctic gale sharpened with hailstones scoured them all day. The barometer read 29.24 inches at noon, rising at sunset.

At three in the afternoon—or six bells, as a seaman would have clocked it, a bell being thirty minutes—Murphy wrote to Grace that she could forget every previous statement he had made about rough seas. It had never been truly rough until that day. They were in the heart of the trackless south Atlantic, far from the trade routes, with South Georgia only 325 miles away, and they had been lying-to under staysail and trysail since dawn. The lee whaleboats were hoisted all the way up to their davit tackle blocks, the seas breaking over the main deck, and the whole ocean seethed with white froth. The gale from the southwest tore the surface to shreds and rolled the *Daisy* on her beam ends. Murphy, however, was an adventurer. To him, it felt glorious, even while uncomfortable. Dark hailstorms alternated with furious blasts of wind, but the sun occasionally broke through the massive round clouds, and then its light on the cavorting waves was a joy and the little silvery whalebirds were exquisite.

The Old Man called it Cape Horn dirty weather, too cold to do anything sedentary and too rough to do anything vigorous—or at least anything beyond what was absolutely necessary. In the morning, braced in the spare whaleboat across the stern, Murphy had photographed albatrosses and other birds until his hands, arms, and neck seemed to freeze around his camera, or into the "Graflex posture," as he called it. To thaw out he went below, where the cabin trapped enough heat to stay above forty degrees. He got out his green and red knitted vest, and vowed to bless the day, should his photographs turn out to be successful.

Continuing south another day, the *Daisy*'s latitude corresponded to that of Labrador. Again, Murphy wrote to Grace of the conditions, saying if she wished to imagine what it was like, she should think of spending a few February days and nights in front of her mother's house on Angell Street in Providence—actually on the street itself, that is. She could imagine plenty of clothing, but would not be free to walk more than twenty feet in any direction. At mealtimes sitting on the curbstone to eat would approximate, and at night crawling into a nice warm sleeping bag spread out on the flowerbed would compare. But on no account was she to think of leaving the open air. At least she would have equilibrium standing up on Angell Street, though. On the ship Murphy struggled to maintain any position as they tossed, even a horizontal one. He bulged with heavy clothes, yet the blood in his feet seemed to congeal while he huddled in the corner of his berth. Whenever the sun did show its face for a few minutes, which it did rarely, he put on his overcoat, pulled on mittens to dance on the quarterdeck for circulation, all the while hanging on to a rope's end to keep from being pitched into the sea.

He was anxious to feel firm ground, to "sleep outside a churn," to walk a brisk mile, and to be sheltered by hills, no matter how jagged, sheer, or cold they might be.

By November 20th, the storm still stewed around the *Daisy*. She tossed about, helpless to do anything except point into the wind. During the night, a heavy sea had broken over the cabin, pouring chilly brine over the companionway and into parts of the ship. Murphy's corner remained dry but the atmosphere around him felt more damp and frigid than ever.

Foul weather subsided to the extent that he was able to develop a dozen negatives that night, thrilled with the images he had captured, having photographed new species. He gloated over his accomplishments and what they would mean to him after his return. "The ornithologists will whoop to see [my pictures]," he wrote. "If the wonderful fortune only lasts, won't we be a happy pair? . . . Just think what fun it's going to be writing up our articles." Even with Grace on dry land he never failed to see his one-man expedition as a joint venture, and she was present in his mind, regardless of the weight of his task.

As the *Daisy* approached land, birds thickened the air. Cape pigeons flew so close Murphy actually caught one in his hands. Later, sooty albatrosses came in more convoys, swinging repeatedly across the quarterdeck. Murphy seized the opportunity and shot one, although not expecting it to come hurtling down into the Old Man's open arms as it did.

"My soul and body!" Cleveland said, but more as a grunt than anything since his breath had been nearly knocked out of him by the sheer size of the bird.

Eventually, the storm ran its course, and the ocean's riot smoothed to heavy fog, colder than liquid air, and stinging the hairs inside Murphy's nose as he breathed.

In the southern hemisphere, November compares to a northerner's May. They were a month from the summer solstice. Each day gathered increasing light in morning and evening alike. At noon of the 22nd, the mist lifted to reveal a two-humped iceberg with a hoary top and emerald walls. Its highest elevation was level with the *Daisy*'s topmasthead. Two right whales, identified by showing a double spout when seen end-on, blew half a mile to the west, in the direction of the iceberg. The Old Man itched to go after them, but the gear had been stowed away during the storm and in anticipation of reaching land.

A large dead whale, distended and probably stinking, also lay afloat, indicating proximity to other whaling activities around South Georgia. Enormous tangles of kelp floated by, again indicating a nearness to land. Murphy was six months from home and, at last, about to reach his long-sought destination. He noted the sound of anchor chain being hauled up from the locker and made ready.

The following day, however, another storm blew in. Captain Cleveland stationed double lookouts at the bow, watching for bergs and growlers, stony blobs of old, worn ice that is mostly submerged. All morning the sea was roughed up. Alternating spates of rain and sticky snow diminished vision. Murphy wrote, "One small whale-chasing steamer was reported, but it paid no attention to our old black wind-jammer."

He strained through long hours of the day to look ahead into the tenebrous mist while the *Daisy* rolled and jerked. A limp wind failed to fill her canvas, but the dull waters around her remained troubled by the memory of four days' storm. More masses of brown kelp and scattered chunks of worn ice lifted on the surface of the sea along with the ship, then fell astern as she pushed through.

The Old Man, close-mouthed as always, told nothing of his noon reckoning, but the signs of land were clear. Everyone on board fell into a fever of expectancy after so many months on the Atlantic. As the gray Antarctic day began to deepen, Murphy thought he saw a flicker of anxiety even on the set face of the skipper himself as he stood beside the helmsman, who peered ahead, and ahead, and ahead.

"Land-ho!"

That welcome cry from the masthead snapped the tension. Murphy rushed to the bow and gazed into an unbroken monochrome of gray. Then dimly, gradually, a long, dark line loomed out. Above it a blur of white blended with the soft sky. Before those on deck could see as distinctly as the men on the mastheads, light faded into a wet and snowy squall.

It was just past three o'clock. The ship stood off. They knew, however, with a thrill of exultation, that their outward voyage was about to end. Through the darkening haze, they had caught a glimpse of the black rocks and the coast hills and the vast snowfields of a wild and alpine land. And not only that, as Murphy learned later, they had made land at a promontory just east of Possession Bay, already six or seven miles along the shore toward their exact destination, and sighted just in time before the storm's curtain fell.

The Old Man celebrated in a way nobody could have predicted. For the first time in the long voyage, he permitted—and, in fact, ordered—a fire lit in the cabin's wood-burning stove. It was not a Barstow-made stove (Grace's father had manufactured stoves under the family name), but was effective nonetheless. The cabin's temperature climbed back up to the high forties.

Murphy retired to his berth, somewhat choked with wood smoke. By the miserable light of an oil lamp he began running over his typewritten summaries of the historical and scientific literature relating to South Georgia.

"We are here," he wrote to Grace and kept thinking that to himself over and over, his enthusiasm not dampened by the haunting knowledge of one previous explorer who had gotten that far only to run his ship onto a rock within a mile of landing. "Tomorrow marks the attainment of what you and I have aimed at for nearly a year, beloved. From this point forward it is proper to consider that I am on the homeward stretch."

A SMALL SPECK at the bottom of the map may be all that South Georgia means to most Americans. Yet Yankee mariners had voyaged to that far-away spot since the eighteenth century, some of them growing wealthy

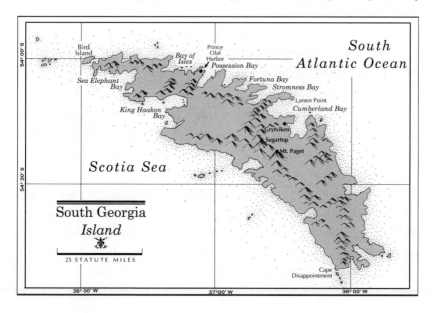

on its spoils. A century before Murphy's voyage men worked South Georgia's beaches, clubbing fur seals. In 1825, James Weddell (for whom the Weddell Sea was named) estimated over a million animals had been slaughtered for their skins.

About the size of Murphy's native Long Island, South Georgia lies in a blustery ocean twelve hundred miles east of Cape Horn. It is one of the broken ring of bleak and treeless bits of ground around the bottom of the earth. The latitude of the South Sandwich Islands, of which South Georgia is the principal member, corresponds to Alaska's Kenai Peninsula, yet the archipelago has an almost Antarctic climate. The islands are the homes of many sea birds that do not nest on the Antarctic continent. They are also the breeding grounds of fur seals and sea elephants. They are the range of the world's southernmost flowering plants.

Not everyone agrees on which explorer first visited South Georgia. Vespucci in 1502? De la Roche in 1675? Whoever it was, it is a certainty that Captain James Cook, in 1775, sailed the *Resolution* into its frigid bays while on his second great voyage around the world.

Captain Cook believed at first that he had reached the *Terra Incognita Australis*, which he was seeking. On finding the ice-capped, lofty region to be merely an island with a circumference of roughly 200 miles, however, he declared the place was "doomed by nature to everlasting frigidness and never to feel the warmth of the sun's rays, whose horrible and savage aspect I have not words."

Cook further observed no one would ever benefit from that land and that it was one which was eminently "not worth the discovery." Then he entered in his journal, "I called this land the Isle of Georgia in honor of his Majesty."

Murphy respected those who had measured and mapped before him. He had with him aboard the *Daisy* every detail Cook and his naturalists had recorded about South Georgia. He felt mystically close that night, in that icy and silent setting, reading the words of men who had cruised the same waters in which the *Daisy* floated.

For Murphy, November 24th opened clear and sparkling, a welcome change from the pea-soup atmosphere through which the *Daisy* had been groping. A gauze of thin fog adhered to valley glaciers and the bases of the steep, bare coastal ranges, reddish brown where sunshine hit. White ridges and ice-sheathed pinnacles gleamed beyond in sharp detail against the bluest of skies. Murphy honed his vision for anything that moved on or near the shore, scanning for each defining element of the drama he felt in himself for the sheer fact of being there.

A gentle breeze pushed them along all morning. They passed close by several dazzling, water-worn icebergs, in whose crevices the swelling seas had frozen into mushroom-shaped sprays as tall as the ship's masts. Great flocks of seafowl flew about, the same as Captain Cook had reported 137 years before. Murphy noted blue-eyed shags with pure white throats and breasts, albatrosses and petrels wheeling over the sea, and flocks of terns and screaming kelp gulls keeping to the rocky shore.

The *Daisy*'s men slanted a course east and south toward the coast, seeing four more of the little whale-chasers chugging out of fjords on their way to open water. As the brig passed the light on Cape Saunders, two large steamers showed up in Stromness Bay. These signs of human activity puzzled and vexed the Old Man, who recalled South Georgia of former years as quite outside the human—and therefore lawful—world. Murphy scanned the shore. Drawing close he made out only the manlike shapes of king penguins with occasional earth-colored mounds that looked to be slumbering sea elephants.

The brig finally came to the entrance of Cumberland Bay, a protected body of water on the island to which they had steered all this time. The skipper was disturbed by what he interpreted to be an incorrect plotting of a light and a beacon on his chart. Furthermore, the wind had died and the brig could not make headway, which set the Old Man off all the more. Frustrated, he ordered Mr. da Lomba ashore with a boat's crew, assigning Murphy to accompany them as some sort of official. Whatever his role was to be, this overjoyed Murphy. Placed in the bow of the boat as he was, he would have the privilege of being the first of their crew to set foot on that remote ground.

Stromness Bay, photograph taken by Carl Skottsberg.

Although the powerful backdrop of land had appeared at first close enough to touch, it was a pull of some miles, rowing to shore. As they gradually approached, the hills emerged, covered with a mossy carpet, and, on their lower slopes where snow had melted, with patches of rank, green tussock grass. Beyond these coastal ridges, the great range of perpetual whiteness rose far into the pale blue vault against a few streaming wisps from behind the peaks.

Not seated as an oarsman, Murphy indulged himself in the surrounding spectacle. Sea birds put on a stunning show. He saw petrels doing what they had evolved to do, spiraling toward the zenith to become indistinguishable specks against thin cirrus clouds. Since some of these approached, or even surpassed, the limit of his vision—which was in perfect working order—Murphy estimated that they soared to an altitude of a mile above the bay—five thousand feet above their starting point!

Albatrosses, too, and giant fulmars, Cape pigeons, and whalebirds shared in the performance overhead. Finally, Murphy pulled his focus lower and studied a bizarrely strewn landscape. Whalebones lined the shore of Cumberland Bay. Spinal columns, loose vertebrae, ribs, and jaws piled in heaps along the waterline. He counted a hundred skulls within a stone's throw and could only guess at how many thousands more had—attached to their flensed carcasses—been borne out to sea by the tide.

More through their sense of smell than anything, the men in the *Daisy*'s whaleboat turned their attention toward an unexpected settlement as they rounded the point that protected the entrance to King Edward Cove. The odor of decomposition increased, the cove acting as a giant caldron so filled with the rotting flesh and macerated bones of whales that they not only littered the bottom but also encrusted its rim to the highest high water mark. At the head of the cove, below a pointed mountain, a whaling station belched smoke with steamer ships swarming and a raft of carcasses yet to be worked over. Entrails and fragments floated out to sea.

Near the entrance of the cove, a frame building flew the Union Jack. The rowers pointed their boat in that direction, and upon landing, were greeted by a gentleman in tweeds who welcomed them to Grytviken. He was Mr. James Innes Wilson, "His Majesty's Stipendiary Magistrate, representing the Government of the Falkland Islands in the Dependency of South Georgia." Accompanying Mr. Wilson was the customs inspector, Mr. Hardy. These two were the sole officials of the Crown. "Jointly or severally, they served as governor, postmaster, port captain, health officer, police force, judge, jailer, the cook and the captain bold and the mate of the Nancy brig, etc.," this last bit being Murphy's playful reference to W. S. Gilbert's cannibalistic spoof on Coleridge's Ancient Mariner.

But Murphy was baffled. All along Captain Cleveland had spun yarns about this land being uninhabited. He thought people merely holed up or stopped off while on a hunt—whether for fur seals, sea elephants, or whales. Yet here was a thriving, permanent—and civilized—European outpost of some three or four hundred people living orderly lives. That implied there would be regulations. The *Daisy* would have to be

Near Grytviken a raft of whale carcasses floats in the middle of "Boiler" Bay.

"received" into the harbor as at any other port in the world. Murphy anticipated how this would rile the Old Man.

But Murphy was delighted. Given the existence of a settlement, he immediately realized he could probably get letters out to Grace. Almost before introductions were complete, he asked about mail service and was told that one room of the magistrate's residence was a full-fledged Empire Post Office, which meant it could accept Murphy's notebooks as a registered parcel, and that mail generally arrived at and left the island once a month. He beamed at the thought of sending letters whose stamps would bear the southernmost cancellations in the world.

Thinking it his last chance, he dashed off a letter to Grace before returning to the brig, "We made South Georgia yesterday. It is wonderful beyond description. . . . There are only a few minutes and I don't know what to write. . . . I didn't know there was any chance of sending a letter from here. Drop a line to Mrs. Cleveland saying the Captain and all hands are well and that he sends his love."

Officer Hardy then boarded the whaleboat to row off with them for the necessary formalities and to pilot the *Daisy* to safe anchorage. Just at that moment Captain Cleveland's weather-beaten craft rounded the point, however; she was already in tow behind the whale-chaser *Fortuna*, which had picked her up in the outer bay. The *Daisy* dropped anchor in the very center of King

The sailors' church in Grytviken had just been built. It was the southernmost church in the world.

Edward Cove. Murphy, Hardy, and the others went aboard to find the skipper "in a funk and a highly apprehensive state of mind. He had no liking for the civilized look of things."

That evening, having learned they would be at anchor for several days before sailing off to the Bay of Isles, Murphy wrote again to Grace, "It is infinitely sheltered and soft and peaceful here, despite the acrid whaley smell. In the morning, my darling, some heavy registered mail, addressed to you, will receive the postmark of South Georgia. The stamped covers should be a philatelist's delight. Sell 'em!"

Chapter Twenty-Eight

CAPTAIN CLEVELAND'S WORST FEARS were confirmed when he went ashore in the morning to call on Mr. Wilson. Law and regulation had indeed reached South Georgia. On his earlier voyage, the Old Man had assumed the land there and all its associated wildlife as his own personal property, slaughtering whatever suited him. Now, there were rules. Port charges must be paid by any ship entering Cumberland Bay. A sealing permit was required, and the permit came at a price. Furthermore, an export license would be necessary to take away any sea elephant oil. Add to that the recent protection placed on undersized and female seals, and the Old Man was undone. What right did these cursed "limejuicers" have to bleed him white?

It seems British law was also putting a stop to the reckless waste of whales. An abundance of humpbacks had historically led whalers to take only the blubber and cast the carcasses adrift. New regulations, however, required the operating companies to process the bone and flesh into fertilizer—either at their shore stations or on floating factories. Fortunately, the fertilizer, once manufactured, was worth almost as much as the oil.

South Georgia's history as a hunting ground began in 1790 when American ships first arrived from Nantucket and New Bedford. Over the next thirty-two years, more than a million seal skins were taken. Ships like the *Daisy* came and went as if they owned the place; men slaughtered whatever they wanted, wherever they wanted. In 1904, however, Carl Anton Larsen arrived and stayed. The community he built was what so surprised Benjamin Cleveland.

Larsen had first visited South Georgia in 1894 on his way to exploring the Weddell Sea. He was no upstart in the region. The Larsen Ice Shelf is named for him. Before establishing his whaling station at Grytviken, he had commanded three exploration ships, including the *Antarctic* with the famed Swedish geologist, Otto Nordenskjöld. Through no fault of Larsen's, the *Antarctic* ended up in circumstances not unlike Shackleton's ship, the *Endurance*, being caught in pack ice and crushed, leaving the men to winter over and make their way to safety under the most extreme conditions.

Early in his career Larsen noted the huge number of whales in southern waters. Finally, at age forty-four, he left his native Norway and returned to the region, this time on a vessel carrying a prefabricated whaling station and workers' accommodations. With him were eleven crewmembers and sixty-five other men, all of whom were prepared to stay. The station was up and running within five weeks. By the time Murphy arrived its population had grown to several hundred.

Early sealers had left their refuse on shore, including two big iron trypots at the settlement that became Grytviken. From these evolved the name, which translates from Norwegian variously as Cauldron Bay or Pot Cove or Boiler Harbor. Larsen's outfit, the *Compañía Argentina de Pesca*—so named because it was financed in Buenos Aires—quickly became the foundation of an industry that settled other fjords of South Georgia's northern coast. Between Captain Cleveland's first venture to the island in 1907 when he had had the place essentially all to himself, and his arrival with Murphy, some twenty other stations and factory ships, both British and Norwegian, had begun operations.

Captain Cleveland and Murphy were invited to meet the station managers. The Old Man characteristically took advantage of having his very own naturalist in tow, swelling with pride to be on a mission for as august an institution as the American Museum of Natural History in New York City. Murphy's presence—if not erudition—elevated what might have otherwise seemed like an ordinary blubber hunt. At the same time Captain Cleveland tried to keep his young scientist under his thumb, fearing

Murphy would become too forward and soak up more attention than Cleveland himself. In particular, the Old Man was quick to answer questions addressed to Murphy.

But that day Murphy beat him to it.

They were greeted warmly by Captain Larsen and ushered into a snug room where they met the German physician and Norwegian clergyman of the station, an Argentinean meteorologist, two station superintendents, one of whom was Captain Larsen's son-in-law, and two secretaries.

Murphy's illusions of the rough Antarctic life were quickly shattered. Luxuriant palms and blooming plants lined the walls and sills. Through the billiard room window and its lace curtains, he saw a pink-cheeked young woman hanging clothes to dry. The salon where introductions were made contained a piano, a mahogany table, more plants, several painted portraits—including King Haakon of Norway—and caged, singing canaries.

The two captains, Larsen and Cleveland, exchanged a few sea stories before the Norwegian turned to Murphy and said, "Professor, how long have you been going to sea?"

Without giving the Old Man a single second to forestall Murphy's direct reply, the "professor" was off and running with, "All me bloomin' life, Sor. Me mother was a mermaid; me natural father was King Neptune. I was born on the crest of a wave, and rocked in the cradle of the deep. Seaweed and barnacles be me clothes. Every tooth in me head is a marling spike; the hair of me head is Eyetalian hemp. Every bone in me body is a spar, and when I spits I spits Stockholm tar. I'se hard, I is, I am, I are!"

With a horrified gasp Captain Cleveland muttered, "My soul and body," but the other eight men filled the room with loud, Norse guffaws. Murphy's recitation was nothing but what all plebes at Annapolis were required to reply when asked by upperclassmen how long they had been in the U. S. Navy, but only Murphy knew the ditty's origins.

A uniformed butler then served an eight-course meal with beer to accompany it and Havana cigars at the end. Murphy almost regretted not

LEFT TO RIGHT: *Captain Cleveland, Pastor Löker, and Dr. Lampert.*

being a smoker. After the fine dinner he was convinced the greatest health risk in that environment of "hardship" would be an attack of the gout.

Communications were in English, although it took Murphy a few minutes to realize what they meant with questions about the "Dicy." Murphy explained to the German physician, Dr. Lampert, that "Daisy" meant *Massliebchen* to which Lampert and the others replied that the Norwegian word would be *Prestekrave.* Murphy's hosts spoke French and Spanish in addition to English and their native languages.

With piano accompaniment, they all sang from a book of English university songs. Then the station whistle blew, and dinner was over. Pastor Löker, Dr. Lampert, and the secretary who had been playing the piano invited Murphy on an afternoon walk around the area. Off they went, the young men, leaving Captain Cleveland "to recover from the most sumptuous repast he had guzzled for at least six months."

They hiked some miles, first along a shore white with whale bones and littered with dozing sea elephants. Murphy poked one or two in the ribs, awakening them to pose for photographs. Gentoo penguins, in response

Bones and decomposing carcasses littered the beach.

to the approaching hikers, ran up the beach, making themselves easy for Murphy and the others to capture. The birds liked to be scratched on their backs, after which they muttered a sort of thanks as they waddled away. When held without being scratched, they delivered painful nips. In addition to whales' remains, dozens of sea elephant skeletons broke through brittle, decomposing skins, the carcasses having been harvested only for their jawbones and huge ivory teeth.

Eventually, the men came to a wide and deep meadow, shoulder-high in clumps of tussock grass where a small herd of horses greeted them. They were the natural result of an expedition having left a few on the island two years before. The horses had bred and run wild. Unsheltered, unbroken, and sleek with rich spring pasture, they were able to withstand the climate on their own. The Norwegians didn't feed them. Murphy wrote, "They were not shy, and one handsome young stallion with a shaggy mane and fetlocks walked up, nibbled my jacket, and allowed me to warm my hands by whacking his neck."

Feral horses.

Captain Larsen had introduced reindeer from Lapland. They grew fat, bred, and were increasing in numbers, having no wolves or other predators to worry about. Sheep and rabbits did not do as well. The only other land mammal to have established itself was the rat.

The hikers arrived at a glacial outwash where they removed their boots and socks to wade barefoot through the bracing waters. Across the other side, they followed a raging torrent up a gorge to a lake, ascended a ridge of foothills and soon reached fresh snow. Looming above them was the island's jagged main range, including Mt. Paget rising 9,600 feet above the Atlantic and Sugartop at 7,643 feet.

In the time it took for lunch and the walk, no fewer than fifteen humpback whales were drawn up and flensed in Grytviken Harbor. "The Old Man was nothing short of goggle-eyed over the big-scale butchery of modern whaling," Murphy wrote.

As it happened he was observing mechanized slaughter at its zenith. Earlier that year Grytviken had laid claim to the largest harpooned blue

Blue whales in the foreground have already been stripped of their blubber at the Norwegian whaling station in Grytviken.

whale on record (then or since). It had measured 112 feet and was estimated to weigh more than 100 tons—a beast the *Daisy* could never have handled.

Murphy was goggle-eyed, too, over the high degree of refinement at this remotest of remote outposts. After his months on the *Daisy* he was unprepared for Grytviken. The men working there were young, good-looking, strong, and graceful in soft leather suits. They removed their hats when greeting each other as if encountering a lady. They even raised their hats to the black crew members of the *Daisy*. They appeared to have no race prejudice. "In ability, intelligence, and everything else, they put our miserable crew to shame. But, of course, they are better fed, better clothed and better treated. The Negroes on the *Daisy* are the first they have ever seen, and those who have cameras bring them off to our brig in order to obtain photographs of live men with black skins."

The place was virtually self-sufficient. Transport ships brought materials for the whaling activities, provisions for the men, and coal to fire the steam boilers that powered bone saws, winches, skinners, and drive shafts for the machine shops. Industry filled the bay with smoke and stinking vapor. Everything felt orderly and well established, with docks, a marine railway, dwellings, dormitories, a carpentry shop, a cooperage, a forge, blacksmiths, a machine shop, cattle and poultry shelters, a library, chapel, infirmary, and a powerhouse for electric lights and a telephone system. Alcohol was prohibited among the workers. Except for the woman whom Murphy had seen hanging out the wash, the only women allowed were managers' wives and daughters. Captain Larsen's family had recently left.

Back on the *Daisy*, Murphy took out of his letter bag an envelope marked "For Bob's first visit to the penguins." It contained a fanciful sketch by museum colleague, Dwight Franklin. Then Murphy turned in early. After months at sea the afternoon hike had worn him out. He anticipated a good night's sleep on the flat waters of Cumberland Bay. Tomorrow would bring another sort of outing.

Chapter Twenty-Nine

MURPHY'S EVER-PRESENT ENTHUSIASM and charm worked in his favor. Captain Larsen invited him to get a close-up view of modern whaling, and since Murphy had no official duties aboard the *Daisy*, he was free to accept. He boarded the *Fortuna* to see how the Norwegians went a-hunting.

A cold current from the southern ocean hits South Georgia's far shore, splits around the land mass in either direction and meets itself in a giant eddy thirty or forty miles northeast of the island. This water is rich in tiny, shrimp-like crustaceans known as krill, of which there are about eighty-five species ranging in size from under half an inch to more than five inches. Dominant around South Georgia is *Euphausia superba*, the Antarctic krill, each about two inches long and weighing a third of an ounce.

The Southern Ocean supports five hundred million tons of these animals in swarms as dense as twenty thousand per cubic meter — possibly the most abundant species on the planet. Clouds are sometimes thick enough to turn the ocean's surface pink, the color of their bodies. Krill is both predator and prey in the food chain, feeding on ice algae, with its filtering, rake-like leg tips, and in turn becoming the principal food of the humpback, finback, blue, and other baleen, filter-feeding whales.

The *Fortuna* steamed out of Grytviken four hours before reaching the feeding grounds, and then suddenly whales were everywhere, mostly humpbacks and finbacks. Murphy could distinguish them — even at great distance — by their spouts. Finbacks blew tall, vertical exhalations while humpbacks exploded short, bushy bursts. Humpbacks were the preferred catch, fat and small enough to handle easily. Most of the skeletons littering Cumberland Bay were those of humpbacks.

The captain and gunner of the *Fortuna* was in his early twenties, younger than Murphy. His mate, a steward, and seven or eight others completed the crew. Naturally, Murphy compared their operation to the *Daisy*, noting espe-

Dwight Franklin's fanciful view of how Murphy and the whales would get along.

cially that the lookout was protected by an enclosing cylinder and not just the thin iron hoops that Cleveland's men had to cling to "like spider monkeys."

The *Fortuna* rolled and tossed, with water spraying across its main deck. Fortunately, the vessel was built for such sloshing, with high combings to keep the spray from pouring into the hold. The gunner stood on a platform at the bow, which was reached via a catwalk above the wet deck. Murphy watched from the bridge.

Three men under the mate's supervision loaded the short, thick cannon that was the whale gun. Mounted on hinges and a turnstile, it could be pointed in any direction. Its charge was a muslin bag filled with a pound of coarse grained black powder over which a handful of hemp oakum, a rubber wad, and a mass of cotton fiber were packed as a cushion to prevent the discharge

The Fortuna's *hundred-pound harpoon opened like the ribs of an umbrella.*

from breaking the harpoon. The harpoon weighed a hundred pounds; its shank filled the barrel of the cannon, with only its steel barbs projecting. The hinged barbs were held closed with lashings of lightweight rope, which would break when the harpooned whale tugged the line, causing the barbs to open like the ribs of an umbrella to hold the harpoon fast to the whale's flesh.

The tip of the harpoon was threaded to accept a cast iron point that contained a three-second fuse and a powder charge that would explode inside the whale. The bomb point was, of course, spent with a single use, but the harpoon was forged from fine Swedish steel to be used over and over, requiring only minimal and occasional straightening by a smithy between uses.

The *Fortuna* had been the first steamer ever to hunt whales in southern waters. By the time of Murphy's visit in 1912, Captain Larsen had increased the size of his fleet. That morning eleven boats in all—some from other stations—were within sight of each other. Harpoon guns went off almost continuously.

The Norwegian steamer, Edda, *has one whale on the harpoon line at the bow and another whose flukes are already chained through the after hawspipe, amidships.*

A pair of humpbacks approached the *Fortuna* with another steamer bearing down in competition. Captain Andersen swung his cannon and fired it with a great blast and cloud of smoke. Then Murphy heard the crack of the bomb exploding. By the time smoke cleared a dead whale had already turned belly up at the end of an intricately constructed harpoon line consisting of a nine-yard leader and a forty-fathom length of the best Italian hemp attached to 500 fathoms of Manila line that ran over a snatch block, which was connected to steel springs. "The whole outfit represents a sort of gigantic counterpart of the rod, reel, and sensitive hands of a trout fisherman."

A winch hoisted the sinking humpback to the surface. A sharp pipe jabbed into the body cavity allowed air to be pumped inside to make the carcass float. The flukes were then severed with a cutting spade to keep the body from spinning when being towed tail-first. From start to finish, the entire operation took less than fifteen minutes and was without moment. The whale never had a chance. This left Murphy feeling that he had witnessed murder. The limber body floated along the port side. Hunting resumed. Within thirty minutes Captain Andersen shot another humpback.

Occasionally a second harpoon would be required and more rarely, a third, fourth, or even fifth. If a single bomb exploded in the thoracic viscera, death was almost instantaneous. But sometimes the only target above the surface might be the tail end as the animal began its downswing after spouting and inhaling, and an explosion at the muscular end of the whale was not so efficient. For each harpoon embedded in the carcass, a notch was cut on the edge of the fluke stump. This would inform the flensers at the shore station how many pieces of hardware to remove before applying their long-handled knives to the blubber.

"Blue whale, dead ahead!" the *Fortuna*'s lookout cried in Norwegian, and all eyes were on the feeding leviathan. "Half speed," came the command down the speaking tube.

The gunner ran to his platform at the bow while the harpoon was made ready. Everyone watched to see where the whale would breach. Engines were cut to quarter speed. Soon, the water would run red again.

"Under the bow!" shouted the lookout.

A flash and a deafening detonation split the frosty air. This time Murphy saw the iron fling its wild tail of line and penetrate the hulk. Three seconds later came the strange and muffled crack of the bomb. Had it reached the lungs? Murphy wondered. No. The shot was too far back for an instant kill. The wounded whale gathered what little strength remained. Muscle power towed the *Fortuna* forward while the winch pulled and the propellers whirred at full speed astern.

Murphy wrote, "No being can reveal more marvelous grace than a whale. Do not think of them as shapeless, as I once did, because of seeing only bloated carcasses washed ashore on Long Island beaches, with all the firmness and streamline of the body gone. Envision, rather, this magnificent blue whale, as shapely as a mackerel, spending his last ounce of strength and life in a hopeless contest against cool, unmoved, insensate man. Sheer beauty, symmetry, utter perfection of form and movement, were more impressive than even the whale's incomparable bulk, which dwarfed the hull of the *Fortuna.*"

It would have been difficult to measure the whale, and there was no reason to, anyway. If it was average for the species, it was about eighty feet long. Its body was tapered, with the head being about a quarter of the overall length. A single ridge extended just forward of the double blowholes to the tip of the snout. Its body was smooth and free of parasites except for a few barnacles attached to the edges of the flukes, flippers, and dorsal fin. Several dozen grooves—or pleats—ran from the lower jaw to the belly.

The end of November marked the beginning of summer feeding when blue whales were gorging themselves, each animal consuming four tons of krill each day —about forty million crustaceans. Instead of teeth in the upper jaw, baleen hung in a series of several hundred fringed overlapping plates. The throat grooves allowed for expansion when huge gulps of water were taken into the mouth so the water could then be expelled through the baleen plates to trap the krill.

Blue whales are gigantic. Captain Cleveland's men, working in open boats with hand harpoons, could never have gone after a whale that size. But Captain Larsen had steam and diesel, and most blue whales tried out at 120 barrels of oil. This carcass was valuable.

If Murphy was overwhelmed by the catch, he kept it to himself. To the Norwegians, it was business as usual. Thirty minutes later a humpback came along, but the gunner missed his shot, and then a fog bank closed in. A neighboring boat winched a dead whale to the surface; foghorns began to sound, and it was time to head in.

The *Fortuna* ran at half or quarter speed, straining through the spongy gray atmosphere to avoid colliding with any of the many boats doing the same. The show was over. Murphy had not much more to do than relax and eat.

In sharp contrast to the grub routinely slung on the *Daisy*, the day had begun at half past six with coffee all around, followed by a stout breakfast. At noon, there was barley soup with greens, and a pot roast of beef with potatoes. Plenty of sugar and condensed milk were available for coffee, which was served again at mid-afternoon, along with wholewheat, white, and rye bread, liverwurst, cold ham and beef, butter, and maple syrup.

During the fog Murphy saw more birds than he could believe existed on earth. In his words, "There were millions and millions of petrels and albatrosses, filling the air like the snowflakes of a blizzard. The albatrosses were grouped . . . with giant fulmars mingled. . . . Now and then the huddled albatrosses would suddenly become interested in others around them and would begin to bill and bow, spread their wings, bob their heads, and caress each other by nibbling. The reaction worked rhythmically, for the initial movements of one bird would spread rapidly through a group, and within a few moments all of them would be spinning on the water, each paying attention first to one neighbor and then to another."

With nightfall came supper. They had a choice of boiled or fried penguin eggs with fried potatoes and pickles. The eggs were fine gastronomically, but aesthetically left something to be desired since the white remained translucent, even when cooked. By eight o'clock Murphy fell asleep on the cabin lounge and was dead to the world until the *Fortuna* chugged past the *Daisy*'s anchorage at half past one in the morning. Murphy called out for the watch to row in and pick him up in the dory. It was two o'clock before he turned in for the night.

Chapter Thirty

NOVEMBER 28TH, 1912, was Thanksgiving Day. As an American celebration, it had meaning primarily to Murphy and Captain Cleveland and not the Cape Verdeans, West Indians, or Europeans at the whaling station. Nevertheless, the skipper ordered the flag hoisted and the steward to serve what would pass as a feast. Murphy wrote, "We even had roasted turkey, except that it was penguin instead of turkey, and it was not roasted. Worse than that, it was not very palatable. Penguin flesh is to be chosen only to save one from starvation." His bigger regret, however, was that the plum duff for dessert was not laced with some of the captain's rum and set afire to create the illusion of a real banquet.

Murphy longed for something special with which to mark the day, so he decided it would not be sinful to remove just one item from his Christmas box. In fairness to making an early advance, he reached in without looking, ready to take what chance would hand him. What he withdrew was serendipitously labeled Choice Figs packed in *Turkey*. At last, he had come up with something that seemed to match the date.

In anticipation of a steamer arriving from Buenos Aires and because Murphy did not know how long Captain Cleveland intended to remain at anchor in Cumberland Bay, Murphy began to finish up his letters to people at home. He tied a parcel of his notebooks to send to Grace by registered mail. He wrote to her, "Anything you don't understand, just guess at. I'll enlarge considerably on those nights to come, when we will talk and talk, until the sun rises. . . . I sometimes get wild to hear from you, and almost allow myself to hope for a letter. . . . If we had only known ahead of the Cape Verdes and the Post Office here, we might have been

Floating blue whales wait to be processed at Grytviken. A stripped carcass lies in the back.

always less than six weeks apart. But forgive me; I'm so happy that you can hear from *me*. . . . I don't care much about public news, except as to who was elected. It is *you* I want to know about, and after that about everybody we love. I hope [my brother] Ed is making a good job of his senior year. I'd give anything for some information as to what you are doing, but I know in my heart that no matter what else you are doing you are always loving me. Send my love and good news to Mt. Sinai, and greet all our friends for me, I hope so much that everything is well with everybody in my far-away land."

As it turned out the *Daisy* did not try to sail for another ten days and would not succeed for three more after that.

The day prior to Murphy going out on the *Fortuna*, sixty whales had been brought in by the Grytviken fleet. A virtual pod lay afloat at the shore station waiting to be processed. By the next night, all but two or three had been converted to oil and fertilizer. This level of production was what had allowed the station to ship more than 2.5 million gallons of oil the year before, and it would probably exceed that volume by the close of the current season.

Seven more stations were operating in other South Georgia fjords. Murphy extrapolated the massive scale of the slaughter. Seeds of horror at the carnage began to germinate, but they had not burst through the surface. Meanwhile, Captain Larsen extended an invitation to tour the shore station, and Murphy was eager to compare modern methods to those that Captain Cleveland and his Yankee predecessors had employed for nearly two hundred years.

Carcasses were hauled out of the water onto an incline, where the Norwegians used sharp, curved flensing knives on five-foot handles to slit the bodies end to end, unlike the spiral of blubber the *Daisy*'s crew cut. Steel cables and winches were then used to pull longitudinal strips of skin and blubber off the carcasses. The men wore special spike-soled boots so they could walk up, down, across, and over the greasy, slippery dead animals while they worked. It was much different than flensing from a cutting stage on a ship tossing in the wind and a carcass rocking in the waves where it floated

On December 4th, the *Fortuna* alone brought in nine bloated whales, and she had left a tenth afloat and marked with a flag at the feeding grounds. A whale's blubber insulates even after death, and the continuing warmth promotes rapid decomposition, which, in turn, produces gas that more than compensates for the leakage of any air pumped in at the time of death. When they reached port, the animals were enormously swollen like giant balloons. Each humpback was worth about $400, making the total catch for one steamer in one day to be $4,000. Eight more whales were brought in by another steamer later the same day, and more would arrive by nightfall.

The finances of the operation were dazzling, even to a man with a growing disapproval of the butchery. Companies paid their owners from sixty to one hundred and thirty percent on their money invested. Murphy learned that it took about $10,000 to ship and set up a plant; $25,000

Five hundred fifty barrels of oil await shipping at Grytviken.

would buy the first steamer; $7,000 would pay for food and salaries for forty men for six months. After half a year the first shipment of oil could be sold for $86,000—or $44,000 more than expenses and enough to buy a second steamer and double the work force. At the end of the year, a dividend of thirty-five to forty percent could be paid. Murphy fantasized about going into business with Grace. "By the second year we reap 100 percent and after that we can have pie every day and take *two* Sunday papers if we want to." Eight companies were working South Georgia's coast—why not a ninth? "The poor whales just wait to be shot, and when you have one fast alongside, you've got some money."

Meanwhile he had his own work to do. Weather was sunny and clear. The harbor was only partly frozen over, and snow came every day or two. In between flurries the air felt mild, and the hills looked soft, green, and summery. Murphy scaled the mountains and struggled through glacial passes, collecting birds, eggs, and plants. Lakes and lakelets dotted the land. He created something of a sensation by using Indian snowshoes to cross the valleys' soft accumulations. Nobody there had seen such contraptions, although everyone was capable with a pair of skis.

Murphy and Mr. Correia walked through the Bore Valley to a divide with a stone cairn. The pass was a thousand feet above the sea and was the same route used by seabirds when flying to the neighboring fjord. Murphy found it odd to see terns and skuas inland and at such altitude.

Above West Fjord lay five clear, cold lakes whose outwash tumbled over rock and flowed through meadows of green and spongy moss. Offshore were masses of stone—some as large as cathedrals—that had fallen from the coastal hills. And above everything were thousands of speckled Cape pigeons and larger black petrels, which the Norwegians called shoemakers "because they sit at the door of their shops and sing." Murphy did not know about Norwegian shops, but the only place he had ever seen birds singing near doorways in New York was on stage at the Metropolitan Opera House. That day on South Georgia, the shoemakers had "their shops everywhere in the thick, black humus under the tussock grass. In some areas I have found a burrow beneath practically every hummock, and from underground I can hear the trilling of the owners."

But speaking of underground, Murphy could not escape the presence of Norway rats, introduced a century before when New England sealers first visited the island. The entire setting would have seemed idyllic if it were not for the rats, but any uprooted vegetation exposed their subterranean runways and revealed vast graveyards of clean-picked bird bones, thousands upon thousands of bones. At the west end of the island was Rat Harbor, where men from Tristan da Cunha had once tried to introduce rabbits, but they never had a chance. Any that did not succumb to the climate were eaten by the rats.

Working against rocky steeps and difficult snowfields Murphy and Correia made their return from the West Fjord laden with spoils. Murphy packed forty pounds of specimens on his back plus his eight-pound photographic set-up. In comparison to the blubber hunters, his hunting felt noble. He was working toward the advancement of science for better understanding of the natural world. His shooting was not for mere financial gain, nor did his collecting activities threaten the continuation of any of the species from which he took specimens.

On an all-day excursion, Mr. da Lomba and Mr. Vincent took their whaleboats to the east end of Cumberland Bay where the Nordenskjöld Glacier tumbles into the sea. The men were in search of elephant seals; Murphy took inventory of the glorious sights. As they approached the wall of ice, everything gleamed under brilliant sunshine. He scrambled up alongside the glacier, collecting some fulmar nestlings and banding the legs of others. The birds were remarkably approachable.

They returned to the brig just before dark, the bottom of their whaleboats aslop with elephant blubber. They had with them also "approximately a bushel of penguin eggs, all freshly laid, *we hope.*" The Old Man had some hot ginger tea ready, and he and the cooper surprised Murphy with a rack they had built especially for drying bird skins.

Another morning, during heavy snowfall in which visibility was limited to a hundred yards, Murphy and Correia set out about half past nine. The snow eventually became rain then ceased altogether, and brilliant sunshine illuminated many small insects playing in and out of the freshly dusted tussock grass. At a cove along the shore, Murphy found a natural rock arch, about fifty feet wide. A brook flowed under and entered the bay. There, they met a dozen dozing sea elephants, "mostly cows and large pups, which were heaped one upon another like a mound of sausages. It was my first opportunity to see the brutes at a time when my bloodthirsty shipmates were not standing around with lances, aiming to murder them."

In between outings there was time for visiting. Murphy had coffee with the meteorologist; he ate dinner and relaxed by the fire with the British Magistrate, Mr. Wilson, who had put on a dinner jacket in honor of the birthday of some member of the royal family and generously opened a bottle of port for the occasion. Another night he broke out a bottle of Scotch, "his national nectar."

Murphy also called at the Argentine Meteorological Bureau to visit with Eric Nordenhaag, whose hospitality included coffee, cakes, candied ginger, and five years' worth of valuable weather data. South Georgia, Nordenhaag explained, may lie in a stormy area of perpetual low barometric pressure, but the lowest readings were not typically coupled with the most violent storms. He calculated an annual mean pressure of 29.33 inches of mercury (compared to New York's annual mean of 30.04) and his observations showed rapid and dramatic changes.

Of course, temperature fluctuated seasonally. Since 1909, the mean had been 34.4° at sea level. February showed as the warmest month with a mean temperature of 41°; June and July were the coldest at about 28°. In three years, the lowest reading had been 10°, and the warmest, 69.3°. Cloudiness measured seven on a scale of ten, with most of the overcast occurring in summer (December and January).

In exchange for this information, the Swede learned how to skin a king penguin and prepare the skin to be shipped home. Murphy then broke the seal on his can of tea, although he found the coarseness of Nordenhaag's coffee mugs to be incongruous with the fine Formosa leaves that Grace had packed.

Murphy received visitors on his own territory too. Dr. Lampert, Secretary Willberg, the British Magistrate, and half a dozen others had all boarded the *Daisy* a time or two. After the early callers saw that he had nothing but West Indian yellow sugar crystals, they sent out a two-kilo box of loaf sugar from the station. Additionally, Murphy bought (and hid) a case of Norwegian condensed milk to guard against future famine.

The skipper made his own trips ashore. He completed his "acrimonious but inescapable agreements with the British magistrate" and had replenished his supply of ship's clothing from Captain Larsen's slop chest. Murphy, too, visited the station's stores and bought for five dollars "an exceedingly well-tailored dogskin jacket, lined throughout with red flannel."

A revelation to Murphy and the Old Man was that the Norwegian supply of oilskins was dusted with wheat flour. After passing through the tropics, the *Daisy*'s oilskins had come out of the cask in a solid block, and the garments had to be "pulled one from another by the strength of wild horses." The layers of Captain Larsen's coats, pantaloons, and sou'westers came apart without sticking, all for having been dusted as they were packed.

Murphy and the skipper went together to call on a factory ship that supplemented the work of the shore operation. The Norwegian captain gave no indication of any particular aesthetic sense, so Murphy was surprised when they entered the man's cabin. It was filled with potted plants, many of which were in bloom. This confirmed a pattern characteristic of the Norsemen; Eric Nordenhaag's hut, where he lived alone with his dog, had been full of roses, "separated only by window panes from the blizzards that howl outside."

Only a few sea elephants lumbered on the shore of Cumberland Bay. Nevertheless, the Old Man issued a couple of shotguns and a few shells. Shore parties came back with small quantities of meat and blubber. The boiled tongues were delicious, but Murphy put the rest of the flesh in the same category as penguin meat. The *Daisy's* crew also killed ducks for the galley, including the native teal, found nowhere else in the world. It pained Murphy to see these little birds shot willy-nilly for food. He had received from Mr. Wilson, the magistrate, a special permit to collect birds for scientific purposes. The only species that was off limits—even to Murphy—was the upland goose. As for penguin eggs, anyone was welcome to those as food—and the penguins themselves if anyone could stand to eat them.

The upland goose is not native to South Georgia but is a species of the Falkland Islands, a thousand miles to the west and where the birds were considered a pest by sheep ranchers. Mr. Wilson had introduced the species to Cumberland Bay two years before. Six or eight pairs lived in West Fjord.

In addition to penguin eggs and elephant meat, the men caught fish in the kelp beds and helped themselves to whale meat at Captain Larsen's station. Murphy thought humpback meat was far superior to sperm whale. The skipper also instructed the steward in the preparation of

PERMIT TO TAKE SEALS,PENGUINS OR BIRDS,UNDER
REGULATION I OF THE WHALING REGULATIONS,
SOUTH GEORGIA.

I,JAMES INNES WILSON,Stipendiary Magistrate at South

Georgia,one of the Dependencies of the Colony of the

Falkland Islands,do hereby,in exercise of the powers

granted to me by His Excellency the Governor under

Regulation I of the Whaling Regulations,South Georgia,

grant permission to Captain B.D.Cleveland,Brig"Daisy",

to take seals and penguins or birds <u>when in actual need</u>

<u>of them for food</u> or at any time when required for a
                        during 1912/13.
scientific purpose.(Wild Upland Geese excepted)

                                    J.Innes Wilson
                              Stipendiary Magistrate.

Government Office,
King Edward Cove,South Georgia,
28th.November,1912.

                    Note: Kindly report hereafter the number of
                          seals taken for food or scientific purposes
                          under the above Permit before the 1st.
                          January,1913.

muctuc, a "delicacy" enjoyed by whalemen from the Bering Sea. Murphy described the process, "Obtain a chunk of blubber from a freshly killed whale. Slice it neatly crisscross, from the outer side, using a sharp knife. You should then have black squares measuring an inch on a side. The blackskin of the whale is about a half inch thick, and under this the firm, white blubber begins. So you cut through a half inch of this blubber, producing several quarts of one-inch cubes, each of which is half ebony and half ivory. They look like big, bi-colored dice without the dots.

"Next you boil your cubes in a large pot of sea water until a fork will slip easily into the black or white halves. They are then sufficiently tender, but are still firm enough to keep their cubic shape. The cubes are drained and packed into Mason jars, which are filled with vinegar and capped. They look very pretty, but the Old Man says they will not be ready to eat for a month. Nevertheless, he is already licking his chops."

DECEMBER 6TH, returning from a trip into the mountains, Murphy came into view of the harbor and was distressed to see the *Daisy* at anchor with its Stars and Stripes at half staff. He rushed to the station and learned that an accident aboard one of Captain Larsen's boats had cost its gunner his life when the recoil of a harpoon gun had broken its mountings. The twenty-seven-year-old man had died instantly, leaving a wife and four children to learn of the sad news. Rather than bury him in the grim little graveyard above the harbor, Captain Larsen ordered his body prepared for shipment home.

Everyone in Grytviken spoke of the anticipated arrival of the *Harpon* from Buenos Aires. Mail closed December 4th. On the 10th Murphy was off on borrowed skis, trudging up and sliding down a glacier with the secretary and the doctor of the station. He did not ski as fast as the "natives" and confessed to "skiing the bridge of my nose once or twice."

Suddenly, a distant whistle broke the air. The long-expected steamer had announced her entry into Cumberland Bay. *"Harpon!"* Murphy's companions yelled in unison and began to make tracks for home, leaving their visitor far behind.

All work stopped. The *Harpon* carried sixteen bags of mail, including thousands of letters to be distributed among the stations. The letters contained news of family and of war. The Balkans were in conflict. Anglo-German tension was rising. Given that the South Georgia population included men from Scandinavia, Britain, Russia, and Germany, political discussions were lively as newspapers were quickly scanned.

To Murphy's delight he learned that Wilson had, indeed, been elected in the United States. Captain Cleveland called Murphy "all kinds of a Democrat and undesirable citizen." The Old Man had the flag poised to raise for Roosevelt but was a good enough sport to fly Old Glory for President-elect Wilson, even though he had never expected to live long enough to welcome a Democrat into office. Murphy whooped for joy and wrote, "Three cheers for the sanity of the American people! Long live the Constitution, and down with pretenders! Here's trusting that President Wilson will justify us."

Out on the *Daisy*, Murphy received word that there was a letter addressed for him. Mr. Wilson had sent the messenger even before reading his own letters from his own wife in Scotland. Murphy's delight was boundless; he barely knew up from down, although the news did not surprise him. For several days he had nurtured the belief that the steamer would bring him something.

He jumped into the *Grace Emeline* with a greenhand at the oars and leaped out the instant the dory's bow kissed the beach. He ran to the magistrate's office and found his mail next to a waiting armchair beside the stove. Grace's letter was embellished with a pressed four-leaf clover whose stem was woven into the first page of laid-finish, ivory-colored paper.

> Beloved Husband: The loneliness rather grows than diminishes, I am well, . . . I try to stand straight & breathe right. . . . I play my scales every day. . . . I massage my face. . . . I cried when your letters came. I didn't know such letters could be written. The last five reached me August 10th. . . . I sobbed for hours & took my first & last veronal powder. The next day I got back my philosophy & my

trust in God. . . . It is very hard to write to you. There can be nothing satisfactory except to be together. As I want to share every thought & deed with you, I can say nothing, for I know not where to begin. You can at least know that I am well & worship you. Poor lonely boy, you are so brave & good. . . . "The long-wished for day of return" about which Darwin wrote, is something so heavenly that, though I live in the thought of it, it seems very far away. [Your] letters have slept next to me many nights.

Evening, Sept. 6, 1912, Dear Husband: You told me not to write much & not to mail my letters till after Election Day. The whalers may go out earlier, so I am going to send this now. I can say nothing—there is too much. . . . [The visit with my sister and her husband in Pennsylvania] went off beautifully. I rested & walked & rode somewhat. You should have seen me drive their car! I am an expert chauffeur now. The babies were a great comfort. I must try to jot down little things you want to hear. Everyone is well. I had a lovely visit in Mt. Sinai in July. [Your sisters] & I swam a mile. . . . Everyone is specially kind to me. Though the days are happy, the buoyancy of fresh memories has died down, the time ahead seems impossibly long, & there is a heavy ache. I only pray that you are happy. Could I be sure of that, the ache would be eased. I am well, & am reading & enjoying the "Beagle." The Progressive Party made huge strides. A tremendous convention, amidst hymn & prayer & enthusiasm for all that is right, nominated Roosevelt. He is wildly popular, yet a strong undercurrent favors Wilson, who is comporting himself splendidly. He announces himself to be independent of party promises. Taft is out of the running. . . . The old emperor of Japan died. Rosenthal, a gambler, about to disclose dealings between the gamblers & the police, was murdered. Because of the disgraceful "system" (police) the prosecution is dragging along. Congress broke the Hay-Panncefort treaty by granting free passage through the Panama Canal to American ships.

I am going down to Mt. Sinai next week. . . . Mrs. Cleveland was well last time I heard. I am going to take a trip to Florida next winter. I shall be near home, waiting & ready, after March, though I will not expect you till July. I wear my locket with your picture night and day. I wake with your name on my lips. I am learning sacrifice and patience. Husband, read all the longing & ache & loneliness & love in my heart. Yet, dear, my days are happy.

September 10, Dear Husband: Your debts, excepting your grandfather's, will be a thing of the past at the end of this month. . . . I played our hymn for those at sea on September first at the afternoon church service. I played Largo, & Traumerei, for offertory & prelude. I start lessons soon. My eyes are very strong. I keep a careful diary of each day's doings for you. [Your sister] has started school. She fits in here perfectly, & is splendid company. . . . Mother is delighted with her. . . . I am the first girl to swim Laurel Lake, I hour 22 minutes, with a hard wind. Two boats followed me. . . . I can do the underwater breathing now.

Your letters go everywhere with me. I can hardly wait for [my birthday] to open your box. . . . Strive for absolute accuracy in all your scientific notes. . . . I glory in the acclaim you will receive on your return. Oh, it is splendid to do such work, to accomplish, & then come home to recognition. "Concentrate & keep well," must be your motto. . . .

The four leaf clover brought the letter to you. One leaf is for Faith, & one is for Hope, & one is for love, you know. And God put another in for Luck. . . . I send half carbon copy & half the original letter, so that, whether you get this from Norway or Argentina, you will have the paper my hand touched. . . . I would love to send you fat letters such as you sent me. . . . I have read the amusing description of the deserters & H. M. Magistrate to many people. It is great . . . Good wishes to the Captain. Your own wife, Grace.

These would be the only letters Murphy received from his wife during his year at sea.

Chapter Thirty-One

CAPTAIN CLEVELAND'S MEN had long since developed the practice of presenting Murphy with whatever specimens and scientific oddities they came across. The evening of December 10th Johnny the cabin boy brought aboard five young goslings of the forbidden upland goose.

Murphy was greatly distressed, but nothing could be done that night, so he put the birds in a basket and kept them warm. The best that could be done was to try to reestablish them with their parents, but Murphy was pessimistic. Too much time and disruption might have irrevocably separated the young geese from their natural world.

Morning brought a blinding snowstorm. Nevertheless, Murphy and a crew member set out, able to see but a few yards ahead in the dense blast. They headed for the West Fjord lakes, where Johnny reported that he had scooped up the goslings. It took two hours to reach the ancient moraine. Upon arrival, as if by divine intervention, the sun burst through. Fog rolled out of the lowlands and the soft fresh snow receded as if heated by an oven. The landscape softened into tints of green and warm moistness.

Full of doubt that he had gotten there in time, Murphy withdrew one of the goslings from their basket, knowing a solo bird would peep. He took it to the pond where Johnny had visited, set it on the ground, and backed away. Immediately, a response came as a low, throaty cluck. A mother goose swam directly forth with a gander following at a distance. Murphy quickly put the other four goslings at water's edge and backed away again. At first the fluffy birds scrambled in Murphy's direction.

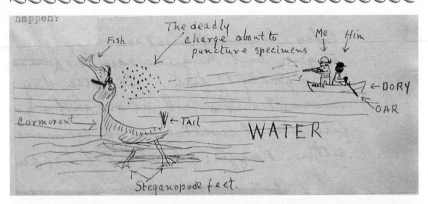

Murphy drew a picture for Grace of how he had collected two specimens with one shot.

Then they heard the familiar sound of their mother and turned their five little tails toward shore to paddle home. Murphy wrote, "The flotilla swam joyfully around a point of land—mama on the left, papa on the right, guarding the lively little ones from the great skuas which were flying above with a strong passion for young goose. It was one of the prettiest sights I ever saw, and I'm sure the five children were the first of their tribe of *Chloephaga picta* to spend a night in the cabin of an American whaler."

This incident did not deter Murphy from continuing to collect specimens from other species. After returning to the *Daisy* and concluding dinner with peach pie, he aimed his shotgun at a cormorant and got both it and the fish in its mouth—all in a single shot, after which he wrote Grace to brag about it.

Snow had turned to sun had turned to rain. Captain Larsen's outfit had been bringing in enormous whales. One sulfur-bottom—as blue whales were called when yellow diatoms parasitized their normally white bellies—had measured ninety-five feet and yielded 180 barrels of oil.

But that was not the business of Captain Cleveland's old windjammer. He was aimed for sea elephants. It was finally time to leave Cumberland Bay now that his doings in Grytviken were over. His men were already starting to heave the first anchor from the muck of King Edward Cove. Murphy would have just enough time to head for shore and accept Mr.

Wilson's invitation for one last "wee sma' nip of the auld kirk," after which he would post his last letter home. By the end of the day all parties would be over. Contact with the wider world would once more be severed.

Rowing back to the brig, he reflected on how things had gone. He had stowed a good collection of plants, invertebrates, fish, rocks, seal skulls, whale embryos, and more than a hundred birds. He had been introduced around town by the Old Man at his own level, always generously presenting Murphy as "a scientific man." This had opened doors to relaxed drinks and conversation among the worldly and knowledgeable men of the station. For an island that had been said to be unpopulated, Murphy wrote to Grace that it was lonelier between Providence and Pawtucket than on South Georgia.

After much song and toil, however, the *Daisy* still floated on the waters of Cumberland Bay. Wind had picked up. "We had one anchor atrip, only to have to let everything go again when the williwaw suddenly raked down from the mountains with such terrific force that the *Daisy* heeled over under bare spars. . . . Never before have I felt winds so strong. . . . All the whale-chasers were driven into the bay for shelter."

Nobody could leave the brig. The storm continued into the next day. Murphy occupied himself with back issues of an English-language newspaper out of Buenos Aires, thoughtfully supplied by Captain Larsen. He read of Grand Central Station's completion, that a Zeppelin had flown over the Baltic Sea, an airplane had carried mail across Long Island Sound, Herschel Parker had reached Mt. McKinley's summit, Caruso had opened New York's opera season, ladies wanted the vote, and Harvard beat Yale for the first time in eleven years. He also read of the growing conflict that would become the First World War. "Two years ago," he wrote, "President David Starr Jordan, of Stanford University, had me nearly convinced that there could never be another war. . . . I still try to believe that [he] was right."

The morning of December 13th broke clear. The brig glided out of Cumberland Bay under tow by one of the whale-chasers. "Old Glory, the Union Jack, and the Blue Cross of Norway dipped thrice in gracious

Three joined photographs show Grytviken on the right, Mt. Paget in the middle background, and the meteorology station at the far left on the low point of land.

farewell. Whistles blew, hats and handkerchiefs waved, and the crew of the *Daisy* gave three long cheers." They rounded the point, leaving milky snow water behind and headed into the blue outer bay. The steamer cast them off and pointed its bow toward the feeding grounds. Mountains, which had been sharp and sunny, were soon erased by fog. A calm set in.

The skipper ordered three whaleboats lowered with full crews to tow the brig slowly ahead. The risk of drifting to the lee shore was great, and ice floated everywhere, massed by the recent storm. Without momentum from the wind they had no way to avoid the bergs and rocks. For a time it seemed the vessel scarcely moved, despite the will and brawn of eighteen men at their long oars. It was just as well they moved slowly, because one of the greenhands mysteriously went overboard. Fortunately, the men on the quarterdeck succeeded in throwing him a line and hauling him in before the temperature of the water won his life. He would probably not have survived had the brig been required to come about for the rescue.

Oddly, another sailor experienced a crisis, this man having a fit of some sort on deck, falling down and losing consciousness, jerking his

limbs. He had had no such previous attacks, so Murphy surmised it was not epilepsy. He attributed it instead to the substandard conditions on the *Daisy* and the poor general health of many of the men when they had boarded six months ago "due to their own fault and to plenty of other causes." Murphy began to fear they would not carry everyone back alive to the West Indies by the time their journey ended.

That night, after an impenetrable fog becalmed them once again, the captain ordered whaleboats lowered into the black. The sea was full of growlers, and the brig had to be towed again. Eventually a breeze came up and the morning rose fresh and sunny. The coast lay forty miles to windward and they were finally underway in earnest.

Winds held through the night and into the next day. The *Daisy* was headed for the large and open Bay of Isles toward the west end of the main island. This was the territory Captain Cleveland remembered as being especially thick with elephants.

Just for the fun of it, Murphy stood a couple of two-hour tricks at the wheel, steering the vessel close into the coast then coming about on an offshore tack, past the entrance to Prince Olaf Harbor. Unlike the green of snug King Edward Cove, the land they sailed near could not have

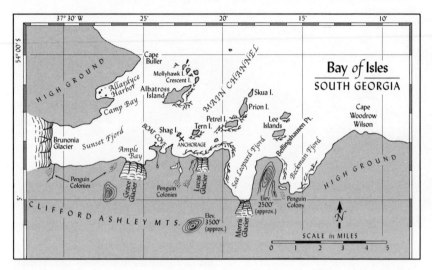

Murphy assigned place names on his sketch map of the Bay Isles, many of which remain in use, such as Grace Glacier, Cape Wilson, and the Clifford Ashley Mountains.

looked more desolate. Bleak and frozen, it stretched white from shore to mountain crest. The ocean was dotted in icebergs, some old and worn into fantastic shapes, having overturned several times each.

The Bay of Isles was as yet uncharted. Save for the body of water itself, no features were named. Murphy was thrilled at the idea of entering virgin territory. "There is not even a map . . . so the first sketch, and the naming of its promontories, glaciers, and islands, will fall to me."

At two o'clock the afternoon of December 15th, they dropped anchor in thirteen fathoms of water after having sailed through tight passages to reach the protection of high cliffs on one side and the encircling kelp fields of two small islands on the other, the kelp acting as a natural breakwater. The Old Man had sailed these waters before, but Murphy was wide-eyed as they barely cleared points of land and seemed about to scrape their yardarms against the orange lichen that grew on the shore's towering rocks.

Islands dotted the bay, tempering the snowfields of the mainland with their tints of green. Wandering albatrosses stood in the lushness of the islands looking like so many scattered flocks of sheep. Penguins and giant fulmars generously populated a nearby mainland beach. Heaps of sea elephants lay here and there. The general landscape, however, struck Murphy as depressingly dull. Everything felt cold and gray.

Murphy wasted no time scrambling into a whaleboat with some of the crew who were rowing to shore on the main island. Seeing the landscape up close was full of pleasant surprises. The tussock grass was more green and lush than it had appeared at a distance. The island abounded in sheltered hollows and fresh ponds.

The men got to work lancing elephants. Murphy split off. Right away he saw sparrow-sized pipits *(Anthus antarcticus)*, the world's southernmost land birds and the only songbirds native to South Georgia, and he, for the first time, met innumerable albatrosses face-to-face on their own territory. He also slew his own elephant with a lance—not primarily for its blubber but for its skull. "Rather an ugly job," he wrote, "although I did it as neatly as possible."

The next day and those following were full of activity. With assistance from three sailors, Murphy began to set up his camp. He selected a tent site in a mossy gulch that faced across a cove to the waterfall from a gla-

Grace Glacier.

Murphy's camp at the Bay of Isles with his dory beached in the landing cove in the background.

cier that so stunned him with its beauty that he named it for Grace. A colony of nesting albatrosses lay a stone's throw in one direction and a group of elephants in the other. He regretted the certainty that the pod would not be wallowing in the shallows for very long. The *Daisy*'s gang would soon "shed their blood and leave them as hideous stripped carcasses to undergo slow rotting in the cold."

The men carried up large smooth stones from the beach and built a wall on the down slope and leveled off with more stones and uprooted turf pulled from the grassy hummocks. Once the site was flat and smooth, they erected the tent and brought a table, a chair, and an oil stove from the brig. This constituted a workshop. Penguins waddled up as if to say hello.

The tent was small. Murphy was disappointed but resigned to make it do as his temporary laboratory. He set his mind to collecting. He rowed to an unnamed island where he shot five teal and five pipits. As far as Murphy knew the American Museum of Natural History had no such pipits as part of its collection—nor did any other museum in the United States. Yet the birds were abundant around the Bay of Isles and their relationship to similar species found in South America was of interest. Dedicating a few of them as "martyrs to science," he drew a bead on the unsuspecting birds. It was tricky, because they were so tiny and so tame it was hard to get enough distance not to "blow them to atoms, even with the small auxiliary shell in my shotgun."

He much preferred to aim his camera. Shooting pictures never involved matters of conscience. He turned his lens to the albatrosses, which were so great in number he assigned their name to the ground on which he and they stood: Albatross Island. In addition to these grand birds, he found nesting giant fulmars whose Latin name, *Ossifraga gigantea*, translates to big bone breaker, but whose common names among sailors were related to the strong smell of musk emitted by the birds. "Stinker" was perhaps the most polite. These birds could nest safely on the ground, since they had no natural predators.

A sudden blizzard blew up, which had Murphy jumping in the whale-boat with the others and pulling stroke oar for home only to have the sky blue up again. It felt strange to have the sun shining long past eight o'clock and stranger still to go to bed while the sky was still light. It was December 18th. The longest day of the year was approaching.

The island closest to the *Daisy*'s anchorage supported a colony of shags, or cormorants. Their undersides gleamed white and their iridescent blue backs contrasted with large orange warts at the base of their bills. A pair alighted on the brig's foreyard "from which both birds watched the activity on board with evident curiosity but no trace of fear."

While the hunters slew, skinned, and stripped elephants of their blubber, Murphy prowled the beaches. The waste of his shipmates' massacre bothered him, because most of what they killed was not used. The skin, which "might make a single piece of leather large enough to line the tonneau of a motor car, is flayed off the blubber in small quadrangles and wasted. Then, after the beast has been deprived of blubber, the huge, red carcass, with its meat and bone, is likewise wasted. The ghastly wastage of former years still lies on the sand and among the tussock hummocks. The birds, such as skuas and giant fulmars, may obtain a brief banquet from an occasional freshly killed carcass, but after the remains have frozen or have dried for a day or two, they no longer serve any active purpose in the economy of nature, and it may be years or decades before such sorrowful remains can disappear."

Snow flurries and winds intermittently kept the men shipbound. Murphy went to his tent as weather permitted, even then its canvas rattling and flapping as he observed and preserved anything and everything he could. "His" pod of sea elephants, for example, was in plain view from his table and chair. He watched enormous bulls fighting over a single, diminutive brown cow, the only female among them.

One evening while rowing the *Grace Emeline* back to the brig through whitecaps and combers, a sea leopard surfaced near the dory just off the cormorant rock. The seal was easily identified by its long, slender body, its humongous gaping jaw and long, sharp teeth. Murphy knew its species, *Hydrurga leptonyx,* as an especially ferocious one, a half-ton aggressive hunter living on warm-blooded animals, as well as fish and krill. The food of choice is penguin meat, chasing or grabbing a bird while swimming, then thrashing the capture back and forth until the skin peels away. The seals are also known for playing with their catch, much as a cat will bat at a mouse. Murphy hoped to reencounter the one he saw that evening.

Returning to land, Murphy worked all morning in his tent, skinning teal and sheathbills—or at least he thought it was still morning. Captain Cleveland came in to say it was three o'clock and did Murphy not want dinner? After that he began to take his dinner ashore with him when he rowed off in the morning. He ate albatross egg sandwiches or cooked a duck breast on his little stove. Then he made tea using his cherished tea ball that Grace had packed for him. The larder in his tent included lump sugar, pilot bread, condensed milk, and maple syrup.

He took great pleasure in how he set things up and he enjoyed the associated solitude. His mind was free to drift without interruption. He sang out loud, philosophized, and dove into his thoughts, which included much dreaming and reminiscing about Grace and home. He sensed utter privacy as he worked. "Across the cove I have a wonderful glacier, about a quarter mile wide. The beautiful blue ice rises up more than a hundred feet, and hourly, or more often, great bergs break off and crash down into the sea with a noise like a presidential salute. Then the waves spread out and dash on the shore below me. Johnny penguins and King penguins trot along the little ice brook that flows a few steps from my stand and bull elephants gurgle and fight all day long. Skuas come down and peer at me through the open door. They clean up my refuse and eat the cast away carcasses arsenic and all. Giant petrels, terns, gulls with white-bordered wings—all cross and recross above me. All these things I can see while I sit here on the job." (Arsenic was used to preserve the skins.)

With the sun not breaking through for several days, Murphy's camera lay idle. A strong gale blew up, accompanied by great ocean swells. Rugged water made rowing the dory difficult. Murphy's arms and back were growing hard and strong with the new routine of traveling back and forth between the *Daisy* and his station on land. Each time he reached the brig three or four men stood by with coils of rope in case the toss of the sea might prevent Murphy from making fast on his first try.

His landing on shore was equally wild. Surf broke violently on two rocky points that flanked his cove. Kelp grew to thirty or forty fathoms at the opening and flattened the water within. Once ashore it was but a short walk to "Camp Chionis," so named for *Chionis alba*, the snowy sheathbills that were in their nesting phase there. These birds depended on other species, steal-

Captain Cleveland holding a pair of Leach's petrel chicks.

ing most of their food directly from penguins and shags or eating eggs, small chicks, carrion, feces, and other such delectables.

The air temperature hovered right around freezing. To keep himself warm in the tent, which was only eight or ten degrees higher than the outside, Murphy wore two suits of medium weight woolen underwear, woolen stockings, and gabardine riding trousers, over which he wore high leather boots that could be extended all the way up to his hips or lowered to knee level. If he were setting out to walk very far, he substituted stout shoes. If the weather looked especially threatening, he added an outer layer of oilskin trousers over his boots. On his upper body he wore a heavy wool undervest, a gray short-sleeved sweater, a heavy double-breasted blue flannel shirt (wool), a windproof Russian vest, his college varsity sweater, and, finally, his recently-purchased dogskin coat, which was sometimes topped with an oilskin jacket. Depending on the weather, he wore a gray felt hat or a sou'wester. His belt was always fitted with two knives, and also, "two pairs of heavy woolen mittens when they're not on my paws." He preferred knitted mitts to leather, because he could wring water out of them and still depend on them for a little warmth.

Despite its sheltered location, his tent seemed often at peril. December 21st was the longest day—and Murphy hoped the windiest—of the year. He lashed the canvas door tightly closed, but the whole structure fluttered and rocked. At noon Mr. da Lomba rushed up to say that the immediate recall flag had been hoisted on the *Daisy*'s masthead. They ran to the boat cove where men were already piling the *Grace Emeline* full of stones. It had become routine even to half fill the thirty-foot whaleboats with sand or cobbles whenever they were going to be left for any time on the beach.

They finished securing the dory, sprang into the whaleboat, and pushed off with two men at each oar. "If the blizzard raged any harder it would blow the hills down," Murphy wrote. "The gale was blinding, and there seemed to be as much salt water in the air as in the sea."

Right about the time they were pulling for the safe haven of the tossing brig, Captain Cleveland recorded the barometric pressure at 28.75 inches of mercury. This compared to the Great Galveston Hurricane of 1900 when winds had reached 100 miles an hour. The Old Man sensed the approach of the southwesterly gale even before it arrived. At three o'clock snow began to fall, or rather, snow began to be driven parallel to the surface of the churned-up sea.

The storm raged well into the next day. When the wind dropped off Murphy went ashore to photograph king penguins incubating their eggs, but he was up against the crew who seemed determined to snatch up every fresh egg they could for the ship's larder. Any egg that was not fresh, the men broke in hopes of inducing the deprived penguin to produce a more edible one. Murphy complained to the Old Man that his men were doing their best to destroy the very resource he had gone to study, but he did not receive a satisfactory response.

Also disappointing was the discovery that the storm had broken one of the ropes supporting his tent. The back had fallen in, the canvas had torn, and snow had ruined a few skins. After emptying the dory of sand and rock and washing the boat, he took whatever skins he could salvage out to the brig

Murphy was frustrated. He had finally arrived at his true destination and it seemed to be one headache after another. Would he ever get a day's work without interruption? He wished for the refuge of a room in one of the whaling stations.

Chapter Thirty-Two

MURPHY HAD NO REASON to expect Christmas to be different from any other day. Few of the crew had any concept of a New England Santa Claus celebration, and Captain Cleveland was not exactly the jolly type. Nevertheless, the night before, Murphy suspended a stocking from the bookcase at the foot of his berth. It was the nearest he could come to a chimney. In his letter bag he had several envelopes dated December 25th, 1912. He tucked these into the stocking and turned in.

What he woke to in the morning surprised him. The captain's voice filtered through the haze of sleep. "Merry Christmas!" rang loud and carried an unexpected buoyancy. Murphy rushed to Grace's letter and read her message several times over before opening his other greetings. One friend had sent photographs of Long Island ducks and shore birds, the images of which pierced with a stab of nostalgia. Dwight Franklin, his colleague from the museum, had sent a cartoon of Murphy's supposed goings-on with the penguins. Grace's mother had generously tucked in a check with her letter, which Murphy "decided not to take to the bank today!"

Grace also sent a calendar with a page for each day. "I shall take infinite pleasure," Murphy replied to her in his journal, "in tearing off the dead records of days past, crumpling them up and tossing them overboard. Ultimately they will melt away . . . until no date remains to separate you and me." How Grace had obtained a 1913 calendar in May of 1912 was a delightful mystery and an effective Christmas surprise.

In addition to her letter, Grace had put together a package of dainties: maple sugar, hard candies, preserved ginger, sweet biscuits, concentrated soup, milk chocolate, and glacéd fruits. She also included a teacup and a second box of peppermints for Captain Cleveland, the first having been given him when Grace departed from Dominica. As it turned out Ada Cleveland, the captain's wife, had packed in her Christmas box for her husband, not one but *six* boxes of the very same kind of mints. Apparently Benjamin Cleveland's fondness for sweets was no secret!

For dinner they ate boiled potatoes. These were a rare treat, given that the supply was very low. They also had apricot pie—a nice change from dried apples.

Murphy enjoyed no such weather on Christmas day as Dwight Franklin had imagined.

The skipper opened the first jar of the *muctuc* he had prepared at Cumberland Bay. Murphy tried a little but felt it had been "a definitely over-advertised dish."

Murphy spent the afternoon on deck working on skins that he and Mr. da Lomba had brought out to the *Daisy* the day before when they had scouted out a king penguin colony not yet plundered by the crew.

King penguins (*Aptenodytes patagonicus*) are big birds—each standing about three feet tall. They typically colonize in vast groups along rocky shores. Murphy estimated the population to be around 350 adults and yearlings. It was the height of egg season, which occurs between November and April. From courtship to fledging of the chick, the breeding cycle is usually fourteen months, so they typically breed twice in three years. They have no nests. Rather, the birds Murphy saw were on bare rock, incubating single eggs on top of their feet and beneath a pouch of fat and feathers. Male and female parents traded off on the task of

James Weddell wrote of king penguins in 1823, "In pride, these birds are perhaps not surpassed even by the peacock."

keeping the egg warm. Later, they would share in brooding the chick after it hatched—about fifteen weeks from egg laying to fledging. Chicks would be entirely on their own after nine months.

The odor of accumulated droppings was hard to ignore, but Murphy found the birds to be highly gregarious and in fine voice. He began by making several photographs, then with his shotgun he sacrificed an assortment of females and males in various stages of molt and maturity. Fortunately, Murphy and Mr. da Lomba had only a short distance to carry the dead birds before finding a comfortable place on the ground on which to skin them. With ten specimens at forty pounds each, it made for quite a haul.

Back in New Bedford Mr. da Lomba had bragged to Grace that he could skin a penguin in four minutes flat, but in actual practice the process took him closer to twenty-five minutes (compared to Murphy's ten). Both men worked as fast as they could, however, and between the two of them they had all the birds separated from their feathers in about an hour and a half. Next came the two-mile hike back to Murphy's camp. The ground was rough, and the skins were heavy—even with the flesh and bones no longer inside. Eventually everything was loaded into the dory.

The penguins were "plump as skunks," and the skins had to be scraped clean before they could be packed in the salt and cotton that would preserve them until they reached New York City. Christmas day,

Murphy and a couple of helpers stood on deck and scraped. The job called for muscle and patience. Although the men stuck with it until late in the day, they were able to finish only seven of the ten big skins. As Murphy flung globs of penguin fat overboard, skuas, petrels, gulls, widgeons, stinkers, shags, Cape pigeons, whalebirds, albatrosses, paddies, and terns circled in tight frenzy above.

Although desolate, gray, and wind-scoured, their anchorage presented much to watch—and watch out for. Icebergs and growlers were a continual presence. With very little showing above the surface, growlers in particular posed a risk to the thin-skinned whaleboats and to Murphy's graceful little dory. Many of those he saw were bowl-shaped, with staghorn-like fronds projecting around the rim. Others were more spherical. All were pitted and faceted—like an insect's compound eye. Murphy wrote, "They are devilishly hard to see from the boat. Miles from the ship, and almost as far from land, in murky weather, I have become first aware of the blood-chilling presence of a growler by seeing a submerged thin blade of ice that has just missed the delicate cedar planks between our boat's crew and the hereafter!"

December 26th a chunk of ice half as tall as the *Daisy* drifted dangerously near. If not headed off, its weight and inertia could have ripped the ship's copper sheathing and ground her hull to splinters. Armed with poles, oars, and spars, as many men as could fit there crowded at the bow to push against the ice. Slowly, and with great effort, the gap between brig and berg widened until, eventually, the threat passed astern.

Sea leopards were also common in the Bay of Isles. Murphy was itching to get one of the beautiful, snaky creatures for his collection. Recovering one posed a problem, though. He did not want to shoot one willy-nilly only to have it sink into the depths. December 28th he noticed one at the surface among the brown ropes of kelp under the counter at the stern of the brig. The animal's back made a small island. Periodically, it lifted its head and opened its nostrils to inhale. Now and then it opened its mouth, exposing terrible-looking triangular back teeth that would have been used to seize penguins under water. Taking the opportunity

Murphy finally aimed his .22 and shot the animal in the brain with a long-rifle slug.

"To my great regret and discouragement the creature, which had been floating so buoyantly, sank like lead. I watched it go down, slowly turning over and apparently stone dead. The next sea leopard that I try to collect will have to be firmly ashore or on the ice, because my conscience keeps me awake when I take life to no purpose."

Whenever weather permitted Murphy went ashore to his tent, even if only to write up the notes in his journal. His tea set-up provided warm comfort, and he relished the privacy of his own thoughts. The tent often rattled and pulled at its stays in a pounding of rain and snow.

December 29th broke clear and bright beneath tattered cumulus clouds, but by mid-afternoon the air filled almost solid with falling, blowing snow. Weather changed without warning or pattern. Breezes shifted from east to west then back again—all in the same day. Their anchorage and the grim, gray land provided none of the shelter they had had in Cumberland Bay. No cove, no hill, and certainly no trees served as interruption to the nearly constant wind.

Murphy doggedly persisted, however. He rowed the *Grace Emeline* to the lee side of the rocky islet where he had found the cormorants. He tied the dory's painter fast and let her float while he scrambled up a wall to the flat summit above.

"The islet was a rugged little pile of strata tipped on edge, cut by many gorges in which long strands of seaweeds swashed. On top it was covered with black soil and tussock grass, alive with millions of the tiny, leaping insects called springtails, and here I found my first pipit's nest. It was made of fine roots, partly covered with a dome. No eggs had been laid, but a pipit flew out of it just before I would have stepped on it.

"The blue-eyed shags or cormorants were, however, the principal inhabitants of the rock, nesting on ledges all over the northerly or sunny faces of the cliffs. I filled fourteen pages of a notebook with observations on the behavior of these little-known birds.

"Their courtship was in full blast while the nests were still building. I

244

saw one pair standing side-by-side on their unfinished home, and curt-seying. The enraptured birds would press their cheeks together, bow down their heads, then twisting their necks, put their other cheeks together in the same way and curtsey again. After this graceful minuet had carried on for several minutes, the male would launch off on a short, ecstatic flight, from which he would soon return to resume the lovemaking.

"I sat beside one shag that was brooding a naked, black, newly-hatched young and one green egg (I had to lift her—or was it him?—off the nest to find out what was underneath). She settled back and watched me with blue-rimmed eyes. Her only note was a barely audible croak—such as Keats calls 'a little noiseless noise.' She kept her bills parted, the mandible and throat trembling as when one's teeth chatter, but I doubt that she was afraid. At any rate, she had no cause to be. I can shoot them at shotgun range, but they are safe when I'm a guest in their homes!"

The *Daisy*'s men were not so respectful of life. While Murphy was being delicate with birds, the elephant seal hunt was in full swing. Captain Cleveland's crew thought nothing of sneaking up on a sleeping animal, whacking it over the head, and piercing it through with a lance. Death occurred by exsanguination.

The joke about the *manduc* that had been made while at sea finally became obvious. When the hunt began in earnest, Mr. da Lomba produced seasoned "elephant clubs" from the brig's hold. These herculean weapons were five to seven feet long. The little bludgeons the men had turned so enthusiastically on the lathe those weeks ago looked suddenly like toys and parlor ornaments. Anyone who had made one stored it promptly in his sea chest. No one would have dared approach a sleeping elephant with one of those souvenirs; any blow they delivered would have served only to rile the animal. But when "Long John da Lomba" swung one of his big clubs, he knocked his victims "stiffer'n a loon's leg," as he put it. Those beasts never stirred again.

Until November, the elephant seals (*Mirounga leonina*) had been thousands of miles out to sea foraging for squid and fish, making two-hour dives that descended three thousand feet or more. Then the males came ashore, followed by the females in early December, and collected on South Georgia beaches. It was calving and breeding season. The pups weighed about seventy pounds at birth and would gain six to eight pounds each day until they were weaned at four weeks. Just before weaning each cow would mate again, but the embryo would not implant for another three months. This ensured delivery at the height of the following austral summer.

Elephant seals are huge animals. Bulls weigh over 6,000 pounds and measure more than twenty feet long from snout to flipper tips. The cows are significantly smaller at less than 2,000 pounds. Because it was breeding season, the animals were not actively feeding. They had put on a thick layer of blubber to sustain themselves. That blubber—and the clear, valuable oil that could be rendered from it—was what the Old Man was after. The hunters found elephants in large groups. Each dominant male—or beachmaster—kept a harem of about fifty cows. Larger pods included sub-dominant bulls, also grouped with several dozen cows.

The common name of the seals comes from the bulls' peculiar inflatable nose, which, indeed, has the appearance of a trunk. Both sexes are swift and powerful swimmers but awkward on land. Barely strong enough to lift their bodies off the ground with their flippers, they ventured inland no more than half a mile, leaving a scraping of tracks as they labored themselves forward.

Murphy observed behavior that ranged from a great deal of sleeping to ferocious fights between bulls trying to establish beach territory. Most fights lasted only a few minutes, after which one of the males would slink off. The fights mainly involved pushing and shoving and bumping each other, with occasional bites on the nose and around the neck. Many bulls exhibited scars from past fights or fresh wounds from recent ones. Big and fierce as they may have been among themselves, they were all defenseless against the *Daisy*'s crew.

December 31st eighty-six elephants were killed. January 1st, despite fresh, hip-deep snow, seventy-seven more were stripped of their blub-

Bellowing elephant. In addition to a layer of blubber, the animals are protected with inch-thick skin around the neck and breast.

ber. Murphy wasted "a good many rifle balls in order to prevent the brutes from being tortured by the ghastly lances. A bullet through the brain does the trick instantly, and the bleeding that the sealers regard as necessary for the production of clear and light-colored oil flows just as effectively from a freshly killed animal as from one still living. Cow sea elephants and young males can be numbed by a clubbing on the head, and then so treated with lance thrusts through the chest that they never wake up. The big bulls are, however, almost impossible to stop in their tracks unless a bullet pierces the parietal bone at the side of the brain case, between the huge crest on top of the skull and the massive bony arch below the eye. The Old Man has four Springfield muskets, shooting a 45-70 lead bullet propelled by black powder. These are used only by himself and the officers. They produce a thundering roar and a tremendous cloud of white smoke, and yet they are not as effective as the much smaller modern rifle and ammunition in my own outfit.

"It is horrible business, but, after all, it is what has beckoned the crew 7,000 miles from home, so I suppose that I ought to be tolerant about it."

Days alternated between penetrating cold with horizontally driven, skin-needling snow and majestic bursts of calm and slanting sun. Clear weather was startlingly transparent. Faraway objects appeared deceptively near, and distance became difficult to estimate. From the brig's deck, the range of hills behind the surf-lined beach looked like something Murphy could throw a stone to, yet he knew from his own tramping they stood at least a mile back. At the last light of day, mountain peaks of South Georgia's main range seemed close enough for him to "run and climb in no more time than it takes to think the act, when, actually, many a toilsome mile and rocky gorge and never-thawed crevasse lie between them and me."

Chapter Thirty-Three

CADELA, THE PUPPY that had earned the Old Man's scorn by running in fear from the *Daisy*'s rats, was alive and well, happy to be loaded into a whaleboat, taken ashore, and allowed to participate in the excitement of the slaughter. No longer timid, she lapped at the pools of hot blood. She even rushed at a twenty-foot bull and seized it by the snout. The men shouted frantically, fearing their pooch would be either bitten in two or flattened by the gross weight of the seal. Instead, the elephant gave a toss of his head and sent the dog flying. Sailing fifteen feet through the air did little to discourage Cadela. She picked herself up and started back for more fight but was successfully called off by the crew.

"My soul and body," muttered the skipper. "That bitch ain't afraid of anythin'."

Mr. Almeida looked on with a knowing glance. "Portugee dog," he said, making a jab at the Old Man's earlier assessment.

Cadela was not the only one who had matured. Conrad, who had trembled like a Dominican gecko on his first ascent of the ratlines and who was nearly "scared into the next world the first time he came into close quarters with a whale", had become one of the most fearless members of the hunt. He was not only the youngest of the crew, he seemed to have come from the most protective family. He had been well schooled in comparison to the others. Determined to pull his weight, he had overcome his terrors of going aloft and of doing vigorous battle in a whaleboat. As the *Daisy* had made her way southward, there was no better member of the watch to slide out on the highest yardarms to take in a sail—even in the dark of night and with wind nearly shaking him out of his clothes.

Conrad had grown husky, too. He pulled a strong oar and wielded a deadly lance, and because he used his brain in conjunction with his brawn, Mr. da Lomba predicted he would make a first-class boatsteerer on the next voyage, if he decided to come along—although Conrad was probably better suited to remaining on dry ground and becoming a teacher.

Murphy, also, had built up muscle. Most days he rowed at least a mile—sometimes six or seven. It was hard rowing both in the dory and the whaleboats, not at all like paddling across the flat water of Mt. Sinai Harbor. "You have to lie back and put your heart into each stroke," he wrote, "for the winds are like a strong hand and they always change so as to be against one both going and returning. Sometimes the water is picked up in sheets and dashed over us as we pull across the wild Bay. I wear oilskins and long leather boots practically all the time now. It is a rough life and I rejoice in it, although it is strenuous in every sense. [The wind] has ripped my little silk 'Old Glory' to shreds. A tent is a miserable affair here. All my work I have to do in an outdoor temperature, and sometimes my fingers tingle as I sit and skin the birds. The stove is no good in the tent when the wind blows . . . It has been snowing every day, and frequently raining ice. . . . Now and then the sun takes a peek through a hole in the clouds, but not liking the look of things he neglects us for two or three days. . . . We haven't seen any neighbors yet, except a distant sealing steamer. . . . At 5:00 or 5:30 we breakfast. Then if weather permits I take the dory and go ashore. Unless I need help for working, or rowing in the wind, I prefer to go alone. Sometimes I come out for lunch and sometimes I take bread and elephant tongue, and make tea. I work at Elephants, exploring, photographing, or bird skinning all day, and about 7 p.m. row out again, yell out, 'Ho! Dory alongside!' The men then drop the tackles, and when I hitch them on and call, 'Fore and aft' I'm hoisted out of the boisterous sea until the cranes are swung. I always make myself responsible for every detail in handling my own boat and always do a full seaman's share when in a whaleboat."

Supper was usually served around eight o'clock—sometimes later—making at least a fifteen-hour day, after which Murphy and the others were usually more than ready for sleep. Little time or energy was left over for bathing or grooming. Murphy had not shaved for over a month and did not expect to until after they headed for home.

In addition to his birds, he explored the inner workings—or former workings—of the elephants. This soft tissue investigation was most easily accomplished in running fresh water. Standing in a brook under falling rain and snow he measured a small intestine at 253 feet!

When it came time to work on skeletonizing, he selected eight heads, both male and female. "Salome, the daughter of Herodias," he wrote, "would not dance very far with one of these on a silver charger. It took two strong men to carry the head of a big bull from beach to boat, which they did by thrusting a lance handle through a loop of the tough hide and swinging the burden between them."

If the men found that their prey had wandered inland at all, they filled iron buckets with a layer of pebbles and shook them against the bottom to scare the elephants back to shore before killing them. This saved lugging blubber overland. It was hard enough hauling them from the beach, lashing their stripped fat into rafts, rowing the load out to the *Daisy*, hoisting it on board, and getting it to the trypots.

Thirty-six elephants were killed January 2nd, forty-two on the 4th. Many of the cows had recently hauled up on the beach and were especially fat, which meant they would yield a lot of oil. Captain Cleveland's license from Mr. Wilson in Cumberland Bay forbade him killing any females or pups. But Mr. Wilson was not in the Bay of Isles to monitor the situation, and the Old Man was accustomed to doing as he pleased. It was his nature to disregard cheerfully any agreements made and to slaughter universally—bulls, nursing cows, and any of the playful young calves.

Days went on like that, with forty-two elephants killed January 5th, and forty-six more the next day. Murphy called it a holocaust.

A few living things were left untouched. Jellyfish the size of open umbrellas, for example, pulsated in the kelp fields, their transparent mantles protecting brown central asters. Murphy scooped some out with a net, noticing small crustaceans and fish among the tentacles, curious that the potent stinging cells did not appear to affect the "small guests living among the gelatinous trailers."

Another sea leopard showed up, sleeping on a cake of ice floating near the ship. Murphy whistled. The seal raised its head and gave a yawn to rival a crocodile, exposing saberous teeth, but it did not exhibit any fear. Murphy was fascinated by the degree to which animals responded—or failed to respond—to the presence of humans and their disruption of the natural order. Whenever blubber was put in the water on its way to the trypots, a kind of ice fish known as *Notothenia* massed and nipped at hooks as fast as the crew could tie them on their lines.

The presence of insects in great number was a surprise in that snowy land. Several species of mites, a spider, a bird's flea, springtails, midges, scavenger flies, beach flies, and two species of beetles went into Murphy's collection. The beach flies were common under damp stones and seaweed, appearing to be too sluggish to get themselves airborne, despite fully developed wings. Fifty or more might be found huddling beneath a single overturned stone. When exposed, they walked—rather than flew—to a new hiding place. "What a life!" Murphy wrote. "Yet, no doubt, they are as nebulously happy as only non-human animals can be. Kinaesthetic contentment; no craving for warmth; no inhibitions; no urge without its gratification; no glimmering of an end or of death.

"The most intriguing insects are the springtails, or *Collembola*, which swarm in inconceivable numbers in the vegetal mould among the tussock stalks. I have collected them by placing a saucer of alcohol on the soil. Then the little skippers, leaping pell-mell hundreds of times the length of their bodies, shower down into the saucer as if they were spontaneous creations of the atmosphere. If there are a thousand springtails on each square yard of grassland (a conservative estimate), how many live on all of South Georgia?"

The name *Collembola* is from the Greek word *coll* meaning glue and *embol* meaning a wedge, which refers to the shape of the bug's abdominal structure. Springtails are scavengers. If removed from their damp environment, they are susceptible to desiccation and have even evolved a special organ to maintain water balance. They have also evolved the necessary anatomy to flip themselves through the air as a means of avoiding predation.

On Albatross Island, Murphy walked through hordes of nesting albatrosses. He scrambled to a high cliff and out onto a rocky peninsula extending toward smaller islets that formed a line that had probably at one time connected to the main island. Here were the tall cylindrical columns past which the *Daisy* had sailed while on the way to her anchorage.

Murphy dug out eleven blue whalebirds from their black-soil burrows. He found his first fully occupied pipit's nest with four chicks and a litter of beetle and amphipod remains lining the bottom. Within only a few steps of Murphy, one of the parent pipits flew in, fed its young, picked a beakful of droppings from the nest, and flew away.

Only six feet away was a giant fulmar's nest. Why did they not eat the pipits? And why not the skuas that gobbled up everything else they could swallow? The pipits seemed almost to run over the toes of these big, predatory birds, but they seemed to have no enemies whatsoever.

As relatives of birds he had grown up with, the pipits triggered Murphy's longing for home. Their music was like a song sparrow's but with a longer, softer refrain. Their bright melody seemed to be present around the tent even in the gloomiest weather.

Many of the birds, such as this whale bird, were tame enough for Murphy and the crew to handle.

January 7th came up shrouded in heavy fog—useless as far as Captain Cleveland was concerned. Visibility was no more than the length of the ship until evening when the gray lifted to reveal the western ridge. Neither snow nor breeze marred the night, and Murphy lingered at his tent to behold its beauty. He climbed the promontory above the landing cove, and for the first time saw clearly all the southern stars. Scrambling around in the dark, he startled a pack of roosting giant fulmars. "The clumsy birds, squawking in alarm, dashed over the brink and down the long bank to the sea, like the swine of the Gadarenes."

He was up until eleven that night. From the brig's deck, the high cliffs of the main island, the broken and callused peninsula that defined the Bay of Isles shone, showing their outlines almost as plainly as in daylight. Albatross Island and its columns of rock shimmered luminous in late night light. From the headlands on shore came a sweet, far-reaching chorus of petrel song. Whalebirds, shoemakers, and other petrels joined in. Murphy wrote, "It is all we have here to replace the katydids and the whip-poor-will and the frog orchestra of the peaceful summer nights at home on Long Island."

Maybe the evening struck Murphy as especially peaceful, because only one elephant had been killed that day. Another—a cow—had slipped away in spite of clubs and lances.

But January 8th they were at it again, taking thirteen elephants. Two days later, eighty-four.

Weather often made it impossible to leave the ship. Wind howled without mercy. Captain Cleveland, who had hunted elephants in the Kerguelen Islands, said the New London sealers used to figure a cask of blubber as a cask of oil. They used to run over to Heard Island, mince their blubber, stuff it in the casks, then carry them to Kerguelen for trying out. On the *Daisy*, the ratio was more like 200 gallons of blubber to 180 gallons of oil, leaving little scrap although they had plenty of clinkers to use as fuel.

In addition to collecting, skinning, and skeletonizing, Murphy caught what he could on photographic plates. He and Correia stumbled upon a family of South Georgian teal among the hummocks of grass near the landing beach. The little ducks seemed undisturbed by men's heavy boots coming down on the mud near their stream of glacial outwash. Murphy got within six feet, at which point the teal, quacking softly, waddled off a short distance to hide behind a screen of drooping greenery. They peered back out. All but their bright eyes and yellow bills blended completely with the surroundings.

What Murphy could not capture in photographs, he described in his notes. On Albatross Island he wrote, "At this season many of last year's young albatrosses still linger on the nesting ground. These fledglings are no longer fed by the adults, so they must go without eating—for many weeks, perhaps—until they have molted their gray down and have learned to fly and to catch squids for themselves.

"But, if they grow thinner, they also grow lighter. They stand on the hillsides facing the breeze, spread their long, weak wings, and jump into the air. Poising for a second, they then glide downhill, tumbling head over heels when alighting. In the bright lexicon of albatross-youth there is no such word as fail. They patiently repeat the bumping process until they have reached the bottom of the slope; whereupon they toil upward on foot, and shoot the chute all over again.

A pair of South Georgia teal as Murphy found them in the tussock grass.

"The show put on by the adults is a marvel. The sexes are of different appearance, at least among fully mature birds, and every unattached female now appears to be besieged by several

South Georgia teal skins mounted and ready for display.

Whether helping themselves to albatross eggs or raiding a petrel's nest, as this crew member is doing, Murphy was acutely aware of what each stolen egg represented.

suitors, which dance about her, gobble, squeal, caterwaul, stand on their toes, and puff out their chests. They also click and fence with their beaks, and ardently spread wide their great wings which, as I have now learned, sometimes have an expanse of more than eleven feet from tip to tip.

"The end of all this, of course, is a mated pair. The humus and soil are raked together to form a nest mound that may measure eighteen inches in height, and on or beside this both birds remain until the single big egg appears. Then one begins to sit, and the other flies off over the ocean for a few days of fattening up before relieving guard on the nest."

To Murphy's distress, the men began to raid albatross colonies. Each egg taken, after all, meant one less albatross chick to hatch in the future. Mr. Vincent tried to limit the omelet hunt, but a dozen eggs were gathered in a single day. Considering each was about a pint in volume, that would have been the equivalent of ninety-six chicken eggs. When brought to the *Daisy,* the Old Man pierced the huge shells and blew out their contents. Those—and the shells of king penguin eggs—would sell for a dollar each to the curio dealers in New Bedford and on Cape Cod.

Despite his vexation at the disruption of the nests, Murphy participated in the raid to some extent. He wrote, "The egg of a wandering albatross is good food, and yet from an epicurean point of view it proves a delusion and a snare. I can compare it with nothing

Murphy wrote, "In popular tradition, the first duty of an albatross, as of a whale, is to be large."

better than beaver tail soup, and this entirely because of its effect upon the appetite rather than from any similarity in taste. You boil your egg, which weighs a pound, until the contents are of just the right consistency. You snip off the smaller end, sprinkle with salt, and dig in. It is delicious! But by the time you have progressed halfway to the bottom, you begin to wish that the bird had laid a somewhat smaller egg, and if you have the stomach to scoop the shell clean, you are sure to hope that you may never see another. However, that first rich taste soon wipes out the memory of what had followed, and within a few days you once more fall victim to the insidious temptation that never fails to cloy."

By now Murphy had enough to keep him busy even when shipbound by weather. In addition to skinning birds, he made partial casts of the larger animals. For example, when the crew brought him the head of a sea leopard, Murphy made a mold before removing the skull. This would be useful to the museum taxidermists when they mounted the skin of a whole animal, which Murphy still hoped to obtain.

Though it kept him from going ashore and collecting more specimens for his own purposes, Murphy began to appreciate foul weather for the degree to which it limited the more unrestrained and bloodier hunt. He completed his notes January 7th, "The weather curtain of the day mercifully protected the sea elephants."

Chapter Thirty-Four

PENGUINS ARE THE ANIMALS most associated with the Antarctic. Some live as far north as the equator, but most are found in the Southern Ocean. They are decidedly aquatic, using their wings to "fly" in the sea but never through the air, and are well adapted to their harsh environment. Gentoo penguins, for example—the smaller of the two most common species around the Bay of Isles—can reduce their heart rate from between eighty and a hundred beats per minute all the way down to twenty during a deep dive.

Because of their dependence on the sea, Murphy expected to find nests crowded near the water's edge. He was surprised to see them as far inland as two kilometers and was likewise surprised to see these birds, whose bodies are streamlined more for swimming than for walking, struggling to great heights to build their nests. Further, they seemed to have a preference for exposure to the elements, settling on the most desolate hills they could waddle to. Murphy wrote, "No matter how much available space there may be near the water, no matter how wearisome the scramble up the steeps, most of these penguins select the summits of windy, shelterless ridges for their homes. Many deeply-grooved winding avenues extend through the snowbanks to the highest parts of the colonies. Processions of adults can be seen coming and going at all times between their nests and the sea. They meet and pass each other without a sign of recognition, each bird trudging gravely along on its own business."

The penguins carried and piled stones, pebbles, grass, sticks, and anything available with which to make a circle. Two eggs were laid inside most circles, but the second-laid egg was often smaller than the first. The eggs would hatch after thirty-five days. With enough food, both chicks would survive and be kept warm in the nest for that length of time again.

With undeniable aggression, some of the gentoos fought over stones or took stones and nest building material away from other birds' nests, all spaced more than two neck-reaches apart. This distance was great enough that rival birds could not tangle with each other while still attending to their eggs.

Murphy sat quietly and alone among the hoards to observe the goings on. It had been almost seven weeks since he had arrived at South Georgia. Now his official ambassadorship was underway.

Gentoos (*Pygoscelis papua*) stand about thirty inches tall and weigh around thirteen pounds. Despite the formality of the black and white "clothes" with which they are characterized in cartoons, their backs are actually blue. The breasts are, however, the white of starched shirts. They have coral-red bills, orange feet, and across the crown of the head, they display white markings that extend from eye to eye, looking like earmuffs. These fillets put Murphy in mind of nurses' starched caps.

After an hour or so of observation, Murphy pulled on his leather mittens for protection and seized a passing bird. He lifted it from the ground easily enough, but the struggle that followed was almost a match for Murphy's strength. "The outraged bird screeched, beat a tattoo with its flippers that stung even through thick polar garments, bit, squirmed, kicked, and fought like a demon. The tussle continued for about a minute, and I was just about to give up and drop the furious armful when it abruptly quieted down. There it rested in the crook of my elbow, unhurt, bright-eyed, and as contented as a well-fed baby. I placed it gently on the ground, whereupon it looked up serenely, as though nothing unpleasant had occurred between us."

Murphy concluded that gentoos were "creatures of the moment, not readily holding one mood after the novelty of the stimulus has worn off. One penguin that was at first excited by my sudden appearance in the colony presently lapsed into a yawn, shut its eyes, and fell asleep. I understood, as soon as I saw that ardent cock and hen penguins took naps in the very middle of their courtship antics, that there was nothing intentionally rude in their behavior toward me!"

Murphy continued to visit the gentoo colonies, the largest of which he estimated at 4,000 adults. He followed their thoroughfares where the pattering of leathery feet had worn sinuous grooves up hills as high as three hundred meters above the sea. On one of these expeditions, Murphy discovered the answer to a question he had wondered about, namely, where do penguins go to die. Gentoos can live up to twenty years, but given their vast numbers on South Georgia, the men had often commented on how few dead birds they saw. Now, Murphy stood before their romantic sepulcher.

"Near the summit of a coastal hill I came upon a lonely pond in a hollow of ice-cracked stones. Several sick and drooping penguins were standing at the edge of this pool of snow water, which was ten or twelve feet deep. Then, with a tingling of my spine, I perceived that the bottom was strewn, layer upon layer, with the bodies of gentoo penguins that had outlived the perils of the sea to accomplish the rare feat among wild animals of dying a natural death. By hundreds, possibly by thousands, they lay all over the bed of the cold tarn, flippers outstretched and breasts reflecting blurred gleams of white. Safe at last from sea leopards in the ocean, and from skuas ashore, they took their endless rest; for decades, perhaps for centuries, the slumberers would undergo no change in their frigid tomb."

While Murphy enclosed himself unobtrusively in the private world of nature's rhythm, measuring, cataloguing, and comparing such details as egg size, color, and roundness, the *Daisy*'s crew was hard at it. January 11th they slew eighty-four sea elephants five or six miles east of the brig's anchorage. Because of the distance, the boats returned late in the evening. Precisely half the animals killed were cows and were therefore illegal. Mr. Vincent reported that many other cows had climbed to the top of a grassy plateau, maybe forty feet above the sea, and had escaped the lances by sliding and falling over the brink while the men used their

The gentoos wore grooves in the ice and moraines.

clubs to try to round them up. The fat animals that got away did so as if unharmed by their long tumble.

Weather had been bright for four days running. January 13th a southwest gale raged. Snow hissed into the sea. Everyone on board was stormbound. The men had their work to do with blubber and trypots, alternating in shifts on deck until they needed to go below and thaw out the numbness in their mittened hands. Murphy, however, was at loose ends. He wrote letters. It was at slack times like these that he missed his bride the most.

"Every day, my darling Grace," he wrote, "I regret that I have been unable to send you another letter. From time to time we sight whaling steamers from our anchorage, but they are always miles and miles away, and probably not one of them knows that an ancient windjammer from New Bedford is lying in the lee of these islands. Sooner or later I hope that one may discover us and pay a call."

He also wrote Dr. Lucas, the museum's director. Murphy was eager to set on paper—even if unable to send the pages—all the joys and successes of his expedition thus far.

The storm continued to deliver ice and wind into the next day. Both deck and land were ankle deep in diamond crystals. The temperature dropped so low Captain Cleveland ordered that all work above decks should cease. Whether this was kindness or practicality was not discernable. Either way, it had become obvious that no one could so much as hold a knife in his cold-stiffened hands.

Somehow, in the middle of all this—possibly out of sheer frustration—Murphy went ashore. He was rewarded. Sound asleep on the shingled beach beyond the landing cove and over the crest of the hill that separated the cove from the main bay was a sea leopard. Ever since his first sighting and later his botched attempt when he had shot and sent one to the depths, Murphy had hoped for one of these animals. "If any museum in the United States yet possesses a sea leopard," he wrote, "it is certain to be ancient and hideous, probably dating from the United States Exploring Expedition of 1838-1842. From a museum man's point of view, a sea leopard is just about as rare as a pine on Pine Street!"

Murphy was enchanted with the species. In action they were swift, crafty, and graceful beyond any of the other seals, devouring penguins with ease. The females exceeded the males in length, with the bulls reaching about ten feet and the cows, fourteen. They lurked in waters at the outlets of the penguins' thoroughfares and cruised back and forth offshore near the rookeries. Murphy had seen them make astounding leaps from water to land, resting on pans of ice and wriggling, eel-like rather than crawling to move about.

Murphy tiptoed away, leaving the sleeping cow where she lay, and ran to his tent for his .22 Winchester. He delivered a single long-rifle ball of lead into the brain through the thinnest part of the skull to make a clean kill. Immediately, he set into skinning. Working in intense cold, Murphy thrust his hands between hot blubber and skin, borrowing the dead animal's residual mammalian heat to keep his fingers agile. It took him an hour to get the job done, although a great deal of trimming still remained before salting down could occur without fear of decomposition.

He set aside the skin and made a quick, exploratory dissection of the carcass before abandoning it. Murphy may have been the first to observe some of the species' adaptive anatomical details. For example, he found the trachea to be a flat band. Where cartilaginous rings would have held the windpipe open as a tube, he found straight bars, allowing the trachea to open only when the animal breathed. The formation left plenty of room for the gullet and was probably what allowed for swallowing penguins nearly whole. Murphy found the mangled remains of four king penguins in the seal's stomach, a 140-pound meal.

Next, he gutted and dismembered the carcass. He cut off and discarded the musculature—still depending on the warmth of the flesh to keep his hands warm enough to continue working. What he wanted was the skeleton. Finally, he loaded skin and bones into the dory, looking forward to a moderation in weather when he would be able to work less hastily. He was bent on preserving every detail and delicacy of every last phalanx of flipper fingers and toes.

Chapter Thirty-Five

ADDING TO THE LETTERS he had written Grace and Dr. Lucas, Murphy wrote one to his mother. He did not know when or if there would be a chance to hand off his packet of mail to a passing steamer, but he kept the letters ready nonetheless, periodically adding the current date to the outside of the envelope addressed to Grace so she might have "the latest possible indication that I am still in the battle." He had had no communication with the outside world for the thirty-five days since leaving Cumberland Bay. Murphy felt forlorn and isolated.

He described the weather, comparing everyday storms around the Bay of Isles to the "puny blizzard" of 1898 that had stalled New York's trains and piled drifts higher than a man's head. But he had no point of comparison to describe South Georgia's more severe conditions. To make his point about brutal wind he wrote, "I sank a sea leopard skull in a fishtrap made of iron wire in order that the industrious isopods or sea lice might eat off the residue of flesh and thus share the labor of producing clean white bone . . . in condition for a museum cabinet. I put also a round stone in the fishtrap so that the combined load weighed over fifteen pounds." He attached a cod line to a one-quart tin as a buoy and sank the trap in thirteen fathoms of water, thinking he would leave the skull for two or three days. Before he knew it, however, the wind had blown the can and dragged the tin and its weight two and a half miles across the bay. Mr. da Lomba came across it quite by accident.

Except at night, the cabin stove roared full blast all the time, but incessant cold beyond the stove's reach finally got to Murphy's hands. The Old Man had long since taken off his ring. Now, Murphy's fingers were swollen also. With regret he removed his shiny new wedding band from where it was choking his finger, threaded it with several strands of heavy cord and tied it around his neck.

January 19th blew snow and sleet. Murphy, who had been ashore, got back to the *Daisy* just in time to keep from being marooned in his tent for the night. He kept his sleeping bag on shore for just such an eventuality, but it would not have been his preference to weather a storm under rattling canvas and tugging lines.

The day before, a whale-catcher had come into view in a far corner of the bay, anchored for the duration of the worst of the blast, but there was no hope of lowering a boat until things calmed down. Now, Mr. da Lomba rowed valiantly in the steamer's direction, protecting Murphy's letters in an oilskin bag, but the vessel took off before any connection could be made.

The crew killed fifty-six elephants that day, of which fifty-five were illegal. "Good pickings," the Old Man said, but Murphy winced at the thought of it. For every cow taken, the species' continuing existence at South Georgia thinned. The next day forty-three more animals were killed.

These hunts were not without risk to the hunters. Captain Cleveland occasionally went along with his boats, leaving Mr. Vincent in charge of the deck. On one beach they found an unusually large bull among a harem of twenty-five cows. "The group seemed so contented and stable that it was left alone while the men first rounded up and slaughtered scattered seals. However, when Captain Cleveland approached within thirty or forty paces of the family cluster, the old bull charged him, humping over the sand like a gigantic inchworm. He repeated these tactics whenever any member of our crew came within a stone's throw. After a while a second bull came swimming alongshore and hauled out nearby, but the aggressive and jealous beachmaster at once attacked and drove him off.

"To bull sea elephants, fighting is a profession, and the only known means of settling the wife problem. The average number in a seraglio

The "Beachmaster," photographed by James Innes Wilson, became the model for Murphy's engraved bookplate. Each volume in his library was identified with the likeness of this old bull elephant.

may be about fifteen, but a truly successful gentleman gathers more. In the code of the bulls, the correct number of wives is just one more than you've got.

"Each bull aspires to be beachmaster, even though no beachmaster is ever left in peace. Other bulls, possessed with the urge and personality to win ladies who don't care who is their husband, are forever swimming alongshore and hauling out in the other fellow's preserve.

"The first stage of combat is bluff. Defender and challenger begin by roaring, gargling, strangling, retching, and seeming to be nauseated. Next they rear up like a pair of rocking horses, even though they be still out of each other's reach. Crawling closer, they bump, raking rival necks and chests with their heavy canine teeth. When opportunity offers, they endeavor to clamp jaws and tear. Marquis of Queensberry rules are not observed!

"One of the fighters may trounce the other quickly, or they may carry on until both collapse from exhaustion, to go at it again when they have sufficiently revived. It is rather slow-going for a heavyweight battle, and yet the bulls have a rabidly furious aspect because it appears to be normal for the arteries of the palate to rupture during the violent "gargling," so that the combatants are presently spewing out blood with every breath.

"More rarely, there is plenty of ripped hide, or possibly a mangled snout, or even an eyeless socket. The captain says that about one big bull in every hundred encountered looks as though he had been bounced through a stone crusher.

A sooty albatross and his chick.

"At any rate, the object of such a battle is to win, not to kill. When one bull retreats to sea, the other resumes control or takes over, as the case may be, and peace reigns until the next interloper lumbers ashore."

While the crew continued their greasy, gory work on the beach, Murphy headed off and found two sooty albatross nests. They were built one over the other on a cliff about a hundred feet above the beach. Each was occupied by a brooding bird with its bill tucked under the wing coverts, or small feathers around the base of the larger wing feathers. Murphy scaled the wall to the lower aerie to meet his first sooty albatross "at home." The white eye ring gave the bird a solemn expression. It grunted softly at Murphy's presence and snapped its beak with a hollow chop. Murphy backed off a few feet and the bird snuggled onto its downy chick while continuing to monitor the human intrusion. In a minute or two the chick stuck its fuzzy head out from underneath and snapped its bill at Murphy the same as the parent had done.

Storms continued. Captain Cleveland had never seen South Georgia weather rage so violently. January 21st, everyone was shipbound once more. Perhaps out of sheer boredom and in spite of the *Daisy* pitching and rolling on ocean swells, the steward was inspired to make a cake, rich with the beaten yolks and whites of penguin eggs. The cake tasted so good to the Old Man that he ordered second slices for himself and Murphy and even broke out bottles of stout to wash it all down.

Finally, the sun shone again. One white mountain after another pierced the sapphire sky, seemingly piled all the way to heaven, peak after peak, ridge beyond ridge. Even in good weather it was essential to bear in mind how quickly conditions could change, however. Murphy went out on a slaughtering party with Captain Cleveland across the Bay to Allardyce Harbor. The men killed twenty-two elephants and were ready to return when a dense fog settled in. Seven or eight miles lay between them and the *Daisy*. They could not see any land, not even promontories. Worse yet, the Old Man had failed to bring the boat's compass. Snow began to fall. Things looked serious. Then Murphy remembered a silly toy compass a friend of Grace's had tucked in with a letter almost as a joke. He fished around in his pockets, wondering why he had even bothered to carry the thing. When held level, however, the toy's needle responded and away they went for home. With that and the guidance of gentoo penguins heading for shore, seven men, one boat, and a load of blubber reached their anchorage in safety.

The next day opened up again. Murphy went along with the boats to a wonderful cove where pointed mountains rose on either side. For lunch, while the men bashed and slaughtered, one of the boatsteerers built a fire of stove wood from the brig under an overhanging cliff. In elephant oil he fried fresh-caught fish. Coffee, boiled elephant tongue, and hard bread completed the menu. Everything was delicious. Nobody had plates or forks; they used their fingers to eat with, as if on a Sunday afternoon picnic.

In between times Murphy had his cache of treats. He especially enjoyed the Knorr soups that Grace had packed. Would that he had had a trunkful. The ship's stores were thinning, too. Meanwhile, the hunt marched along. Mincing and boiling continued steadily on board, and whenever the men could get their boats to shore, they chopped up more raw material to add to the trypots.

The first rule of hunting elephants was "Get 'em to the beach," driving the animals as close to the water as possible without actually driving them into the water. There they would be clubbed, and the great arteries near the heart would be lanced through.

Blood surged as from a fountain then the hide was slit lengthwise down the middle of the back. Side cuts allowed flaps of skin to be flayed off. Each man worked with two curved butcher knives and a sharpening steel hanging in a wooden scabbard from his belt. The ring of steel on steel sang a rhythm through the air.

Looking appropriately cautious, a crew member approaches a bellowing bull with a lance.

Each carcass was worked over by four men at a time. With skin removed, an eight-inch thickness of fat would be exposed. This was separated from underlying muscle with sweeping strokes of the blades. The fat was then cut into manageable squares, or blanket pieces, and the carcass was rolled over for its underside to be stripped.

Blanket pieces were floated and strung on short ropes called raft tails, which were towed to the anchored ship. Each raft tail was looped around a hawser that extended from bow to stern along the *Daisy*'s waterline. The blubber was left to rinse in the sea for forty-eight hours or so, until all the blood appeared to have washed out. During this blanching process a little of the oil was lost, and ravenous Cape pigeons stole blubber night and day in an interminable hubbub.

Once hoisted aboard, the blanket pieces were cut and minced, and if the air temperature was above freezing, a further loss of oil occurred during that stage. The trying out process was the same as for sperm oil.

The butchery held Murphy's interest only intermittently. Weather permitting, he liked nothing better than taking off on his own. January 23rd the snow blew on and off then calmed. He hiked the lateral moraines of the glacier he had named for Grace. There he found South Georgia terns on their nests, although the single eggs laid directly on stone chips hardly seemed like much in the way of nests. As incubators, the terns showed distinct tenacity. They could scarcely be driven away for an inspection of what they were sitting on—so firmly committed to their speckled eggs and so lacking any sense of predation that Murphy was able to kneel beside one of the birds and stroke its back and head. Others were not as docile. They made high-pitched calls that brought their mates around who in turn threatened with swoops and dashes near Murphy's face. Whenever a skua flew close, however, the human intruder was no longer of interest, and the sitting terns left their eggs in pursuit of a more familiar enemy.

But it was the penguins Murphy returned to again and again. He grabbed an oar every chance he could to go ashore, and he was getting to know his way around. In particular, he knew his way to the gentoo colonies.

Chapter Thirty-Six

LIKE TERNS, THE PENGUINS were not experienced with land predators of any kind, and so were fearless of humans. Carnivorous skuas—the hawk-like gulls—would steal eggs and chicks if given the chance. The gentoos rushed at every skua that landed nearby, and they routinely brayed and barked at any that flew over—all in protection of their chicks. When it came to themselves, however, they needed no protection when on land or ice. The ocean was different. Sea leopards lurked.

Cadela's presence provided an interesting illustration of penguin instincts. Whenever the terrier pestered a group of gentoos near the water's edge, the birds invariably ran up the beach for safety rather than diving into the sea where they would, in fact, be out of the dog's range. To a penguin's brain (such as it is) land means refuge and water means danger no matter what. They have not evolved an effective response to dogs and men—only to sea leopards, and any threat apparently translates to those sharp-toothed seals. Even after Cadela had seized a penguin by its tail and had swung it around and around, when released, the dazed bird scampered inland. Murphy concluded from this, "The surest way to keep gentoos ashore is to try to drive them to the water."

Penguins have often been credited with intelligence—maybe due to their upright posture and apparent tameness. Captive birds sometimes become downright companionable. Despite appearances, they are capable of very little actual thinking. Like bees or ants, they depend on instinctive behavior—even when repeated experiences should have taught them better.

Murphy stood knee-deep in the Bay of Isles. At thirty-six degrees, the water was clear and brilliant in sunshine. Four gentoos swam around and brushed against his leather boots. They rolled from front to back, surfaced, and even leaped. Most likely they were feeding and not actually interested in the pair of human legs about which they swam. After a time three of them walked out of the sea, shook the water from their spiny tails, and turned to watch Murphy watching them. When they waddled up the beach he followed.

Ordinarily they fed far from shore, eating krill and opossum shrimp. Flipper-wings pushed the birds through water with amazing power and speed. Toward dusk countless penguins often zipped past the *Daisy*, presumably on their way from deep feeding grounds to their regular landings. Their habits were so predictable, the men had come to depend on the birds' sense of direction whenever dense fog descended. Homeward bound, they invariably pointed the boats toward a smooth shore.

Impressed with their swimming abilities, Murphy clocked the birds' speed. With a stopwatch he timed them at about thirty feet per second—almost twenty miles per hour, although it was not a steady rate. Periodically they leaped out for a gasp of air.

Of their courting habits Murphy wrote, "They give up eating and remain ashore hungry, but too much in love to realize it, for periods of at least two weeks. The lady gentoos select nesting sites, after which they await the attentions of suitors bearing gifts in the form of pebbles or ancestral bones, which make the foundation of the nests. Males and females appear exactly alike, and sex is evidently recognized by a process of trial and error. Cocks sometimes make mistakes, with dire results, by offering pebbles to other cocks. The presentation to a hen is a pantomime of bowing, accom-

Male to male, a bow and a pebble were offered.

panied by soft hissing sounds and later by either angry or joyous trumpetings, according to the outcome. The hen is the builder of the home, the cock the bearer of bricks, and acceptance of the first pebble is the symbol of success in wooing. Today a cock bird laid a pebble at my feet, a compliment properly followed by ceremonial bowing and, I hope, by mutual sentiments of high esteem."

Murphy also looked in on the king penguins. In particular, there was a rookery near the glacier that Murphy had named in honor of Frederic Lucas, the director of the museum. Murphy collected six adult birds that appeared to have neither eggs nor young. He skinned them on the spot. The work went quickly because he had discovered how to take advantage of the skuas' scavenging habits.

Murphy sewed up the slits in the skins, turned them inside out, and tossed them on the pebbles. Almost instantly, thirty or forty skuas appeared, ready to pick off every clinging bit of flesh and fat, completing the job faster and more thoroughly than Murphy could. When he had first brought back such skins to the *Daisy*, the Old Man wondered how the task had been accomplished so well and so efficiently. All Murphy had to do was keep a watch on the skuas to make sure they would not carry the skins away or nip holes in the tough hides.

Murphy wrote, "The skua is cock-o'-the-roost at South Georgia. It is capable of killing and eating any bird no larger than itself, and of plundering the nests of all the others. It can drive Cadela into hiding and is just as quick to assault a man who happens to approach the neighborhood of its nest. When I go up into the grasslands behind the shore, I am never left long in doubt regarding my invasion of breeding territory. The old skuas become quite frenzied, swooping at my head so that I have to duck, and varying their attack by standing on the ground close by, wings pointed upward and heads downward, and screeching at the top of their lungs. Today, when I was banding a skua chick in the nest—he protesting lustily all the while—both parent birds struck with their wing quills the barrels of the gun that I held up as a protection against their furious stoops.

"Energy is apparent in every movement—in their restlessness, rapacity, the quantity of food they can ingest in a few moments, and in the volume and continuousness of the screams that issue from their throats. They look like small eagles much more than like relatives of the gulls. They make the most impressive picture when they stand with wings held upright, in the posture of those on ancient Norse helmets. They are then the apotheosis of defiance, and they fairly split the air with their shrill cries.

"They are as close to wholly intrepid as birds can possibly be, and, when I sit beside my inside-out penguins skins, they will actually crowd against my legs in their eagerness to pick at the fat. They snip it off in small bits with the hooked tips of their beaks, swallowing the pieces one after another as rapidly as a chicken gathers strewn corn. During the process they are also quick to attack each other, springing up like game-cocks and pulling out feathers half on the ground and half in the air.

"When they deign to notice me at all, they glance up with bright, fearless, unsuspicious brown eyes, accept from my fingers any food I offer them, and show no concern over the loudest shouts, whistles or hand claps. Then I quite succumb to their charm and, regardless of the rapine and cannibalism, I subscribe to the principle that such supremacy of might must be deserved."

Chapter Thirty-Seven

WHILE MURPHY WAS NOTING the pecking order of skuas and penguins, a struggle of the human variety was shaping up. Back on board the *Daisy*, the steward was in irons.

Trouble began when the skipper went to a locker where he thought he had five gallons of West Indian rum in a demijohn. The demijohn was in the locker but the rum was not. At the point of discovery, Murphy heard the usual rumbling and ominous grumblings he had come to associate with the Old Man's displeasure.

Captain Cleveland summoned Mr. da Lomba who brought the steward to the after-cabin. Without uttering the slightest introduction, the Old Man simply pointed to the open locker and said, "Out with it." The steward sniveled and his knees quivered but he denied all knowledge of any crime.

The lazaret would have been dangerously cold for incarceration, so Captain Cleveland shackled the suspect and sent him to steerage with the command that the prisoner was to have nothing but hard bread and water and that he would break any man who might be found passing along food.

Twenty-four hours elapsed before the steward was ready to talk. Once again he was taken to the after-cabin. This time he admitted to having drawn off the rum. It seemed a few of the Norwegian whalers at Grytviken had supplied him with pint and quart bottles and were willing to barter. The steward had acquired four dogskin jackets, some Eskilstuna knives, and an assortment of other Scandinavian goods. All the items were found in the steward's sea chest and sea bags.

After the interrogation and confession, and the goods had been turned over, the Captain ordered the man unshackled, a task that fell inexplicably to Murphy. The steward was then ordered to pack up his personal property and take it to a bunk in the forecastle, all under the watchful eye of the first officer, Mr. da Lomba. Johnny, the cabin boy, was next called aft and informed that he would be serving as steward until further notice.

To see whether anything else might be missing, the mate made an inventory of supplies and announced that there was bread and flour enough only to last another three months. That meant they could not remain at South Georgia beyond the beginning of April at the latest, since it would take several weeks to reach the first port. Murphy took this as good news; he did not want to be stuck indefinitely at sea. He was thinking they might head for Cape Town as their first port, but it was only a guess, and he knew better than to ask. The Old Man never revealed his plans, anyway. But Murphy's sense of an April departure matched the rate at which the brig's casks were filling with elephant oil. Furthermore, the seals would be returning to the ocean by the end of summer. There would be nothing to hunt for after that.

That evening all was quiet. Weather was calm. The ship did not even rock enough to indicate that it was afloat. Murphy checked his counts and found that, as of January 26th, the *Daisy*'s men had slaughtered 1,094 sea elephants—297 in December and 797 thus far in January. If they had all been big bulls the brig might have been loaded to the hatches with oil by then. But the greater number of the animals had been cows. Some had even been babies, of which Murphy said, "[Those] could have been killed only by men capable of crushing the skull of a friendly puppy."

Murphy's grand tally, of course, neither slowed the hunt nor improved its legality. The next day forty-four more elephants were lanced, forty-three of which were cows. Two days later seventy more were killed, sixty-seven of which were cows and those only recently hauled up from the sea. The shores near Brunonia Glacier where the men worked were littered in bull carcasses from an earlier hunt—maybe a year ago, maybe longer. Because disintegration was slow in that climate, it was difficult to judge how long the remains had been decomposing, but they had probably been left by Norwegian or British companies. Those outfits were known to take only bulls without harming cows or pups.

January 30th broke clear but penetratingly cold with wind. Glacier snouts crumbled into the bay and iced its surface with a fine mush. Pallid sunlight did little to compensate for shivering, but it lit the hills and their inhabitants to a point of brilliance. King penguin colors gleamed with a "splendor not to be forgotten." Murphy wrote, "I have never seen any other animals that appeared quite so chic and magnificent as these royal birds. The movements of the white breasts and golden gorgets stir me as the daffodils stirred Wordsworth."

Murphy had been reading James Weddell's account of visiting South Georgia in 1823. Ornithologists had often dismissed the British explorer's description of penguins, "In pride, these birds are perhaps not surpassed even by the peacock," but Murphy found Weddell's impressions to be in complete harmony with his own.

The Bay of Isles' largest king penguin colony was near the Lucas Glacier, a cold and cheerless site of stone and wind. Southerly gales howled through a slot in the mountains, but the thousands of birds seemed oblivious. Chicks from a year ago had reached full height but still had down attached to their feathers. Murphy thought they looked like college boys in raccoon coats.

The *Daisy*'s crew had helped themselves to most of the eggs in

Juvenile king penguins are covered with soft brown down before their feathers appear.

December. Since then some of the birds had produced new ones. Each sitting bird carried its egg on its feet, typically stretching up to full height when approached. At one point the men had left a pile of eggs on the ground, and some of the robbed penguins slyly re-appropriated what had been theirs to begin with. Other birds gathered up stones to satisfy their urge to incubate. Still others, after losing their eggs, were reduced to shuffling around flat-footed, as opposed to their ordinary walking gait, which was up on the toes.

The kings crowded together during incubation. This seemed curious, since their close proximity seemed to lead to a great deal of quarreling. Murphy described it, "I was watching a dozen birds all asleep, all snoring softly, and all swaying very gently back and forth as they snuggled their eggs. Then one bird woke up and, without provocation, jabbed its sharp bill against the back of another's neck. The latter penguin, grunting vehemently, retaliated by delivering backhand blows with one wing, without turning to face its opponent. The fracas was enough to wake up all the others, which joined in with both rapiers and broadswords until every member of the group was exchanging thrusts and whacks. The mêlée died away about as quickly as it had flared up, and within a few minutes all the sitters were snoring and swaying once more.

"King penguins have an indubitably lofty and martial bearing. Their regimental characteristics, such as standing at attention, marking time with their feet, and marching in single file or in doubles, are almost too realistic to sound true. Their voice also has a military sound, for the call is a series of long-drawn bugle notes, highly musical and almost worthy of being called a tune. When delivering this the king stretches up to his full stature and points his bill skyward, after which the volley rings forth from an expanded chest. At the close of the song the head is tilted forward with a smart jerk and the bugler stands at attention for several moments."

Calm but "dirty" weather marked the close of January. Murphy had a sore throat and aching chest, possibly as a result of exposure. In matters of health, however, it was Mr. da Lomba whom Murphy worried about.

Murphy's photograph of king penguins marching was copied into the painted background of the South Georgia diorama at the American Museum of Natural History.

He had had a bronchitis attack while in Cumberland Bay that might have finished him off had it not been for the physician there. Now, the first officer spent a large part of his time in wet clothes. Tough a man as he may have been, Murphy felt Mr. da Lomba might "remain permanently in South Georgia unless the Old Man puts a stop to his constant and undue exposure." The consequence of Mr. da Lomba having unusually large feet (size 13) was that no boots out of the *Daisy*'s slop chest could accommodate him. The ones he wore leaked. Murphy faulted Captain Cleveland for not providing adequately—especially since John da Lomba had been Benjamin Cleveland's right-hand man on other voyages.

Caring for the men went beyond a humanitarian consideration. As a matter of convenience, the Old Man called the steward out of his exile in the forecastle and restored him to his post. This was not accompanied

*Captian Cleveland's logbook entries for January 30th, and the two days following,
read, "This day begins with moderate weather. All hands on board mincing. middle
breezes from the West. So ends the day. Today begins with very good weather all day
boiled all day with two boats after Elephants they returned at night loaded so ends this
very fine (day) This day begins with very light Easterly winds 2 two boats over on
Cape Bullard side after Elephant at 12:30 PM began to rain and breeze up to 3 PM
beg snowing hard and the weather geting bad at 4:30 thick snow storm the two boats
started to come acrost the Chanel they finely brought up away down by the Ice glacier
and stove both boats lost 2 two guns oars and about everything out of the boats there
the men remained all night at eight oclock in the morning got sight of the crew from one
of the hills."*

280

with any forgiveness. In practicality, his services were required. As for the five gallons of rum, that would be taken out of his hide in New Bedford when the final accounting of the voyage would be made.

Murphy felt better the next day. Conditions were calm so he went ashore. An easterly gale came up in the early afternoon, however, and he had a tough time of it rowing the *Grace Emeline* from the landing cove to the anchorage. Wind shredded the surface of the bay, and by the time he reached the *Daisy* he was drenched to the skin with ocean brine. Some of it was driven through Murphy's oilskin where the creases had begun to wear through, but most of it went down the collar and up his sleeves.

Murphy logged for the month of January three clear days, three days of fog, and eighteen of precipitation in the form of rain or snow or both, three of which were heavy and prolonged. They had experienced ten days of frost and a total of fifteen days in which gale force winds had blown from one or all compass directions. Four days in the month had been calm, two of which were shrouded in fog.

Chapter Thirty-Eight

The FIRST NIGHT of February was the most anxious they had spent since the start of the voyage. Two of the whaleboats, each with a crew of six men, failed to return. Darkness descended. Weather screeched and spit. Nothing could be done except hang extra lanterns in the rigging in hopes of guiding the boats home. It felt like an empty gesture. The men were probably either already on shore or drowned. Murphy sat with the skipper, greatly agitated and worried that there was probably no compass under the thwart of either whaleboat. Murphy felt helpless. He read the last five cantos of Dante's *Paradiso* and then turned in for the night. Captain Cleveland did not go to bed at all.

At midnight the snow ceased; an hour later the wind died, and by three o'clock daylight broke under clear skies. The shore became visible but no boats were in sight. Five o'clock and still no sign of the men. Water was calm, and the atmosphere, transparent. Murphy climbed the mainmasthead. Through his binoculars, he scanned the miles of long coast. On deck, all eyes strained toward the northwest, where the lost crews should have appeared. At eight o'clock Murphy went ashore in the dory. He climbed to the hill above his tent, sat on a hummock, and steadied his elbows on his knees that he might have the clearest possible look though his field glasses.

Far in the distance he saw an indistinct group of penguins. Or were they penguins? Murphy jumped up and waved his oilskin jacket across as much of the sky as he could cover. This alerted Captain Cleveland to lower another whaleboat, and soon enough it was ashore at the landing cove. With the skipper in the stern and Murphy at the after oar, they and four others rowed around rocks and through surging waves. Once or twice rollers came close to swamping them, but eventually they came within sight of the stranded crew: twelve men, Cadela, and two damaged boats.

Wading through nasty surf, the bedraggled bunch—wet, tired, and almost crazy with cold—piled into the single whaleboat, eighteen men in a vessel designed for six. Ten took the five oars, and the rest huddled wherever they could. They pulled for home. Nobody spoke except Mr. da Lomba, who told what had happened.

They had killed eighty-nine elephants and had more blubber than they could carry. After burying the excess for safe keeping, the men had started out for home with the first load. But the sea was too rough for Mr. Almeida's crew, so the two boats made for a protected—but far off—corner of the bay. Just as they were coming into the beach, a sleeper wave—huge and horrible—slammed one boat into the other.

The two officers, Mr. da Lomba and Mr. Almeida, immediately cut their spring lines, but their hands were greasy from blubber, and the waves were knocking them about. Along with the ropes, they inadvertently incised their own palms.

Both boats were stove. All the gear—including the oars—was swept into the sea. Someone thought to hang onto one of the lantern kegs, which had matches. Everyone had to swim and then wade through floating ice to get ashore.

With hard bread from the keg and a splintered plank from a boat's hull, they kindled a fire of blubber. Still, the night was long and miserable. Suffering did not let up until someone saw Murphy waving his oilskin coat from his hilltop.

It took two hours for help arrive, followed by a long pull back to the *Daisy*. No sooner had the men eaten and changed into dry clothes than Mr. da Lomba insisted on returning to Allardyce Harbor to recover the buried blubber. The Old Man agreed to this, but Murphy thought it was a foolish move. In his opinion, "all these men should have been tucked into their berths for the day and the following night. Several of them look fagged out, and one, the Dominican called William Elwin or William Stephens, is in an alarming condition. The Old Man is now sighing for his pilfered rum, which he says that William needs. However, I never knew him to dish out any while he still had it!"

Mercifully, the weather was warm and bright. By half past seven wind had begun to blow, but the three boats were nearing home. Two rode low in the water with the cached blubber, and the third towed the two damaged boats, each temporarily patched with sailcloth but both nearly awash. The inventory was one good boat, one in fair condition, one very much battered, and two that looked thoroughly wrecked. The Old Man, the cooper, the officers, and the boatsteerers all readied themselves to patch up their fleet. A whaleboat could take nearly any amount of rebuilding as long as her keel had been neither "hogged" nor "back-broke."

In the midst of all this, half the blubber of the eighty-nine animals had to be jettisoned. Murphy wrote, "This seemed to tear the Old Man's heart more than any other aspect of the catastrophe. For my own part, I am more inclined to mourn the futile loss of the forty-five of these wonderful animals than I am to weep over the skipper's spilled oil at 50¢ a gallon. His point of view is probably not out of harmony with his calling, however."

Winds the next day made it impossible to lower a boat safely, but there was much to do on board. Half the crew minced and boiled while the other half devoted themselves to carpentry.

Frank, the only boatsteerer not involved in the previous day's fiasco, collapsed in bad health. He had become feverish and *gleety*, a reference to pus and discharge, possibly associated with late-stage gonorrhea. Captain Cleveland managed to pull him through with something out of the medicine chest, but the man was not fit for duty.

One more day and the whaleboats were re-planked and nearly ready to be put back in service. All they needed was paint and they would be as good as new. Murphy was interested in the skill and efficiency of the repairs, but he was also itching to get back on shore. Eventually, weather calmed enough for him to lower the *Grace Emeline*.

He visited both the king and gentoo penguin colonies. Then, since he was close, he decided to explore the Lucas Glacier. Unlike the Grace Glacier, which was too rugged to cross on foot, the Lucas Glacier was smooth, although Murphy kept a look out for crevasses. In general, the ice seemed solid and glassy except for occasional patches of soft snow. Heaps of silt and broken stone had been pushed up along the sides. Murphy wrote, "As I proceeded southward and upward on this vast smooth causeway, which seemed to lead toward a valley or pass in the main mountain range, the bottomless funnels in the ice became more numerous and terrifying. When I finally slipped on a bit of the wet and trickly surface, and began to slide down the barely perceptible slope in the direction of one of the unfathomable abysses, I realized that it was time to stop traversing such terrain alone. I have no hankering to melt out of the seaward end of this glacier a hundred years hence."

What Murphy really wanted to do was organize a couple of companions to rope together and cross the main island to the wilder south side. Prying anyone away from the "endless murder of sea elephants" was, however, next to impossible. Once in a while the cooper or Mr. da Lomba took an hour or two, but a serious expedition seemed out of the question.

On February 7th, the men returned to Allardyce Harbor and slew seventy-one elephants. Murphy prepared tissue samples for subsequent histological study. He ran pieces of liver, pancreas, kidney, and other glands and viscera through mercuric chloride, glacial acetic acid, and alcohols of decreasing dilution until the tissues were fixed and preserved at full strength.

Every chance he came upon, Murphy tried to coax information out of the skipper about their anticipated return voyage, but the Old Man invariably dodged the question, saying he had not decided on the next step. Murphy did not like not knowing when he could count on arriving home, but he told himself, "There is no use getting hot under the collar about it, because he is built that way and can no more help his taciturnity than his gray hair."

Murphy tried to avoid thoughts of home, but there were moments of powerful nostalgia. He missed having a big, comfortable chair, a fireplace, his familiar possessions. He longed for an evening with Grace when there would be no thoughts of rising for a five o'clock breakfast. He missed having anything like a real evening. On the *Daisy*, supper was not finished until eight, and by then the only way to escape close quarters with the windburned weary men was to crawl into his berth and fall asleep.

The weather turned miserable again. Two boats had returned to Allardyce Harbor, and wind picked up before they set off home. That meant spending the night ashore. This time, however, the men were dry and better equipped. They drew alongside the *Daisy* before noon the next day, loaded with the blubber of forty-nine animals.

Mr. da Lomba described killing the elephants on a cliff above the bay. The men had flensed the carcasses then tossed blanket pieces over the precipice to the beach below. Two cows had escaped by lurching over the edge and dropping the hundred or more feet. One of the cows broke her neck and never moved again. The other hit and "bounced like rubber" before scrambling into the sea.

In the water, sea elephants stay under the surface most of the time, moving themselves forward with wide, graceful sweeps of their hind flippers. Their huge, spindle-shaped bodies weave through tangles of giant kelp with ease.

On land or ice they moved with remarkable speed, heavy and "legless as they are. Given a level surface, they can bob along faster than a person can walk. They arch their backs and jerk their fore flippers in a sort of blubbery gallop, heads jerking up and down, massive sides quaking."

Murphy took great pleasure in observing the animals' behavior. Pups, for example, did not object to being patted and tickled by human hands, but were instinctively contentious among themselves, sparring and trying to look fierce. The older animals were not merely practicing ferocity, however—especially the bulls. They could be lethal. Even cows had been known to kill men when provoked.

Most of the time, he found the animals sleeping, piled on top of each other like so many giant sausages. Slumber seemed to be their main purpose during summer months. Some dozed in coves or ponds, face up with their backs awash, nostrils closed as if under water. Murphy wrote, "A sea elephant's slumber suggests either nightmares or a guilty conscience. The inspirations are irregular gasps, the expirations tremu-

During November the elephants spent most of their time sleeping in the tussock grass and giving off a strong swinish odor.

lous wheezes. The whole body shakes violently from time to time and the fore flippers are forever pawing about, now scratching the sides, now the head, now crossed over the breast so that one hand may be scratched by the nails of the other. The hind flippers are now and then spread fanlike, brandished in the air, or rubbed and clasped together. Whether awake or asleep, the brutes are fond of flinging sand or mud over themselves. All this activity often goes on while they are in such total oblivion that it is difficult to arouse them even by kicking their fat ribs.

"If I approach a wide-awake bull too closely, it will rear up on the fore flippers, thrash its hinder parts about, contract its trunk-like snout into tight bulging folds, open its pink mouth to show the great canines, and finally utter its rather anticlimactical vocal expression of displeasure or warning. The process appears painful, because the first step is a period of nearly noiseless choking. Then the rush of breath seems to squeeze out of the windpipe, the soft palate vibrates violently and forth comes the strangled bellow."

He also observed behavior that seemed distinctly tantrum-like. If a bull became annoyed, it might bash and bounce around, bite at the ground, and snap at anything and everything in its range the same as a small child would kick the floor when he did not get his way.

The men returned again and again to Allardyce Harbor. Cadela invariably went along, although Murphy sometimes did not. On one such occasion, the dog was said to have killed seven mice. More likely they were young brown rats, their species introduced a century before, but the crew failed to bring home the specimens, so the identification could not be verified. The crew did, however, come home with a duckling—a South Georgia teal—still in its downy coat, which Murphy accepted with glee, certain that it was the first such specimen ever collected.

Chapter Thirty-Nine

THE MIDDLE OF FEBRUARY brought nasty weather. Stinging pellets of snow mixed with rain made any sort of useful work impossible. The temperature hovered in the upper twenties. Murphy's first set of oilskins was no longer waterproof, so he drew a second set out of the slop chest. On the new pants he sewed an extra piece of sailcloth over the seat and coated the canvas and his stitching with linseed oil in hopes of keeping himself dry even when sitting on the boat's wet thwarts.

Storms continued for seven days. Even in the southern hemisphere, Murphy thought of February 14th—the day for sweethearts—as a precursor to the beginning of spring. In the early dawn he dreamed of seeing Grace in warm green fields. Then the Old Man's voice broke into the idyllic meadow scene with the announcement that it was five o'clock and time for breakfast. Murphy pulled valentines from his letter bag, and, later, when a rainbow arched across the Bay of Isles he attributed its appearance to Grace as her greeting of the day.

But it was more the 17th of the month that he took special notice of. He wrote, "Clear and fair, as it ought to be on this greatest of [wedding] anniversaries. Mare's tails and shattered cumulus clouds fleck the sky. The westerly breeze is gentle, though a heaving swell is dashing to spray on the rocks. The sun is warm and unusually bright. The Old Man has appeared on deck in a straw hat, which looks extremely quaint against the background of glaciers and perpetual snow. The tussock grass seems a brighter green, the water a richer blue. It is a calm, deep-breathing day. The pipits are singing like skylarks, but I am happier than either the pipits or the sunshine. I have been trying to extract a faint odor of orange blossoms or lilies of the valley from the fragment of your bouquet taken from the letter bag. There is not much of either now, but what a beautiful bouquet it was a year ago today."

Murphy worked that morning in his tent, his mind racing with thoughts of home and how each passing day brought him closer to return. He found himself feeling more and more isolated from the crew. A growing resentment gnawed its way into undeniable conscious thought. Murphy did not like to place blame, but he felt the captain was not living up fully to the terms of the agreement with his sponsoring museums. Those institutions had subsidized the entire voyage in exchange for cooperation and assistance when cooperation and assistance were requested.

Admitting to the concern that he was not getting the help he had been promised, Murphy conceived an opportunity when an exceptionally large bull came lumbering up near the tent that afternoon. "Aha," he thought, "here's my chance to *demand* that the Old Man [assign me some men to] help in roughing out the whole skeleton of a big one I've just killed for him!"

But Murphy had left his rifle on board the *Daisy*. The next best thing was his camera, which he grabbed to get a portrait. Not wanting a picture of the bull sleeping, Murphy whistled a single sustained note to rouse him into a pose. Two eyes opened, which was precisely the desired response. But, the bull came rather too much awake, because, not only were his eyes at full alert, he was flipping from his back onto his stomach, and snorting. With no hesitation whatsoever, he came charging toward the whistler. Murphy barely had time to avoid attack. He wrote afterward, "I dodged aside, but he continued humpety-bump after me, with homicide in his eye."

Murphy set the camera down and went for a lance instead. The bull had traveled to the upper beach with plenty of maneuvering room around him. Murphy—an inexperienced hunter of elephant seals who knew full well that the crew *always* shot the big bulls before lancing—

had the reckless confidence to strike. For five minutes the bull snorted, bellowed, and reared up on his belly, stretching his head a good three feet above Murphy's. One good hurl of the gigantic body and the man would have been crushed had he not been quick on his feet and armed with a lance.

Finally, the bull was beaten, and it collapsed in a pool of blood by the water's edge. Murphy also collapsed, catching his breath for a considerable time before rowing out to the brig for a change of clothes and the assistance he felt he had earned and was his due.

The skipper came ashore with an officer and two boatsteerers to peel off the blubber. When he saw the size of the kill he lavished loud praise. But when Murphy worked up the courage to suggest that he might like help with the skeleton, the captain turned him down. Murphy pointed out that the museums were paying for more than mere bed and board, to which the "old robber" waved him away and said they would get plenty of skeletons later.

Storms returned. Wind, cold, and snow quelled a brief attempt at blubber boiling. Once again, no work could be accomplished. Murphy indulged in the luxury of an afternoon nap. It would be February 21st before he could make it back to shore and then only by the assistance of Victor, the senior-most boatsteerer and by far the strongest member of the crew. Wind blew harder than ever, but Murphy was determined to fetch some mollymauk skins from the tent so he could at least have something to work on in his cabin while weather raged and rocked the brig.

February 24th finally broke clear. The Old Man reacted by rousting everyone out of bed for an extra-early breakfast with the 4:30 announcement that the *Daisy* would be moving to a new anchorage. Murphy rowed to shore immediately and broke camp. He gathered up his specimens and equipment, and loaded everything into his

South Georgia crustaceans.

dory. The glassy green sea had never looked as thick with crustaceans and the dreamy float of ghostly organisms as on that day. Sunlight penetrated the quiet depths.

Murphy felt cheerful to be weighing anchor and heading east. It would put the *Daisy* that much closer to the whaling stations and the possibility of mail. He had seen a large steamer on the horizon just that morning and felt certain the vessel carried letters addressed to him.

The *Daisy*'s sails billowed under a sapphire sky. Adding to the feeling of connection to civilization, they sighted a whaling station in Prince Olaf Harbor—one whose existence was not known to them until that moment. Continuing east, taciturn as always, the Old Man finally gave the command to round the point into the next fjord, the next hunting ground, uninhabited.

One hundred thirty-eight years earlier, Captain James Cook had sailed into that same wild and godforsaken body of water. He rowed ashore with a handful of men, a musket, and a British flag. In the translated words of Anders Sparrman, who accompanied Cook, "With a salvo of musket fire and the hoisting of the flag, the territory was taken possession of for his Britannic Majesty, in whose honor this island (thirty-one leagues long, ten wide, and of less value than the least cottage in England) was named Georgia, and the bay was called Possession Bay."

The *Daisy* dropped anchor near a sandy spit. A steep glacier to the south and headlands to the north would confine most of their boat traffic to what was probably the very landing used by Cook. The whaleboats immediately went to work searching for elephants, and Murphy rowed ashore in the *Grace Emeline* to scout out a good place for his tent, which he intended to erect the following day.

But the next day was scoured with southerly gales. Wind raged all afternoon, williwaws gusting off mountains, ice, and snow. Murphy wrote, "Possession Bay seems extraordinarily cheerless and desolate. It wholly lacks the feeling of spaciousness that we had at the Bay of Isles. From our anchorage we can look toward the sea only through a narrow gap between headlands. In every direction the icy mountains shut off our view. There is little green to strike the eye, and animal life seems to be scanty."

Ever the naturalist, however, he made what he could of the life he did find. Earthworms, for example, were a complete surprise in that climate. He discovered them while digging a hole in which to anchor a tent pole. Also in that boggy but sheltered site, he identified plants not seen around Grytviken or the Bay of Isles: a buttercup, a starwort, and something Cook had called wild burnet. Captain Cleveland knew the burnet as diddle-dee and claimed it would cure whatever afflicts you, "Just make a tea of it and all will be well." Hummocks of grass grew farther apart here, some stalks as tall as six feet and others bitten down by rats, which appeared to have quite a stronghold in the area.

Murphy's library identified no more than nineteen kinds of vascular plants growing on all of South Georgia. In addition to various mosses, lichens, hepatics, and even a mushroom not previously reported, he already had collected specimens of most of the nineteen. Too far south for woody plants, Cook emphasized this lack when he wrote, "Inner parts of the country were not less savage and horrible. The wild rocks

raised their lofty summits, till they were lost in the clouds, and the valleys lay covered with everlasting snow. Not a tree was to be seen, nor a shrub even big enough to make a toothpick."

Cook was also impressed with the calving glaciers. "The head of the bay . . . was terminated by a huge mass of snow and ice of vast extent . . . pieces were continually breaking from them and floating out to sea. A great fall happened while we were in the bay; it made a noise like a cannon."

Kerguelen tea grew on the shores of Possession Bay.

Murphy was already used to the sounds of South Georgia. He described a brook in a wet meadow that had enough slope "to make a pleasant gurgling sound, where I have found eight steel drums of gasoline." These, he came to find out, had been left by none other than Benjamin Cleveland four years before when he and his officers had made a futile attempt to adapt a whaleboat to an engine. The costly experiment had been a flop.

Norwegian and British sealers who routinely scoured the coast, had left the drums intact, honoring the fact that the fuel belonged to whatever person had cached it there. Murphy had no qualms about taking advantage of the windfall, however. He found an immediate use for a small amount of the gasoline by washing some of his oily, fatty bird skins in it.

Weather changed again. A southwest wind blew so cold that none of the *Daisy*'s tough men could hold his face against the blast for more than a few minutes at a time. By nightfall, the wind warmed but was still strong enough to push raindrops to nearly horizontal.

Tucked between storms, the elephant slaughter continued, but the Old Man was disgusted with the results. The men killed forty-three animals that day but they were generally small and thin. The bulls had hauled out of the sea for rutting season weeks—or even months—ago and had not returned to the sea to feed. Murphy wrote, "They look skinny and flabby, the hide hanging in lappets from the snout, the flews, and the wall-sided head, while the blubber yield, as the skipper grumbles, makes it hardly worth the labor of killing and flensing. Most of them are unsightly beasts in other ways also, because they are shedding their hair and have a particularly sleazy and moth-eaten look. Some of the bulls are still surrounded in their wallows by five or six cows, but their generally woebegone appearance indicates that the jolly season has passed, and that they would be wise to go back to their winter migration in the nourishing ocean before the goblins get 'em."

Chapter Forty

MURPHY'S JOURNAL ENTRY for March 1st begins, "May this be the final month at South Georgia!" The entry closes, "Tomorrow, if the weather is favorable . . . we are scheduled to make a trip by whaleboat to the station in Prince Olaf Harbor."

And the weather was favorable. At six o'clock two whaleboats set out under a bright sky. Beside Murphy sat Captain Cleveland, who divulged—in strictest confidence—that he planned to leave for home in two to three weeks, hunting for sperm whales along the way. They would probably reach Barbados or Dominica early in May. This was what Murphy had been hoping for.

The British captains at the Southern Whaling and Sealing Company of North Shields at Prince Olaf welcomed the *Daisy*'s tattered crew but had no letters to deliver. Murphy posted his, hoping they would reach Grace by mid-April. Part of the welcome included the midday meal, which Murphy and the Old Man enjoyed in the dining saloon of the steamship *Restitution*. The crew was invited to join the general mess. Murphy was once more reminded of the contrast between Benjamin Cleveland's stingy operation and that of a full-fledged whaling business.

"How well these people live!" he wrote. "Four captains and I have been devouring dainties and drinking aqua vita, and having a jolly talk. A cheerful, red-haired English captain named Rochester took me over to his big barkentine which has painted ports and the hull of an old-time many-gunned frigate. Her main cabin is a gorgeous example of the passing shipwright's art. Captain Rochester produced three large bottles of Danish Carlsberg beer, for the consumption of which we were joined by the plant's physician, a very lordly looking Irishman.

The conversation turned unaccountably to boxing, a subject that seemed to interest even the elderly doctor. They asked whether Murphy was "proficient with the gloves." He replied that he was not but held out his right hand, offering the captains the opportunity to shake the hand that had once clasped the paw of "Terrible" Terry McGovern, a featherweight who, in Tuckahoe, New York on September 12th, 1889 had knocked out Pedlar Palmer in one of the shortest fights in boxing history. Murphy's hosts appeared positively awestruck at being in such vicarious presence.

Next the men turned more serious. They reported the news that Robert Falcon Scott, in his attempt to reach the South Pole before any other man on earth, had not only arrived to discover that Amundsen's Norwegian expedition had beaten him by one month, but Scott and his men had perished on their return journey. Eight months dead, Scott and four other men's frozen bodies had been discovered November 12, 1912. The team had set out long before Murphy's own journey had commenced. He especially mourned the loss of the expedition's official artist and scientist, E. A. Wilson, a physician, zoologist, and skilled watercolorist who was, in Murphy's estimation, "the best naturalist who ever worked in the Antarctic."

Back at the steamship *Restitution*, Murphy toured Captain Rochester's byproducts operation. Dried and ground flesh, viscera, blood, bones, and whale stomach contents were processed at a cost of two shillings per ton then shipped and sold in England where it was marketed for more than six pounds per ton. Making fertilizer was certainly more industrious than any use to which the *Daisy*'s men put their orts and carrion, given that they simply left huge peeled carcasses littering the beaches.

Next, Murphy walked up to the graves of some American sealers. The men, crewmembers of the schooner *Elizabeth Jane* out of New York, had been buried in 1835 at the top of a little tussocky knoll, a sheet of brass having been perforated with their epitaphs.

Death, it seemed, was in the air. The promontory that divided Possession Bay from Prince Olaf Harbor was pierced along its base by numerous deep caves. Murphy had seen these openings from the whaleboat that morning. What he had not seen was the ancient skeleton of a man that had been discovered in one of these caves only weeks before.

It was a Sunday, and therefore a day of rest for the workers at Prince Olaf Station. Many of them had gone off skiing, up and over the spine of the main island. It so happened they were at the point where South Georgia pinches to its narrowest between King Haaken Bay on the South and the very deep Possession Bay just opposite on the north coast. A trudge of only four miles on skis would have taken Murphy to the other side. He itched to go but knew an opportunity would be unlikely.

Meanwhile the Old Man was negotiating the purchase of supplies from the station agents. They sold him rice, flour, butter, and potatoes— not because they would benefit in any way by diminishing their own stores but because it seemed the decent thing to do as an act of hospitality. These goods were loaded into the whaleboats by late afternoon, and the *Daisy*'s men were underway. They reached the brig at nightfall.

As he had felt after his visit to the first whaling station at Grytviken, Murphy wrote to Grace of his growing disgust, "It is not cheerful to compare our miserable business on the *Daisy*, murdering pup sea elephants and living on penguins and dishwater, with the mode of life of these South Georgian Britishers and Scandinavians, who do things on a grand scale, have proud, upstanding men for crews, and live in a civilized or almost luxurious manner even though they are in a forgotten corner of the world. At times like this it makes my gorge rise to think of our penny-pinching skipper, who is willing to exist like a coolie. The contrast between his daily fare on the *Daisy* and in his rather distinguished white home on Pleasant Street, where the flag flies from a mast in the yard, is appalling. I suppose his point of view at sea must be attributed to the hard life which he began as a twelve-year-old cabin boy. Another element is that our old Yankee whaling has long since passed its day of glory, and the few present participants represent anachronisms of the old calling.

At least the Old Man had the grace to . . . replenish his stock of supplies. There are sea captains and sea captains, and while this trip is a great success for you and me, I think we'll never go again on a windjammer . . . headed by a penny-chaser . . . but I'll soon be home again."

The morning of March 3rd, Captain Cleveland asked Murphy to accompany Mr. da Lomba overland to Antarctic Bay, which lay to the east. The decreasing population of elephants had the Old Man wanting to sniff out new territory. This request suited Murphy just fine. He and the officer put ashore immediately after breakfast.

If Cadela had not consented to going along Murphy might well have missed an opportunity. While they threaded their rugged path the dog took a side route and was greeted by two penguins, which would ordinarily not have been noteworthy, but these made a more strident clatter than Murphy had heard from any gentoos. He caught up to the dog and the birds. "To my delight," he wrote, "they proved to be ringed, or chinstrap, penguins, cousins of the gentoos but far more cocky, pugnacious, and swashbuckling. They were quite prepared to whack the hide off Cadela, if she had dared to toy with them as she does with other kinds of penguins."

Murphy and Mr. da Lomba continued over the ridge and down toward a good view of the neighboring fjord, smaller than Possession Bay and more recently glaciated. Rock formations were smooth and rounded without the pinnacles and knife edges that were characteristic elsewhere. A large and active glacier headed the bay with another, smaller glacier on the far shore. A broad sandy beach arched below with two similar beaches on the other side.

Through field glasses they searched both shores, near and far and counted no more than eight sea elephants and they were small ones at that—good news for Murphy; bad news for the Old Man. Summer was over. It was time to go home.

On the trek back Murphy surprised a sleeping sea leopard, the species that had so excited him around the time of arrival. Now, however, he left the beast alone. There would have been no way to carry any part of the animal back to the brig, anyway. The seal snorted, looked up, opened its jaws to an impossible angle, closed its mouth, and wriggled off snakewise.

Upon returning to the *Daisy*, they learned that the day's elephant take had been only one, despite the fact that all four boats were out and the weather had been favorable.

The trip was winding down. Murphy's hair had grown long and his patience short. He joked in his ongoing letter to Grace that all he needed was her violin case and he could be mistaken with Jan Kubelik, a famous virtuoso of the day who was known for his wild hair almost as much as his musical talent.

Early on, Murphy had taken pleasure in working alone. His tent had provided a retreat where he could sing at the top of his lungs and enjoy whatever daydreams floated through his thoughts. The crew had been a source of entertainment and curiosity on the voyage down, but arrival at South Georgia afforded enough elbowroom for intellectual privacy. The unsophisticated and backward ways of the crew were sometimes tiresome, and the tent provided continuing refuge. With the end of his stay on South Georgia coming into view, however, Murphy's vexation increased with the feeling he had been denied the assistance the museums were promised. The Old Man had continually put off granting him help. *Later*, he had been saying, *we'll do it later*. Now it *was* later and Murphy worked alone.

Pitched against a protective rock slope and with enough greenery at the entrance to give a semblance of lawn, the tent site at Possession Bay was mercifully more sheltered than it had been near the Bay of Isles. March 4th Murphy rowed his dory ashore. He worked on skins, including those of the chinstrap penguins. Later in the afternoon he struck out on a solo climb.

He reached a sharp summit, barely big enough for standing. To the south he saw row upon row of snowy ridges and pyramids, which he described as "a still, white land, beautiful in the sunset light, but fear-inspiring, too, because of its cold and tracklessness." He had no barometer with which to calculate his elevation, but later, after a difficult descent in which he repeatedly sank into snow up to his hips, he took angles from the ship and figured the peak at about 1,700 feet.

March 5th the boats took twelve sea elephants, only two of which were adult bulls.

March 6th, rain all day. A nasty looking iceberg bore down ominously toward the *Daisy*. They lowered a whaleboat, made fast to the chunk of ice and tried to tow it. At first it seemed to move not one inch. Eventually, however, they succeeded in diverting it from its course. Later it ran aground and fractured into pieces.

March 7th, storm and a high, rolling swell.

For three days Murphy had been confined to his dim cabin, sleeping, reading, rereading letters. Johnny gave him a haircut. March 8th, the storm abated in the afternoon. Murphy and Mr. da Lomba lowered a boat and tried to go ashore, but the surf was too high, even for the experienced mate.

March 9th the Old Man gave orders to water the ship. This meant they would be sending casks ashore to be filled with fresh water for the voyage home. Murphy described the process, "The wind is right to let the casks blow . . . toward the beach, where our men retrieve them from the surf. They are then filled through the bungholes in the brook, plugged, rolled back to the beach, and hauled off on a whale line to which many casks are attached by running bowlines. They are tremendously heavy to handle ashore, but since the density of fresh water is less than that of salt, the filled casks float just awash in the bay. The chine hooks are caught alongside, after which the casks are hoisted to the deck by block-and-fall, and lowered into the hold."

March 10th, more water. Weather was difficult. Murphy took the *Grace Emeline* ashore only to swamp the dory in the surf. While preventing the hull from being smashed on the rocks, he lost the oars and thwarts. Later in the day one of the whaleboats salvaged them from where the pieces had been caught in kelp half a mile away.

March 11th, only two small elephants.

That night, however, things looked up. Everyone on board came awake when a whistle pierced the dark. Murphy pulled on trousers over his pajamas, slipped into boots and an overcoat, and went on deck into the illumination of a searchlight. It was Captain Rochester's whale-catcher *Southern Sea*. The vessel eased alongside and a British officer passed across a packet of mail before stepping aboard the *Daisy* to shake hands. Murphy wrote, "We did our best not to let our feverishness about our mail prevent us from being courteous to the friends who had gone to so much trouble on our behalf," but it turned out the steamer was not inclined to stay long anyway.

All pieces of mail were for Captain Cleveland, including one from Mrs. Cleveland, dated January 12th and another from his New Bedford agents, mailed January 17th. Trying to rise above bitter disappointment over not receiving anything from Grace, Murphy reminded himself how easily all the necessary connections could have been missed. Mrs. Cleveland's January letter gave proof that mail sent from Cumberland Bay in November had made it out, but if Grace had been in Florida when his letters arrived in Providence, for example, she might have been missed the opportunity to send a reply. In nine months he had received only the one letter from her, and, as it happened, the captain's wife reported that she had not heard from Grace since autumn.

Feeling more at the end of the earth than ever, Murphy returned to bed but found it difficult to fall asleep. He knew of an envelope addressed in his letterbag, "For Bob, when he worries about his wife." He opened it in the morning. Grace's message, apparently written while still on Dominica, burst with love and reassurance; it succeeded in bucking up the lonely bridegroom. The very image of her sitting on a bench in Roseau's sunny plaza—months before—anticipating his need for her words of devotion was enough to warm him.

On March 13th, Murphy set foot on South Georgia Island for the last time of the voyage. After having loaded the final effects of his camp into the dory, a moment of reflection inspired him to lower himself to the ground and kiss the cold stones. "It is an icy but beautiful land," he wrote, "where I have learned so much, and upon which I always expect to look back with a sort of nostalgic affection. . . . One sea elephant was killed today. If this represents the end of our slaughter, I shall be truly thankful, and I hope with all my heart that no sealer from the United States will ever trouble these shores again. . . . My business is over except for what I hope to be able to accomplish at sea. There is still much undone at South Georgia, of course, but I can honestly say that I have done my best."

SECTION IV
Seventeen Thousand Miles

Chapter Forty-One

Beastly weather prevented the *Daisy*'s efficient departure. More than once the anchor chain had clanked and groaned up, only to be let out again when wind velocity became too dangerous. By Murphy's review of shipping records, Captain Cleveland's brig was the forty-fifth vessel to leave South Georgia's waters in the century and a quarter since Captain James Cook first reported on his discovery of the island. No one could say how long any of them had to wait out the skies once it was time to go home.

Squalls heightened. Snow blew and stung. Wind sang through the rigging, and the men sang no chanteys on deck while they toiled at the windlass. The *Grace Emeline* hung on her davits, filling with slushy rainwater. Now, finally, on March 15th, the *Daisy* was under sail and crossing over the bar at the mouth of Possession Bay.

There remained only one piece of business before getting underway in earnest. As they neared Prince Olaf Harbor, Mr. da Lomba's whaleboat was lowered with letters to mail. Murphy went along.

As before, the station captains extended an enthusiastic welcome. They said a steamer set for Buenos Aires was due in from Cumberland Bay and that letters would probably reach the United States in a matter of six weeks. Dr. Leach, the gray-haired physician, urged Murphy and the others to stay for drinks, a game of chess, conversation, but any such indulgence would have been out of the question. They hurried off sending blessings and farewells across the water, the echoes of which lingered with an eerie finality.

The brig was standing off. Mr. da Lomba's boat met up with her at dusk, six or seven miles off the coast. After days and days of too much wind, the evening was calm. Birds flew all around—whalebirds, Mother Carey's chickens, and various petrels. Specifically, Murphy identified numerous *Fregetta tropica*, the black-bellied storm petrel, misnamed since it enters the tropics only on its migration. All those in the sky that evening and hundreds of thousands more of the same species had to have nested somewhere in South Georgia's grassy soil, but Murphy had not been able to find a single one on land. Now, they flew all about. Their thick presence stirred a sort of regret. He wrote, "The sight, the whirr and splash and twittering of these incalculable birds, like bats in a vast black cavern roofed with the firmament and floored with the ocean, so stirred my imagination that I was jumpy through the night."

In the morning the brig wove her path between chunks of ice. Pointed mountain peaks smoothed into a distant horizon. Glaciers faded to white blurs, not to be seen again. Murphy's dream had become reality. Now, it was over and thoughts of home occupied his mind. He had only his patience to manage on the return voyage—along with a touch of seasickness. Having been either on land or at anchor for over three months, his legs were wobbly and the reentry was rough.

While struggling toward equilibrium he decided to prepare a diving petrel skin as a gift for the Old Man. Murphy had not turned his hand to taxidermy since leaving for college six years before, and he did not have any glass eyes with him, but he was able to mount the bird in an attitude of convincing flight, and the skipper was tickled with the results.

This is not to say the captain had softened. The Old Man was as hard driving and hard bitten as ever, making no secret of intentionally leaving Possession Bay without putting in at Cumberland Bay to clear his ship and pay the taxes on the seal oil he was taking. He planned simply to sail into the first port in the West Indies and use the last clearance issued before Cumberland Bay, the one from São Vicente at the Cape Verde Islands last September. Such timing would seem completely reasonable for any whaleship. Even if some official knew the *Daisy* had visited South Georgia, he would probably not consider that remote land as a port of

entry. Murphy wrote, "The long arm of international shipping regulations may some day catch up with Captain Cleveland and his co-owners
of the *Daisy*. But he evidently thinks the chance worth taking, because,
although he expects to go to sea until he is 'to the north'ard of seventy,'
he has no intention of ever returning to South Georgia."

March 17th and the threat of seasickness had passed. Using his best
Irish term of endearment, Murphy began his journal entry to Grace,
"The top of the mornin' to you, mavourneen! I am celebrating St.
Patrick's Day by being in the homeward parade, although I'm afraid it
will not be the 'straight wake for home' in which sailors rejoice."

The glaciers' refrigerating breath lay behind. Latitude 49° S, which
compares to the long boundary between Canada and the western United
States, had already fallen astern. The *Daisy* plowed the waves at eight
knots with the sun sinking on her port beam. Murphy had taken off his
heavy overcoat for the last time. He contemplated his pith helmet, which
had been tucked away through the polar summer, and he anticipated the
happy day when he would discard his woolen underwear and thick socks.
The tropics beckoned.

The Old Man borrowed Murphy's copy of *Divina Comedia*, with Italian text and its English translation on facing pages. All the way through
Hell and *Purgatory*, and halfway through *Paradise*, the skipper's entire
comment was, "Dante had a head on him."

On March 19th, in mid-ocean, the sea turned rough but with not
enough wind to stabilize the ship. Anything not lashed to something
solid rolled around, including dinner out of Murphy's plate and into his
lap. Impressed with the crew's natural ability to deal with the Atlantic's
unpredictable action, Murphy observed, "The Portugee can balance the
most rolling of beans, once he gets it on his knife!"

March 20th, latitude 47° 20' S. West wind, light rain.

March 21st, latitude 45° 50' S. Very rough. Seas slopping across the
deck. Birds all around. It was Good Friday, so Murphy read the Gospels.

March 22nd, latitude 43° 20' S. Bright and mild with winds that
favored the northward course. They were creeping up the globe. For the

first time since November, Captain Cleveland ordered lookouts aloft to search for whales, but all they saw was a shark.

The next day was Easter. Murphy imagined the spring scenes Grace must have been enjoying, the scent of crocuses that would have already popped up and opened in the grass around the Barstow house. He opened three cards from his mail bag, one was from Grace, another from her sister, and a third from the minister who had performed the Murphys' wedding ceremony.

March 24th, latitude 43° S, as far south as Boston is north. A storm forced the *Daisy* to run eastward. Birds dotted the sky. With assistance, Murphy caught twelve wandering albatrosses by using bent nails as hooks. He kept a mature male, two females, and a yearling as specimens. The others he set free after banding their legs with identifying numbers and the address of the American Museum of Natural History.

He killed the four specimen birds and hung them by the legs to cool prior to skinning. A squid with a body more than a foot long, dropped out of one of the birds' gullets. Happy to have his specimens produce specimens, he scooped up the squid and preserved it in formalin. After skinning the birds, Murphy turned over the carcasses to the cook for stew.

On March 25th, thick overcast blanketed the sky, and no sighting could be made. Wind raged and tore at the sea. Every sail of the mainmast and most on the foremast were furled under a "ripsnorting southerly gale." In a high following sea, each mountainous wave loomed from behind as if to crash down on the brig but would instead lift the stern up, up, and farther up, before sliding under her hull and passing harmlessly on either side.

Through that night and into the next day the vessel had carried only the lower foretopsail and no other canvas. After nightfall, the wind moderated. Men were sent up into the blackness to loose a couple more sails.

March 26th, latitude 38° 50' S, comparing to Chesapeake Bay. Winds were light. The skipper gave Murphy permission to lower the dory onto subsiding ocean swells. A wealth of birds littered the twilight. Of the young wandering albatrosses he wrote, "[They] were having a wonderful social jamboree, meeting in gams on the water, raising their long wings and bills, screaming and squealing at each other, just as I saw their parents do on the whaling banks off South Georgia last December." Aware that it might be his last opportunity, he shot at birds until he could no longer see through the dark. Aiming at a moving target in a bouncing dory, his rate of success was low, but he managed to return to the brig with three sooty albatrosses and five species of petrels, one of which was new to his collection.

Weather turned so rough it became difficult to sleep. The ship jerked and pounded. On March 28th, Murphy wrote, "As I seesawed on my thwartship bed, I was wrenched and bruised, and my skin was tugged and stretched by the force of gravity until my head ached and the miseries were all through me. I could hear the seas swooshing aboard and the spray slapping the deck above. At least I had a dry corner, whereas many another man on board not only had the water above him but also felt it dripping into his bunk."

Finally, it felt more restful to be up than to try to sleep. Objects crashed and sloshed. A kettle flew over its rack and scalded the steward. Murphy held on tight with optimism. With luck they would cross the Tropic of Capricorn in no more than a week. Part of that luck would include the absence of whales. Murphy wrote, "I hope they will continue to keep their snouts down out of sight," but he kept this hope to himself, since the captain would have considered it unspeakably disloyal from anyone on board.

The afternoon of March 29th a large, sleek tomcat surprised Murphy on deck. "Come now," he wrote of his reaction, "cats are not produced by spontaneous generation, and we certainly found none at South Georgia." Then he remembered the kitten taken on board in October. It had disappeared into steerage at the first whiff of cold weather. Its reappearance bore proof that someone had taken care of the animal or that the *Daisy*'s rats had been enough to see it into maturity.

The next morning was calm and distinctly summery in feel. Their latitude corresponded to Savannah, Georgia. Murphy had another surprise. The spiders he had experimented with while in the Sargasso Sea were alive and well in his cabin; they had survived the cold of the far south. Cockroaches, however, had not. Murphy had seen no activity in that population since November.

March 31st, latitude 29° 31' S, Murphy stripped off more clothes and cleaned house. With his pith helmet protecting him from the heat of the sun once more, he set up his canvas chair on deck. "Today's latitude," he wrote, "corresponds with that of northern Florida, the blue Canary Isles, Cairo, the Himalaya Mountains, and Lower California. It is hard to keep patient."

April 1st marked another month gone. The Old Man found Murphy in his berth and called him to the quarterdeck to see the bizarre sight of a penguin riding the back of a loggerhead turtle. April fool!

Chapter Forty-Two

WEATHER CONTINUED OFF AND ON with wind shifting from north to east to west then back again to north, sometimes reaching near gale force and raising a sharp sea. Rain came in bursts.

Mr. da Lomba was on watch during the early hours of April 4th. He sent the helmsman down the companionway to call Murphy awake. Mr. da Lomba had never sent for him in vain, so Murphy scrambled up on faith that the disruption would be worth his while. Groggy as he may have been, it turned out that Murphy would not have chosen to miss the scene for any price.

St. Elmo's Fire is a phenomenon not limited to ships at sea but is named for the patron saint of sailors because it is often observed at sea. Any tall, piercing object such as a church spire or a ship's mast can gather luminance when a gradient of electrical charge exists between the ground and the atmosphere. Somewhat akin to the aurora borealis or aurora australis, the glow is not fire at all and it carries no danger. Traditionally, many have considered it a good omen, since it often occurs at the end of a thunderstorm and signals the arrival of better weather.

Columbus, Darwin, and countless other sailors have described the phenomenon. The Greeks called St. Elmo's Fire *Helena*, and named the rarer double form after the two stars in the constellation Gemini: *Castor* and *Pollux*—not surprising that they chose stars significant to marine navigation.

The glow danced and snaked around the *Daisy*'s rigging that night, sending thrills running up and down Murphy's spine. He wrote, "The hair of my bare head also stood on end, but I cannot say whether this was due to mental exaltation or because I, like the ship, was spurting a brush discharge of electricity into the atmosphere. . . . The *Daisy* was agleam. . . . Pale blue spherical glows tipped both masts, the upper yardarms, and the end of the jib boom. At first they shone in the calm and intense blackness with a steady light of somewhat indefinite outline. But, when a puff blew out of the northwest, the fireballs lengthened and flickered into tapers, emitting a fizzing, crackling sound, as though the timbers from which they streamed were afire. I was spellbound until rain began to fall again and the celestial lights went out, whereupon I returned to my berth."

Later that day, the *Daisy* slipped into the tropics. The temperature felt perfect. Murphy wore a clean white shirt, and the crew pattered about in bare feet. A Portuguese man-o'-war passed alongside. Weather was warm enough for a general cleanup.

Below decks, the berths, lockers, and cupboards were emptied and scrubbed. Walls and ceilings received a soap and water treatment. Above deck men dangled in boatswain's chairs and swabbed the length of both masts. Each part of each spar got scrubbed. Deck planks were scoured.

Murphy watched in amazement, because not only was the crew more vigorous than he might have imagined, the "household cleanser" was urine. He described it, "A collecting barrel is lashed to the bulwarks near the fo-castle and twenty or thirty gallons of its contents have been applied, along with elbow grease, from stem to stern of the *Daisy*. As though the fluid was not already sufficiently potent, the mate added a good quantity of blubber ash from the furnaces beneath the try-pots. This residue is rich in lye, so altogether we have had a mixture fit to burn paint off wood, not to mention skin off muscle and bone. The cleansing was followed by a free-for-all water fight when the men rinsed and showered the craft with innumerable wooden buckets of sea water. Fearful and wonderful are the traditions of Yankee whaling!"

Next came grooming of a more personal nature. Under a hot calm a frenzy of shaving, bathing, and barbering took place both fore and aft on deck. Johnny trimmed Murphy's hair to a prisoner's length. Roderick, the twenty-two year old greenhand from Barbados, who had worked as a tailor's apprentice, mended Murphy's clothes. He regretted having neither doeskin nor white duck with which to make what he considered proper repairs to Murphy's suits.

Roderick had been the man to pitch Pinhead's iron knuckles overboard. He had never been to sea before this voyage, yet he seemed to have learned every chantey that could be sung. That evening, during the second dogwatch, Roderick coached Conrad, Feddy, Elise, John Paul, and a few of the other Dominicans in a new song. The Portuguese sailors did not fall in; they seemed to stick with a handful of New Bedford favorites. Murphy wrote, "On most ships [songs] are led by the 'doctor' (meaning the cook), but on *Daisy* the cook, who is not even called doctor, is a silent bird. Mr. Almeida is our usual tenor hero during cutting-in and anchor-weigh." Roderick's new song began,

> Ho! for Japan and wideawake!
> There's plenty of whales for us to take.

> And now the whale is on the run.
> The iron holds fast, but his flukes we shun.
> His flukes we shun for they'd break our bones
> And send us down to Davy Jones.

> And now the doctor's made some duff,
> Likewise horse-pie, but not enough.
> So we'll fill our bellies with blubber and tar
> And sleep our watch on the capstan bar.

> And now the ship is bound for home,
> And in her teeth she carries a bone.
> When we get there we'll raise the hair,
> Get soused, and love the girls for fair.

The men brought whale bone on deck to work on at idle times. Now that the *Daisy* was passing through the southern horse latitudes there was plenty of idle time. This area of calm is a subtropical high pressure belt relating to equatorial air that warms, rises into the atmosphere, and

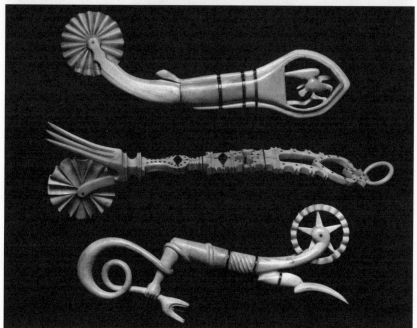

Scrimshaw is a craft believed to have originated with American sailors. After the voyage Murphy became a collector of pieces like these fine examples.

expands. With increased volume the air mass is deflected toward the poles. It cools and spills back down to the earth's surface at about 30° latitude in each hemisphere. Where it falls, pressure is high, weather is hot and dry, and wind is typically scarce. Spaniards noticed the pattern in the early days of sailing to the West Indies. Becalmed, desperate to move, and fearing the depletion of their fresh water supply while waiting for wind, some captains have been reduced to ordering that their animals be dumped overboard as a means of conserving drinking water, hence the term, horse latitudes.

The pigs were long gone and the only live animals on board the *Daisy* were a dog and cat sniffing around. The men whiled away their time with whale bones, working the long pieces into walking sticks with files and the hand lathe on deck. One sailor patiently etched the image of a whaleship onto a big, polished tooth. Murphy had seen scrimshaw in New Bedford, including ornaments and useful objects, some of which combined sperm whale ivory with bone, wood, silver, and mother-of-pearl. Scrimshaw is a uniquely American craft that rose with the Yankee whaling era and died when it died, leaving behind a record of whalers-eye views of ships and whale hunts, sweethearts and reminders of home—all scratched into tooth enamel. The fine lines were blackened with carbon.

Murphy had stowed several whale teeth in his personal collection but did not try his hand at the sailors' craft. Instead he scampered up to the mainmasthead and swept the horizon with his binoculars. In the far distance he made out the faint purple peaks of Trindade about forty miles ahead. The Old Man had said nothing about a stop, but Murphy hoped for one.

It is a small and rugged heap of volcanic rock between Brazil and Africa—just five miles long and not much more than a mile wide. Lying in the middle of the Atlantic as it does, the island historically gave vessels headed for Cape Horn a nautical reckoning. Legend had it that pirates had not only hidden out there but had buried the plunder of Peruvian churches. If so, the famed astronomer, Edmund Halley, failed to unearth the treasure when he visited in 1700. People have never settled there for long; the permanent population consists mostly of thousands upon thousands of birds: petrels, greater and lesser frigate birds, red-footed boobies, brown noddies, white terns, and sooty terns. Green sea turtles use the island's beaches for nesting. Land crabs scuttle. Tree fern forests flourish.

Mr. da Lomba had been ashore on an earlier voyage. His wandering had taken him to a cluster of stone-marked graves in a green valley beneath the island's towering mountains, phonolite like Fernando de Noronha.

The morning of April 7th, Trindade lay many miles to the west. Wind was down. That night the brig apparently drifted, because the next morning the elusive gray stack bore north and east—but much closer now. Finally conceding to the calm that he was stuck in, the Old Man issued a command to stand by for lowering. Murphy made ready to scramble into Mr. Almeida's boat.

The pull for shore would be about eight miles. Fired with enthusiasm, the men drew closer and closer to the thunder of surf breaking against rock and cliff. The air was calm, but a groundswell heaped huge surges of water on the tough coast ahead.

They approached from the south near a peninsula of basalt columns that they skirted in search of a place to land. But the few beaches they saw were terrifically narrow and each was barricaded with sharp and dangerous outcrops. All the while the whaleboat rose and fell with such dreadful intensity that even some of the most seasoned sailors became ill.

Murphy felt fine. This was the adventure he had hoped for, with its promise of exploration and discovery. Man-o'-war birds wove in and out. Fairy terns and Trindade petrels circled at a distance. A booby flew right between two oarsmen in the boat. Murphy scanned the rocky heights. Tall peaks, spires, towers, pillars, eroding scree slopes, and drainage channels made a jumble of relief. One of Murphy's references had put the island's topmost point at about 2,000 feet and another said closer to 3,000. Either way, the topography was dramatic. A cylinder of rock at the west end, known variously as the Ninepin of Halley, the

Monument, or the Priest, rose directly from the ocean to a height of 900 feet. From its pitted walls tens of thousands of feathered sprites looked out from their niches "like saints of a cathedral spire."

Since no safe landing became evident, they fished their way back to the brig. Murphy wrote, "Here, as at Fernando Noronha, we lost many of our prizes because of sharks, the lines often coming inboard with nothing but fishes' heads on the hooks. Even one of our largest garupas was nipped in half. It gave me a rather awesome feeling to see a huge head come over the gunwale with its jaws still gasping but no tail behind the gills!"

They caught some of the smaller sharks, too. Murphy examined them and found that their ugly mouths "harbored curious, extensible leeches." The sailors attracted less fearsome swimmers alongside the boat

The Ninepin on Trindade Island.

by throwing scraps of fat into the water. In all, they landed about two hundred fish, divided among nine species.

Murphy did his best to take it all in. Even the flies caught his interest. They were "flat, triangular feather flies, which live as parasites in the plumage of boobies and man-o'-war birds. . . . They scuttled sidewise like crabs, adroitly dodging capture, and seemed bent on getting on the underside of whatever they alighted upon, whether a gunstock, one's hand, or a thwart of the boat. These flies were the only insects we saw."

But it was the birds that caught his imagination, "filling the air and covering the rocks. The noddies were incredibly confident and curious, hovering round our heads, even alighting upon them, and peering into our faces so closely that one had to look at them cross-eyed. It was the simplest matter to catch them in the hand as they fluttered among us." He tagged four petrels with American Bird Banding Association rings and set them free with the hope that the birds would one day come into the clutches of some other eager naturalist. Of the fairy terns, like those he had seen at Fernando de Noronha, but here even thicker, he wrote, "The most delicate and wraithlike of birds are these white terns; when they fly against the glare transmitted from a bright sky, the dark line of their wing bones is projected like an X-ray shadow through the feathers."

His journal continues, "Boobies soared among the pinnacles a thousand feet above us. Man-o'-war birds, flying overhead, seemed all head, wings, and tail. There are two species at Trindade, and both were more interested in the brig offshore than in our tiny whaleboats. The man-o'-war birds are notorious pirates in their feeding habits, but I saw a troop of the smaller kind fishing for themselves. Half a dozen of them hovered in a row over a school of surface fish, and faced in a direction opposite to that in which the fish were moving. While the birds poised close over the water, they beat their big wings slowly. Then at the right moment they struck downward, swinging their long bills like scimitars back under their bodies, the hooked tip seizing a fish from the rear. They seemed to catch three or four a minute, and yet made no commotion among the moving school of the victims."

He collected the rare petrels endemic to the island, both the black and the bicolored forms. The skins would be the first such specimens for any museum in the United States. Then, as luck would have it, immediately after reloading both barrels of his gun and having discharged one shot already, he saw in the distance a bird whose appearance was entirely new to him. A fortunate long shot spun it down to the water, and the whale-boat reached it before the sharks did.

Murphy was, of course, delighted with the opportunity to observe and collect more seabirds. Of the one he could not identify, which he found to be the handsomest of all, he wrote, "If by chance [this petrel] should prove new, I will stand to sponsor as fine a bird as any biologist could wish for. But it is possible, of course, that the petrel may have been described since the British Museum Catalog was published." He later concluded that the bird was a known species exhibiting a previously unknown plumage phase.

Five o'clock and the sun was slipping down the sky. Two merchant vessels had skimmed the horizon that day, a four-masted ship going south and a German bark flying skysails headed north. These canvases above the royals indicated a light, favorable wind. As Mr. Almeida's crew pulled for home, and the rough lump of Trindade grew smaller with distance, Murphy looked regretfully at what might have been. One of the legends is that anyone who drinks the water from the natural springs on the island is bound to return, but Murphy had not been near enough to have a sip. "It was aggravating to be unable to land," he wrote, "through the whole day, while our little boat skirted the seething edge of ocean, I gazed longingly at the tree ferns far above, and could not help thinking that there may possibly have been unknown land birds there, among the spires of the fascinating unattainable mountains."

Chapter Forty-Three

MURPHY HAD ACCESS to Captain Cleveland's records, some of which he had, in fact, volunteered to maintain for the Old Man. One aspect of interest was how charges were made for what came out of the ship's stores.

Sailors withdrew whatever they needed from the slop chest as they needed it, whether it was a new pair of pants or a needle and thread with which to sew up an old pair (of course, an officer had to oversee the withdrawal). No payment was made at the time of "purchase." Rather, in the style of sharecroppers, a charge was entered against the man's account, which would be deducted from his pay at the end of the voyage when the final settlement of the net proceeds would be made. Naturally, the ship's owners made a profit on the goods. Murphy thought this was fair, but he noticed certain inconsistencies in the cost of the same kind of item from one account to another and from one day to another. He concluded that the amount charged depended more on the Old Man's state of mind than on the item's original, wholesale cost or to whom the item was sold. According to the captain, the law allowed owners to make a twelve percent profit. Murphy thought they might have exceeded the legal limit from time to time, but he reminded himself that at least the profits were supposed to be figured into the net proceeds and would thus be theoretically distributed—at least fractionally—in the shares of every member of the crew when everything would be tallied.

An example of one account was Attenaze Jean-Baptiste's, the six-foot greenhand from Martinique—

April 25, 1912	1 box cigarettes	$ .35
Aug. 3	1 pair blankets	2.45
	1 jacket	3.25
	1 denim jumper	.75
	2 pairs denim pants	2.50
	2 cotton shirts	1.50
	1 cap	.95
	1 oil hat	.85
	1 sheath and belt	.30
	1 knife	.40
	thread and needle	.15
Aug. 6	1 oil suit	4.00
Sept. 6	1 pair shoes	2.50
Sept. 10	1 tin cup	.15
Sept. 12	1 lb. Tobacco	.60
Sept. 28	pot and pan	.30
Oct. 13	2 pairs wool pants	5.50
	2 wool shirts	3.50
	2 wool undershirts	2.00
	2 pairs drawers	2.00
	2 denim frocks	2.00
Oct. 31	1 pair mittens	.60
	2 pairs woolen stockings	1.50
Nov. 17	1 pair leather boots	5.00
Jan. 28, 1913	1 oil suit	4.50
Feb. 3	1 pair mittens	.60
Apr. 1	1 cap	.75

With the *Daisy* having approached and then reentered the tropics, there was less and less need for woolen socks and undershirts. The crew was working barefoot once again, and the slop chest was visited infrequently.

Also, with increasingly agreeable conditions, an ailing greenhand, William Elwin from Barbados, began asking to be carried on deck in the afternoons to rest on his blanket in the clean, warm air. Until the sight of this man on deck, Murphy had not thought about him one way or the other since that horrible February night when the two whaleboats crashed into each other and broke at the Bay of Isles. Elwin was one of the men who had had to swim ashore in the icy water and wait out the night while huddled around a greasy heap of burning blubber.

To Murphy's knowledge, the twenty-one-year-old man had simply folded himself back into life in the forecastle after that wretched event. No conversation had been made among the officers about the man's condition, and Murphy had no reason to miss his presence.

When Elwin turned up sick and gaunt on deck, however, Murphy's thoughts flashed back to how the man had looked the morning of the rescue, and he realized Elwin had probably been suffering the entire time since experiencing the shock of Antarctic temperatures, both in the sea and on land while waiting for rescue. Once he pieced the situation together, it struck Murphy that Elwin's ailments—such as they might have been at that point—should have been brought to the attention of Dr. Leach before departing Prince Olaf Harbor. Whether Captain Cleveland knew of the man's condition at the time was not clear. Now, the most the Old Man could do was to offer a stimulant of some sort from the medicine chest, and even at that, the skipper used the opportunity to curse the steward yet another time for having pinched the rum.

But the captain was too late with his stimulant. On April 10th, Elwin's shipmates carried him into sunlight for the last time. They laid him down; he gasped a few times and died. Murphy felt for a pulse, but there was none.

He and some of the men wrapped him in his blanket and laid him on the carpenter's bench, where Mr. da Lomba and the boatsteerers sewed his body in canvas. He would be draped with a blue flag and left through the night on his final watch.

At eight o'clock the next morning Captain Cleveland ordered the sails to be hauled aback. The American flag was hoisted to half-mast, and the section of bulwarks at the waist of the ship and beside the cutting stage was removed. Elwin's body was laid on a hatch, and a bag of sand was attached to the winding sheet.

"I am the resurrection and the life, saith the Lord . . . began the captain. The crew crowded around in solemnity and curiosity. Most of them were unfamiliar with the Anglican *Book of Common Prayer*, from which the Old Man was reading, but it seemed they found the formality appropriate to the occasion of committing a dead man's body to the sea.

For a man walketh in a vain shadow, and disquieteth himself in vain: he heapeth up riches, and cannot tell who shall gather them.

According to Mr. Almeida, Elwin had disposed of his few effects four days earlier. Murphy considered whatever "riches" Elwin would have had coming to him at the final settlement of the voyage. A greenhand's meager share was only 1/185 of the profits. Murphy wrote bitterly, "If they yield a hundred dollars to the heirs or assigns at the final division next summer, someone will have failed to enter sufficient costs against his account."

For as much as it hath pleased Almighty God of his great mercy to take unto himself the soul of our dear brother here departed, we therefore commit his body to the deep to be turned into corruption, looking for the resurrection of the body (when the Sea shall give up her dead), and the life of the world to come, through our Lord Jesus Christ; who —

Right at that point Mr. da Lomba made a gesture, and six of the Dominicans tipped up their end of the hatch cover. The remains of William Elwin plunged feet first into the sea. At the sound of the splash, Captain Cleveland left off in the middle of the prayer and snapped the book shut. The Lord's Prayer, the Collect, and the Benediction were left unsaid. Instead, he bellowed the command, "Haul down the clews of the foresail! Raise up your wheel!" and the *Daisy* was once more under way, resuming her course in the trade wind.

That evening, the Old Man consulted Murphy about how he thought the sailor's death should be recorded in the ship's log. In truth, Murphy thought Elwin had died as the direct result of abuse and neglect, pure and simple. But he modulated his response and suggested the captain

Oath of Master to Death or Loss Overboard at Sea of a Seaman or Mariner.

Consulate of the United States of America at **Barbados. W. I.** ,

May 9th. 1913. 189 .

I, master of the **Brig "DAISY".** , of **New Bedford.** ,

do hereby make oath, in due form of law, that **William Elwin.**

died at sea, on board the said ship, on or about the **16th.** of

April 1913. , 189 , on the voyage from **South Georgia**

to this port.

Benjn D Cleveland

Subscribed and sworn to this **9th.** day of **May 1913.** , 189 .

[SEAL.]

Chester W. Martin
U. S. Consul.

William Elwin never recovered from his overnight on the beach in South Georgia.

might attribute the death to *exposure*. Even that went too far, however, so they finally "compromised" on rheumatic fever, which had been the captain's euphemistic diagnosis all along.

That a man had been dying more or less under Murphy's nose without his awareness came as a shock to him. He did not see himself as self-centered, yet there he had been existing in relative comfort, no more than 125 feet away. In his words, "It has rather bowled me over," especially in light of new information that another sailor, twenty-six year old Antão Dias, was ill.

Murphy had no contact with the forecastle but knew from Mr. Almeida's description that it was a dark and miserable hole—damp, smelly, and often wet. What a place to die, he thought, "so far in space and time and comfort from all that is dear to one." Murphy at least found a little hope in the fact that Elwin's shipmates had done their best to care for him with what little they had to use.

Antão, or Ferleão as he was called, was better known to Murphy than Elwin had been, and learning that the man was sick, he went forward to visit. Although no diagnosis was made, the formerly strong oarsman lay wasting away as he apparently had been for a month or more, suffering from bouts of internal bleeding and eventual confusion. Murphy, who had already begun to miss Ferleão's good-natured, hard-working presence on deck, regretted having consumed all his beef tea while in South Georgia. Murphy, Irish-white and living in an era of sharp racial divide, hunched in the dimness of the forecastle with the blackest man on board, wishing with all his heart that he had one last remaining jar of the stuff to spoon into Ferleão's mouth. As it was, Murphy sat helpless, having nothing to offer but a few words of kindness to cheer the man on.

For three days Murphy visited the forecastle until, on the fourth day he wrote, "Ferleão, whom I now see daily, is going out like the last flickers from the wick of a whale-oil lamp. He seems completely listless and at peace. The tenderness and consideration of his shipmates is a revelation of man's innate mercy. They know that he has only days to live. Their role and responsibility are something quite apart from the quarterdeck and cabin. They vie with one another, like nuns, to give comfort. They feed him, wash him with warm water from the galley, keep him clad in clean shirt and cotton trousers, and neither balk nor gag because of vomit, blood, or excrement.

"It is easy to call men black, lazy, dissolute, or any other name to which you choose to attach opprobrium. But saintliness is, nevertheless, where you find it, and charity shines in the peak between *Daisy*'s bluff bows."

Five days later, at about noon, Murphy and the Old Man stood together on the quarterdeck, elbows leaning casually on either side of the companionway when Johnny the cabin boy came aft and announced quietly, "Ferleão, he say he going to die today."

The Old Man spat out an oath. Murphy wrote, "[He] banged the painted canvas with his fist, and told Johnny to get below and bring no more foolish messages from the forecastle. His show of temper was, however, nothing other than an attempt to rustle up a confidence which he could not feel, because as soon as the cabin boy was out of sight, the captain turned to me and whispered weakly, 'When they say they are going to die, they always do.'"

Just before the ship's bronze bell struck seven that evening, the steward found Murphy and the captain standing in the moonlight. Ferleão was dead and, in fact, already cold. Two men had been sitting close to him, but Ferleão's light had gone out so silently and calmly, they had not even noticed the change. They said he suffered no pain. Murphy wrote, "He was an obliging, gentle sort of fellow, black as coal but with a white man's features. I'm glad to say that I gave him a few clothes and helped him keep warm in South Georgia."

Ferleão's shipmates had bathed him and dressed him in clean clothes that morning. For his sea burial they put the man in his "long togs," meaning a store-bought suit. They bound his head in clean, white linen and stitched him into sailcloth. The Portuguese had a more elaborate ceremony for one of their own than the West Indians had had for Elwin. After that, the captain opened his prayer book as before.

And as before the Old Man snapped the book shut, mid-sentence the minute the body plunged into the sea. No Lord's prayer, no Benediction. Just an order to hoist the sails and resume their course.

Murphy wrote about three blue sharks—each seven feet long—and a smaller one of a different kind that had been swimming around the *Daisy*'s stern since dawn, "The old conviction that these hated brutes had come expressly for the corpse was breathed about the ship." But the sharks paid no attention when the shroud went overboard. In reference to the very moment following the plunge of Ferleão's body into the depths, however, "Many necks craned over the bulwarks as the body plummeted. Afterwards I heard numerous soft discussions as to when Ferleão would reach the bottom, or whether he would ever reach the bottom at all."

The deaths in the forecastle annoyed Captain Cleveland but did not seem to trouble him to any lasting degree. It was April 21st. Several of the sailors and two of the boatsteerers exhibited signs of what Murphy judged to be a form of beriberi, a vitamin deficiency characterized by pain and edema. But the Old Man wanted to head to the "Twelve-Forty Grounds," a traditionally rich area centering around 12° N latitude and 40° W longitude where sperm whales were usually thick.

Topping up the *Daisy*'s casks might not have been foremost in the men's minds at that point. The crew's time would be up the end of the month. Murphy suspected they might refuse to hunt after April 30th. Some had already suggested this to the cooper—even if it would mean going in irons. A few daring hints were made that the crew might *ratten* the whaling equipment if forced to continue, which meant they intended to damage machinery as in a labor dispute. This would have been one step below mutiny.

Chapter Forty-Four

THE *DAISY* HAD FINALLY PASSED north of the horse latitudes into the southeast trades, where air is drawn back toward the equator to replace that which had risen in the cycle of heating and cooling. Wind was brisk. In one twenty-four-hour period they had progressed northward by three degrees of latitude, or a little over two hundred miles. Murphy kept a constant eye on the readings. He wanted to get home.

And, apparently, so did everyone else. Conversations on deck turned to women. Murphy overheard their graphic fantasies. By now English had become the common language, so he could understand much of what was being said. One of the officers bragged about his past adventures. Murphy wrote, "[He] has roamed the African coast sampling the wares it offers. He now enjoys gloating—and whetting the appetites of the others—over detailed reminiscences of his prowess among fat-buttocked Hottentots and the Angola women whose labia reach halfway to their knees.

"Today, just as the [bristly] moonface of Mr. Almeida appeared above the forward companionway, the aforementioned officer asked, 'Do you like a fat woman or a thin one?' Mr. Almeida snapped, 'Any goddam thing!' and ducked back below decks."

Still, there were whales to hunt. At one point all four boats were lowered and gone so long that two of them disappeared over the horizon. Murphy wrote, "I wish the miserable whales would stay out of sight, particularly if they have no intention of being caught." But later he added, "In the afternoon I regretted that I had not gone off with one of the boats, because any excitement being experienced was far from this stationary brig."

It would have been the lesser of two evils, had Murphy gone along. While he read Shakespeare on deck, the crews were making fast to a total of eight whales, all of which had to be towed slowly and painfully from horizon to brig. The boats were not back until well into the evening.

The carcasses were all small but with eight of them chained alongside, the labor of cutting-in would be grueling nonetheless. The men were happy when Captain Cleveland deferred the process until morning; Murphy was not. He saw it as one more irritating delay. At least he could loaf while the others toiled. He read; he wrote in his journal; he observed the captain indulge in one of his odd pleasures: eating putrefied fish.

"After our big haul of fish at Trindade, he selected for himself a good-sized sarugo, which is a kind of grunt, and also a garupa about two feet long. These were gutted and washed, after which the skipper tied them firmly with cod line to the main shrouds, where they have hung in the sun this past week. They soon began to smell somewhat like strong cheese, and then considerably worse. I don't like to go near enough to learn more about them, but they have obviously cured to a point at which the flakes of muscle come off at the slightest touch. In other words, the carcasses would fall apart of their own weight but for the fact that they have begun to dry out and shrink.

"This is the stage for which the Old Man has been avidly waiting. He now walks past . . . pulls a small chunk out of one fish or the other and eats it with the greatest gusto."

The cutting-in took all day. Before the carcass of the largest bull was cast adrift, the fourth mate severed its penis at the base and hoisted it on deck, where it became "the object of much noisy and ribald admiration." But the officer had a distinct purpose. He skinned the organ and laced strips of the black, shiny hide onto several of the whaleboats' oarlocks. This would muffle the oars and act to silence them when sneaking up on a whale. Previously the tholepins—or wooden pegs that stabilized the pivot point of the oars on the gunwales—had been softened with braided cordage. But the whaleskin was better; the black rawhide would shrink as it dried and would be longer-wearing.

With the tryworks fired up once more, air around the *Daisy* blackened with smoke. Many of the men were sick. Some showed signs of scurvy. Frank, the boatsteerer who had earlier been stricken with buboes, was nearly incapacitated with some sort of illness.

They were five degrees south of the equator. Murphy began watching the night sky for evidence that they really were progressing toward his home hemisphere. "The lady in the moon has almost righted herself," he wrote to Grace and "the Southern Cross begins to look as it did from Dominica. I try to be cheerful in such thoughts, but why oh why, did your letter never come? It is discouraging to be penned in an old hulk that must rely entirely upon the gift of heaven."

On April 18th they passed Rocas Reef, an atoll described in Captain Cleveland's Pilot Book as a desert island containing nothing but coral rock, sand, sea birds, and a few introduced coconut palms. When he climbed to the masthead, however, and had a look through his binoculars, Murphy made out the shapes of a little house, a second building, and a water tank. Fernando de Noronha was sixty miles to the east. Barbados was 1,700 miles away. At the rate they had been moving, they would reach that port in five or six weeks, after which he could catch a steamer bound for New York.

Murphy had all the time in the world to read, dream, and observe. Feeling a strong desire to be alone, he climbed up to where he could stretch himself out flat in the belly of the lower foretopsail. It was like a hammock, rocking and swaying him under the stars. Nobody knew he was there. He had found his solitude, listening to the waves, water lapping the ship's sides, the rigging as it taughtened and eased with the wind. Out of this reverie he was suddenly jolted awake by the sound of the ship's bell—ten o'clock and time to feel his way down the ratlines in the dark.

Under daylight, Murphy took his canvas chair atop the cabin and traveled with Darwin in the *Beagle* through the Galapagos Islands, across the Pacific to Tahiti, then on to the Indian Ocean. Murphy revered

Darwin. "How I long to see with the eyes of that matchless man of science," he wrote. "When I come home, I must study more geology. I want to be able to grasp something of the whole scope of nature in the lands and seas I visit; to be broad, not narrow, to be both a naturalist and a humanist, not a mere specialist. In technical work a man of this age must specialize, but in a reconnaissance of a part of earth's face, whether soil or sea, I want my comprehension, like that of Charles Darwin, to be able to interpret the underlying significance of clouds, hailstones, argillaceous rock, hot springs, cacti, land planarians, ice-borne boulders, carrion beetles, wingless flies, graminivorous birds, nest-building fish, viviparous reptiles, dodders, omnivorous rodents, sessile-eyed crustaceans, insect-eating plants, and foraminiferous protozoans! Nature is a chain, a million-knotted web of fishnet of life. Nothing exists of or for itself, but only in relation to other organisms, as Darwin seemed to know more thoroughly than anyone else."

The next day was dead calm. Murphy felt he could endure the poor food and myriad discomforts as long as they were moving forward, but calm was almost unbearable. Scurvy became more evident. Murphy had been eating a lime or two each day, but at least two of the Dominican greenhands had bleeding gums and loose incisors. Vitamin C comes from fresh food, and that had run out long ago. Half a dozen other men had discharge from their eyes, and their faces looked swollen. On top of this, the cat died, apparently from the heat, and poor Cadela lost her playmate.

On April 22nd, after several days of calm, Murphy tried to keep his mind occupied by cleaning his guns and fiddling with an albatross skeleton. He even resorted to shooting rats in the sea after someone else had tossed them overboard from the cage trap. He changed his clothes, took a nap, and waited for the diversion of supper. That night a steady rain came up only to add to the misery of getting nowhere. Murphy wrote, "Now many little rills are running and dripping from the ceiling of this miserable mousetrap of a cabin. Tin cans swing gracefully under some of them, and when they overflow, Johnny empties and rehangs them, but there aren't tin cans enough in a grocery store to catch all the leaks."

Chapter Forty-Five

IN CONTRAST TO THE TEDIUM of calms was the ever-present fascination with birds. At the close of daylight on April 23rd, a brown booby flew around the *Daisy* and finally alighted on the gunwale of the spare whaleboat across the stern and snuggled down for the night. He was not the least wary of Murphy; the bird merely "tucked his head into the groove of his back, where the scapular feathers cover its bill," after which nothing seemed to disturb him, including the ruckus and barking of a late-night rat chase. ("The rat, by the way escaped, jumping down the twelve-foot steerage companionway without touching a step.")

It could be said the booby got a free ride while standing on one foot aboard the *Daisy* but there was no wind and, therefore, the ship did not move. The bird slept unruffled until 5:30 the next morning when a sailor went to the stern to fetch a bucket and unwittingly scared it off.

Of the calm Murphy wrote, "The brig lay innocent-like upon the placid ocean, and a piece of cork alongside in the evening was still there this morning—although it was nearer the stern, proving that we had progressed somewhat. But sh! A breath of air, which almost deserves the name of zephyr, is coming out of the northwest. I am below, where it can't see me write this, and I'll pretend not to notice, and talk very quietly, and maybe it will increase."

But the transitory stir of air did not last. By evening the *Daisy*'s bow swung helplessly toward the southwest under a pink and heliotrope sunset. The brig lay half a degree south of the equator, about thirty-five miles. If they could only make it into the northern hemisphere Murphy would feel confident in the belief of actually reaching home.

April 25th, dead calm again except for a brief squall followed by a double rainbow whose reflected arc completed the image of a perfect circle shared by sea and sky. Then it too was gone.

Not until four o'clock did they finally slide over the equator. A pleasant breeze picked up. Murphy wrote, "I hardly dare speak of the little catspaw, fearing its inconsistency. But anyway we are moving, and the beloved Dipper is overturned in the heavens on our right. We can follow the pointers toward the spot at which Polaris lies just under the horizon, ready to pop up and guide us home. I'll begin to look for it about the day after tomorrow, if this breath continues to blow us northward."

Murphy organized and packed. He put his winter clothes, plant specimens, traps, rifle, cartridges, blankets, and other equipment in the Brooklyn Museum's trunk and stowed it with the understanding that it would be left undisturbed until the *Daisy* reached her home port in New Bedford. His personal luggage was pared down to the absolute necessities of his steamer trip from the Caribbean to New York.

At that time of year they could expect to move out of the doldrums and into the northeast trades at about two or three degrees above the equator. They had already traveled one of those degrees. Murphy estimated a couple of days and they would enter the sweep of the "steadies." Twelve days beyond that would probably get them into port, "not allowing for whales." Each sperm whale sighting meant a delay of several hours while the boats lowered and chased. A capture meant a delay of at least a day if not two for the cutting-in and boiling. His estimated a Barbados arrival of May 17th.

Sure enough, April 28th, at 2° 36' N latitude, wind blew steadily all night. Murphy advanced his estimate to May 15th.

April 29th was Murphy's 26th birthday. Among the cards he found in his letter bag was one from Grace in which she said, "Our separation shall be only a night between two summer days, and a night full of the stars of memory and hope." Murphy replied to her in his journal, "What a letter bag! What a bride!"

As if in celebration, they came into a school of albacores and caught one large enough to feed all hands. He wrote, "[F]resh fish is a blessing for men in the precarious condition of most of our crew. The ship's food has not affected me badly because I am very careful of what and how I eat, but I admit that the craving for fresh food, whether plant or animal, is a constant gnawing. Physiologically this low-protein diet ought to benefit me if not carried too far, because when I get ashore and eat judiciously of fruits, vegetables, eggs, fish, and meat, I ought to begin to build up actively at once. I haven't the slightest symptoms of scurvy although many of the crew have it." He went on to describe the keg of West Indian limes that had been discovered in the ship's run. The rinds were discolored, but the pulp remained sound. Their tartness set Murphy's teeth on edge, but he ate them.

Another albacore was caught and trade winds continued. Murphy advanced his estimated arrival at Barbados to May 14th.

On the last day of the month Murphy began his entry, "April is gone, and the warblers are arriving at Neutaconkanut Hill in the early morning. Do you remember the spray of apple blossoms that I picked for you, there, two years ago at sunrise? How I would like to be there or in the cedar woods along [Long Island] Sound!"

That night he saw the first twinkling of the North Star. The trade wind sang like a deep-throated conch shell, and phosphorescence flashed in the watery holes left by flying fish as they darted aside the furrow the *Daisy* plowed through the sea.

Mr. Almeida was added to the sick list.

May 1st, the water thickened with Portuguese men-o'-war—more than Murphy had ever seen. Several of the men on board had tangled with their stinging cells as children and held great respect for the jellyfish. Murphy counted fifty on what he estimated to be no more than an acre of water. The Old Man said that was nothing. He had once seen as many as one per square yard, which would have been 5,000 in an acre. Their luminous sails looked like jewels bobbing on the surface. Murphy, observing them safely from deck, was struck more by their beauty than their stinging potential. "Its float, or bladder," he wrote, "has a crimped upper ridge and gleams in the sunlight with various delicate tints of blue, purple, pink, and yellow, the general effect being like the opalescence of ancient Roman glass. The fleets today [are like] fragments of a rainbow, scattered over the sea."

May 2nd, 9° 14' N latitude and tearing along on course. Mr. Almeida's condition improved, although he still looked soft and pasty. Murphy finished reading *Pilgrim's Progress*. He packed the remainder of his bird skins for shipment from Barbados to New York. The heavy and imperishable specimens such as skeletons, rocks, and items pickled in alcohol would remain on the *Daisy* until she docked at New Bedford.

Barbados lies roughly 13 degrees north of the equator and 59 degrees west of the Greenwich Observatory in London. The *Daisy* had only two degrees of latitude and ten degrees of longitude to go. Murphy advanced his estimated arrival by one more day, putting it at May 9th. He also began to imagine where Grace might be at a given time and what she might be doing. She could have still been at her mother's in Providence, waiting for word, or preparing for his homecoming in New York, or even waiting to greet him somewhere in the West Indies. He wondered whether she too was picturing him, flying toward her in a sailing ship shoved along by the trade winds. Again, a faint cloud passed through his thoughts: why had he not heard from her a second time in South Georgia?

Captain Cleveland began periodically tasting the seawater, convinced that he could determine from its salinity how close they were to the outpourings of the Amazon. Murphy was skeptical. He put a little on his tongue and declared it strongly brackish, if not downright salty. At the beginning of the sixteenth century, however, a Spanish explorer, Vincente Pinzón, filled his casks somewhere in the vicinity of where the *Daisy* was and reported on his return to Spain that the tropical Atlantic was composed of fresh water.

Breakfast and dinner that day reached an all-time low in what Murphy called "hog-trough meals." That afternoon, however, they hooked a sixty-pound dolphin, which improved things for supper, along with some superior baked beans.

May 4th, a West Indian sailor drew a knife on a Portuguese boatsteerer and stuck him in the ribs. Like all other sheath knives on board, its tip had been blunted. Nevertheless, the blade not only broke the skin but forced some of the boatsteerer's shirt fabric into the wound. The offended man, enraged more than injured, grabbed an ax from the chopping block, but a dozen men rushed to prevent him from swinging it.

The sailor was put in irons in the lazaret, but the Old Man seemed uncharacteristically impassive. "On the contrary," wrote Murphy, "he has recently become softspoken, peacemaking, and as genial as a bishop at a tea party, even paying a compliment now and then to a sailor doing a job. All of this signifies to me that he has made up his mind to get into port as rapidly as we can, and, of course, he wants everybody to arrive with a heart full of contentment, brotherly love, and the kindest memories of our happy voyage."

They caught another dolphin and turned it over to the steward. To Murphy's disgust the slabs of flesh were cooked in foul-smelling elephant oil, which the steward said was the only remaining fat.

Light wind continued steady. Murphy fell asleep that night, content that they would have moved sixty or seventy miles nearer his "heart's desire" by morning. He was now hoping to see Barbados Thursday, May 8th.

In the season of molting plumage, he had been giving away his tattered and excess clothing to the steward, the cabin boy, and other members of the crew. Each morning he began with clean—but worn—socks then gave that pair away at the end of the day. He had also been bathing and shaving regularly. He shampooed in rainwater. His moustache was gone, much to Johnny's dismay.

By now Murphy was up and down the rigging, standing at the masthead, scanning for signs, prickling with eager anticipation almost to the point of making himself ill.

May 7th, the last full day at sea. Birds signaled the proximity of land. "Just think," Murphy wrote, "we are only as far from port as Montauk Point is from Brooklyn. We have only the length of Long Island to sail!"

Murphy could not work, could not concentrate. He went to sleep that night hoping to wake to the sight of land.

The morning of May 8th emerged gray and pink with a good breeze. At four o'clock the faint beam of a lighthouse had reached the *Daisy* with its intermittant flash. Murphy climbed to the masthead before breakfast. With Mars still bright overhead, night's darkness gradually faded as a hint of day-blue flowed across the eastern sky. As on his first—and all subsequent—climbs to that towering lookout a hundred feet above the deck, the vessel's exaggerated action jerked him back and forth above the waves. Feeling uncharacteristically seasick, he clung to the thin iron hoop while simultaneously straining to see the broad white beaches and green expanse of cane fields that he remembered from almost a year ago. A sliver of sun crept above the rim, yolky gold in the *Daisy*'s wake. They were heading west on their final course.

Murphy touched the now-familiar oilskin folder beneath his shirt, the waterproof pouch that contained the last of Grace's letters—one that would remain mercifully unread. It had hung around his neck day and night since July 18, 1912, with a message he was to resort to only if circumstances made it seem certain that he would never be able to return home. But now all danger of his voyage was past. The letter would remain sealed.

It was noon before they dropped anchor in Bridgetown's Carlisle Bay. The port doctor came aboard and began his medical inspections. Murphy was declared physically fit. Next, a Mr. Lewis of the *Daisy*'s agents called across the water from an approaching boat, asking specifically for Murphy. Mr. Lewis was aware that a letter from Grace was being held at the American Consul's office. Not quickly enough, Murphy and Captain Cleveland were in the agent's boat and racing for shore. Murphy wasted no time in hailing a carriage and getting himself to the Consul office, where Chester Martin handed him an envelope postmarked April 8th, 1913.

Murphy sat, lost to the world. He read, smiled, laughed, and wept from relief. All his letters from South Georgia had obviously reached her. She, in turn, had sent her replies by registered post. This explained why they had not reached him. For the sake of "extra safety" they had most likely been delayed at each step of the journey, while Mrs. Cleveland's, which had been sent by ordinary mail, would have gone by the first means of transportation at every postal link.

Murphy had asked the cabbie to keep his horse and carriage waiting. The next stop was the cable office to send Grace the news of his arrival at Barbados. Since he could not expect a reply to his message any sooner than the next morning, he headed into the streets of Bridgetown to find lunch.

He ate pâté de foie gras, a magnificently turned omelet—delicate and foamy—and soft fresh rolls with lots of butter. He washed it all down with a whiskey and soda. Next, he scanned a month's worth of American, British, and French newspapers, astounded by how much had occurred during his absence from the world.

Murphy took a room at the Hotel Balmoral at the rate of $2.00 per day. The next morning he wrote Grace, "Your [cable] came this morning, and I am happy. I am bound here for a week, because the *Guayana*, sailing tomorrow, has only a [shared] berth. I would take it nevertheless, but for the fact that the later steamer will get me in almost as soon, and give me a chance to get some clothing. Only one of my old shirts can I close around my neck; I have only one old suit, and am short on all else. . . . I'll get in touch with you by cable or wireless so that you'll know of my coming a few days in advance. God bless you, dear. You are a brave wife. After reading your letter, I no longer have any doubt that the long months we have given up were for the best, and that we can build on them for the rest of our days."

On May 9th, a "Certificate of Discharge of Seaman" attested that the brig

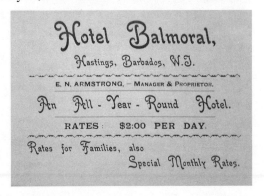

"Daisy," whose description of voyage or employment had been a "Whaling cruise" and whose port of registry was New Bedford, had discharged R. C. Murphy, whose character was judged to be "Good" and his ability also "Good," in Barbados, W. I. with the cause for discharge listed as "Mutual consent." The document is signed by Benjamin Cleveland, Master, and Chester Martin, American Consul.

Murphy wrote to Grace, "Two weeks from today, God willing, we'll be together again." He would travel on the *Vestris*, a steamer that would go direct, taking only six days.

THE LAST PAGE of Murphy's journal ends with an Irish poem. His brother Ed, who accurately anticipated the most difficult aspect of a bridegroom's months at sea, had included it in one of the notes he tucked into the wealth of Grace's letter bag. Both being Murphys, the brothers knew that *mavourneen* and *machree* meant darling and dear.

THE SEEKERS
Says she:
'Tis a long way ye've traveled, mavourneen,
'Tis a long trip ye've made on the sea
For the sake of a slip of a girl like me,
To be gettin' a kiss no better than this,
'Tis a long road ye've traveled, machree.

Says he:
'Twas a long way and a lone way, me true love,
But 'tis millions of miles, as He knows,
That a hungerin', wanderin' sunbeam goes
To be gettin' a kiss no better than this
From the lips of no sweeter a rose.

(Form No. 18—Consular.)

CERTIFICATE OF DISCHARGE OF SEAMAN.

AMERICAN CONSULAR SERVICE,

Barbados. W. I. May 9th. 1913. , 19

Name of ship, Brig "DAISY".

Official number, 6752.

Port of registry, New Bedford.

Tonnage, 383 net.

Description of voyage or employment, Whaling cruise.

Name of seaman, R. C. Murphy.

Place of birth, New York.

Age, 26. years.

Character, Good.

Ability, Good.

Capacity, Assistant Navigator

Date of entry, June 10th. , 19 12. Date of discharge, May 9th. , 19 13.

Place of discharge, Barbados. W. I.

Cause of discharge, Mutual consent.

I CERTIFY that the above particulars are correct, and that the above-named seaman was discharged accordingly.

Robert Cushman Murphy _Benjin D Cleveland_
Seaman.   Master.

Given to the above-named seaman in my presence this 9th. day of May , A. D. 19 13.

Chester W. Martin

American Consul.

Epilogue

O N MAY 9 TH, Murphy rowed one last time to the *Daisy* where she lay at anchor in Bridgetown's roadstead. It was time to bid farewell to the men with whom he had shared space for so many months. He would greet some of the crew again when the *Daisy* arrived at New Bedford at the end of the summer, but others would have been discharged at Dominica by then. He wrote, "[These men and I] stand as close to a relationship of warm esteem as is possible for comrades whose paths are not likely to cross again. It touches me to realize that I have never had so much as an irritable glance from one of them through all their trials. They were always willing to help me far beyond the limits of the Old Man's sanction, and never with anticipation of favor or reward. They have shown no envy of my relative comfort, as contrasted with their own plight. They have accepted me, man to man, even at the oar of a whaleboat. In carrying out their duties by fair weather and foul in mortal combat—wood to blackskin—with mighty adversaries; and, for the most part, in dealings one with another, they have proved their possession of no mean stock of the cardinal virtues, and even of as goodly a share of the beatitudes as more fortunate human beings would dare to claim."

The second and third mates had already been discharged in Bridgetown along with Murphy at the Consul's office. Thirty-two-year old Mr. Vincent and twenty-nine-year-old Mr. Almeida had been aboard the *Daisy* for nineteen months. They expected to find another whaler putting in at Barbados and were ready to sign on. Captain Cleveland paid the officers small advances against their shares of the *Daisy*'s proceeds; the balance would be calculated after the oil had been sold. Mr. Robinson

(Victor) and Mr. da Lomba would serve as the sole officers on the voyage to New Bedford as they cruised through the sperm whaling waters off Cape Hatteras, North Carolina.

After re-outfitting himself with new clothes and catching himself up to life on shore, Murphy waited impatiently to take passage on the Irish-made *S. S. Vestris*. Finally on board and halfway into the six-day voyage he stood on deck, instinctively scanning the expanse of ocean, when two sperm whales breached and spouted in the near distance. From force of habit, a long and mighty *Blo-o-o-o-ows!* issued from Murphy's lungs. By his telling, all passengers rushed to the rail where he stood, and the "swift but cranky *Vestris* nearly turned turtle."

GRACE HAD GROWN UP on a street lined with elm trees and among gentlewomen from the old school who were not hampered by housework. As a new bride all she knew how to cook was fudge. After her return from Barbados on the *Guayana* with Mrs. Cleveland—only four months into her new marriage—Grace took up residence in her old room once again at her mother's home in Rhode Island. Grace's former childhood nurse, Jennie, had been brought back into service to act as a companion for the duration of the *Daisy*'s voyage. Mary, in her ever-present ruffled cap, continued to serve the family meals. Bob's sister Carolyn stayed through the winter, and his brother Ed called at the house from time to time. All this and a trip to Florida provided diversion. Grace had plenty of assistance, company, and entertainment, but she was lonely.

Grace's mother had no patience with the concept of boredom. "Queen Victoria," said Mrs. Barstow, "studied Hindustani after she was eighty. The world is full of things to do." Grace filled her days, but time dragged nevertheless. For her it was a year of quiet growth. She received five letters from Bob in the months he was away and he only the one from her that arrived in Grytviken. She had been a diligent correspondent, however, writing often and sending carbons and originals to any place she thought there might be a chance the *Daisy* would put in and collect mail. For two and a half years after Bob's return, her undelivered letters came back from Cape Town, Buenos Aires, Tristan da Cunha, the Falkland Islands, St. Helena, Ascension, and a peppering of other locations around the Atlantic, including South Georgia, where her much-yearned-for letters reached their destination only after the *Daisy* had weighed anchor for home.

When Grace received her husband's cable telling of his scheduled arrival on the *Vestris*, she did not have enough time to reach Barbados and greet him there. She hurried to New York to set up housekeeping, this time determined to learn something about cooking. By absolute coincidence the very apartment they had given up the preceding May was once again available.

The day finally came for her to go to the dock. A friend escorted her, holding her arm so firmly she felt she could barely move. He explained later that he had feared she would fall off the wharf in excitement without someone there to stabilize her.

Bob rushed down the gangplank brawnier and more tanned than Grace had ever seen him but very much the man she had married. For all they had to say to each other, however, they could barely speak. Those first few days they felt tongue-tied. As Grace put it, "[It] had been a year of idealism and idealization, not of day-to-day reality."

She had lived with the image of him on his stormy island among the nesting albatrosses and the penguins in gales strong enough to blow men down. She imagined him subsisting on not much more than the preserved beef that sailors called salt horse. In her mind he had grown even taller than his six-foot, three-inch frame. Now it was different, and it would take time to find their footing and put their lives back together.

A trip to Nova Scotia began the process. He picked hillside flowers to her delight, and she rediscovered her sense of humor. In the fall of that year, Grace learned she was pregnant.

One week before her due date the following spring, Bob was scheduled to give his first public lecture on South Georgia. Grace's doctor was old fashioned even for the time. He insisted that her attendance at the lecture would be indecent and that, if she went, he would fire her from his care. Alison Barstow Murphy was born precisely one year after Bob's return from South Georgia. Fifteen months later, they welcomed the arrival of a second child, Robert Cushman Murphy, Jr., and three years later, another son, Amos Chafee Barstow Murphy, named for Grace's father and a brother lost in childhood. Grace never forgave that doctor for blackmailing her into his way of thinking. She was furious at missing out on the lecture. It would turn out to be the first of many lectures on South Georgia and other expeditions, although on these later adventures Grace—and often their children—went along.

Bob had returned from the rim of the Antarctic to the chaos of conflict between the world's nations. In the twilight of commercial whaling, the *Daisy*'s owners re-outfitted her and restored the vessel to merchant service, meeting the needs of war. Bound for Europe and laden

with a cargo of beans, the old brig sprang a leak. Ocean water seeped into the cargo; the beans swelled; her deck bulged; and the hull yielded to the expanding load. October 29, 1916, the *Daisy* sank in the eastern Atlantic.

Despite the crusty old captain's prejudice against New Yorkers and anyone else who did not hail from New England, Murphy and the Old Man remained in contact and on good terms. The skipper believed true civilization was limited to a forty-mile swath between Bedford and Boston, but Murphy could maintain something of an equal footing with the Old Man when it came to heritage. Prior to his family's Long Island history,

The Daisy*'s first owners paid $15,000.*

Murphy counted eleven generations of New England ancestry. Benjamin Cleveland could trace only eight.

Captain Cleveland continued to go a-whaling after unloading Murphy's hundreds of specimens. In 1916 he paid $100 each for sixty of the *Charles W. Morgan's* sixty-four shares. A year later, however, on August 8, 1917 Benjamin Cleveland sailed the *Morgan* into Buzzard's Bay for the last time. At age 83 the Old Man was "gathered into his Father's arms." Working his way up from a fourteen-year-old cabin boy, he had commanded ten whaleships and had been principal owner of two.

The *Morgan* returned from her thirty-seventh and last whaling voyage in 1921. In her day she had caught and processed a total of 600 whales. In 1941 she was acquired by Mystic Seaport, where she is displayed as the centerpiece of a Yankee whaling exhibit. Likewise, one of the *Daisy's* whaleboats is on display at the Cold Spring Harbor Whaling Museum on Long Island, thanks to Murphy's diligence at preserving the craft and the history it represents.

Benjamin and Ada Cleveland's son and only descendant was lost at sea around the time of the Old Man's death, but Mrs. Cleveland lived a long life. Murphy kept in touch and saw her shortly before the end at which point she confessed to him that, having reached her early nineties, she

was beginning to dread "the prospect of growing old."

José Correia, the *Daisy's* cooper also stayed in touch with Murphy and participated in several more cruises on behalf of the American Museum. Murphy had taught him how to skin birds. Late in 1913 Correia went by passenger steamer from New York to

José Correia working for the museum on a later voyage.

Buenos Aires from where he traveled on an oil carrier bound for South Georgia for the express purpose of continuing what Murphy had been unable to accomplish. Through the cooperation of Captain Larsen, Correia collected examples of the island's smaller birds at various stages of maturation. In the spring and summer of 1922 Correia shipped a collection of waterfowl skins from the Cape Verde Islands to Murphy in New York. He later accompanied Murphy on an expedition to the Gulf of Panama. José Correia died in 1955 at age seventy-two.

Murphy learned indirectly of others' fates. Some were killed by sperm whales on subsequent voyages. Others, including Victor, the fourth mate, sailed out of New Bedford and were never heard from again. Somewhere along the line Murphy "picked up from the breeze" a rumor that John da Lomba was living as the "unofficial king of the tight little Isle of Brava," a fate so fitting that Murphy hoped it was true.

The *Daisy* was the last ship of her kind to put in at South Georgia, after which all whaling in that region was mechanized. Operations at Grytviken continued into the 1960s. The last American voyage under sail on which whales were actually taken was on the schooner *John R. Manta* in 1925 in the Hatteras Grounds.

Of birds alone, Murphy shipped to New Bedford about five hundred specimens of fifty-five species, together with more than a hundred sets of

eggs. Seven years after the *Daisy* Murphy's research made him the first to establish a connection between patterns of bird life and oceanic conditions. Until then people assumed seabirds moved around at random. Murphy demonstrated that they are as closely linked to their environment as the land birds are. Ocean currents, global winds, climate, land masses, and food source concen-

Petrels skins from Trindade. Murphy prepared specimens in varying stages of molt and maturity whenever he could.

trations are elemental to the birds' cycles—connections taken for granted by now.

Before voyaging on the *Daisy*, Murphy was unclear as to where, specifically, his biological interests lay. Frank Chapman, whose page galleys Murphy had proofread the year before starting college, advised him early on, "Don't be an ornithologist if you can help it. But if you can't help it, go ahead, and the chances are that you will become a good one." After the cruise to South Georgia and an expedition to the bird islands of Peru, Murphy had no doubts. In 1927 he was named curator of oceanic birds at the American Museum of Natural History, the first such position in any museum—probably because no other person had ever known enough about the subject to qualify. He later became curator of the Department of Birds and, later still, Lamont curator.

MANY PEOPLE ASSOCIATE South Georgia with the legendary expedition of the *Endurance*. Twenty months after the *Daisy* set her sails for home, Ernest Shackleton made the island his base from which he took on his final stores before setting out for the Weddell Sea in his attempt to reach the South Pole. Sixteen months later Shackleton was to return. The *Endurance* had been lost to the ice, stranding the men on the floes and forcing them to winter over. Eventually, they made their way north. Twenty-eight men in three twenty-foot boats landed on the bleak shores of Elephant Island. Their only chance of survival was for Shackleton and five others to make the eight-hundred-mile ocean journey to South Georgia in hopes of reaching help from one of the whaling stations. After two weeks of misery and storm in their open boat they landed on the hostile south shore with no choice but to climb up and over the crags and glaciers. In a greatly weakened state, and with only a rudimentary map to go by, Shackleton and two of his men set out. Thirty-six hours later they staggered into Stromness Harbor. Taking one look at the tattered, tired trio stumbling toward them at the Tonsberg Company's station, men ran away as if having seen the devil himself. No one had ever crossed South Georgia or approached the station by land.

Shackleton documented the event in his book *South*, "We came to a wharf, where a man in charge stuck to his station. I asked him if Mr. Sørlle (the manager) was in the house.

"'Yes,' he said, as he stared at us.

"'We would like to see him,' said I.

"'Who are you?' he asked.

"'We have lost our ship and come over the island,' I replied.

"'You have come over the island?' he said in a tone of entire unbelief.

"The man went toward the manager's house and we followed him. I learned afterward that he said to Mr. Sørlle: 'There are three funny-looking men outside, who say that they have come over the island and they know you. I have left them outside.' A very necessary precaution from his point of view.

"Mr. Sørlle came to the door and said, 'Who the *hell* are you?'

"'Don't you know me?' I said.

"'I know your voice,' he replied doubtfully. 'You're the mate of the *Daisy*.'

"'My name is Shackleton,' I said."

It is likely that the station manager, after more than three years since the *Daisy* had been there, confused Murphy in his memory as having been the first officer. The mate, John da Lomba was mixed race and had a distinctly Portuguese accent. Murphy and Shackleton were both Irish. They looked somewhat alike and, in fact, sounded much the same in delivery, each articulate and with the inflections of education in their speech.

Despite the profound hardship of the *Endurance* rescue, Shackleton set out again on his fourth attempt to conquer the pole. But the voyage was not to be. He arrived at Grytviken January 4, 1922 feeling hale but in less than twenty-four hours was dead of a massive heart attack, aged forty-seven years.

News of the death brought the existence of that far and frozen island to many people's consciousness for the first time. In response, Murphy published an article, "South Georgia, An Outpost of the Antarctic," in

National Geographic magazine. It was an exhaustive survey of the biology, geology, history, and climate of the place, including Murphy's own sketch map, which, if Shackleton had had for his heroic climb, would have guided him to the whaling station at Prince Olaf harbor near the mouth of Possession Bay in a matter of three or four hours and not the thirty-six it took to reach Stromness. Also accompanying the article were thirty-nine of Murphy's photographs developed aboard the *Daisy*.

In 1915 Murphy had published a 133-page monograph, *The Penguins of South Georgia*. In 1917–18 he published articles on old-style Yankee whaling, mechanized whaling, and one on marine camouflage in which he compared seabird markings with the artificial camouflage sometimes painted on steamships. Along the way he earned a Master's degree from Columbia University.

As his career built, Murphy went on other expeditions—Baja California, New Zealand, Peru, Florida, Ecuador, Columbia, Venezuela—always recording his experiences enthusiastically in journals as he had done aboard the *Daisy*. In 1925 he published the book *Bird Islands of Peru* and in 1936 the two-volume *Oceanic Birds of South America*, which is considered by some to this day to be the best and most comprehensive book of its kind. Peter Harrison, who is credited with having seen more seabirds than anyone, past or present, and who has written and illustrated his own bird guides, wrote of Murphy's work, "[His *Oceanic Birds* occupies] the most prized and hallowed position on my library shelves, and I do not foresee that another 50 years will alter my feelings. I regard Murphy as a cult figure. He was the forerunner of the modern birder who sacrifices anything and everything, undergoing hardships and deprivation in pursuit of his overriding love of seabirds."

Oceanic Birds won Murphy the John Burroughs Award for nature writing and the Brewster Medal of the American Ornithologists' Union. In all Murphy published over five-hundred scientific articles, nine books, and dozens of popular articles. He was awarded three honorary degrees in the sixty-year career that began aboard the *Daisy*, including the Ph.D. given by his *alma mater*, Brown University.

In 1960 Murphy was invited by the National Science Foundation to return to where it had all begun for him in the Antarctic. The trip was part of Operation Deep Freeze aboard the naval icebreaker *Glacier*. Grace suffered his absence once again, still longing to view the frozen hills herself and to see directly that southernmost part of the world she knew of only by description. In 1970 when Murphy was eighty-three, Lars Eric Lindblad invited him aboard the *Explorer*, the first cruise ship to venture to South Georgia. Murphy's role was to be chief scientist. He had not seen that land for fifty-eight years.

"I'll accept your offer so long as my wife might accompany me," he replied. Grace was thrilled at the prospect. Roger Tory Peterson, also on that cruise, commented, "The years seemed to fall from Murphy's shoulders as the *Explorer* came within sight of that long-ago land." Peterson further observed, "He seemed a much younger man when he delivered his lecture on his experience there."

With the birth of her third child, Grace's deafness had advanced. In those early years of motherhood, she heard nothing without amplification by big, bulky aids. Later, however, not even amplification could help. Despite the discomfort of having worn the awkward appliances and their associated heavy batteries, in her memoir, Grace wrote, "I would wear fifty hearing aids each as big as a piano or build yardarms across my shoulders to hang a hundred on if I could hear my granddaughter play her violin." But after age fifty she could not. Nevertheless, totally deaf and bent with scoliosis, the eighty-one year old Grace boarded Lindblad's *Explorer* with the enthusiasm of a schoolgirl. For a brief moment she was the bride again, sailing with her husband from port to port.

The names Murphy assigned to various land features around the Bay of Isles and that he applied to his sketch map of the region had been adopted. They were in use then as they are today, Grace Glacier, Albatross Island, and Cape Woodrow Wilson among them.

Named for Murphy himself are two mountains, an Antarctic inlet, a louse, a fish, a plant, a lizard, a spider, a petrel, a county park, and a Long Island public school. His modesty was apparent when he said, "As a scientist, I'd as soon have a louse named for me as a mountain." Of the junior high school Murphy felt both deep delight and mild embarrassment at the honor. He said at the dedication, "I am mortally afraid of being cast in the role of hero before the young people of this school, instead of one of themselves grown up, a Long Island country boy who found his niche in the world and has attained a measure of success merely because what he has been doing was all in good fun."

Though never wealthy himself, Murphy moved in a circle of moneyed and influential friends. Slender, tall, and dapper, his appearance and self-assurance helped him travel through life first class. Widely known for his conservation efforts, Murphy dedicated much of his last decade to the preservation of the great cetaceans. His voice was among the first to utter, "Save the whales," and it carried weight because he had been there. A documentary film, *And So Ends*, featured him as a moving force in this effort. Speaking out against the mechanized killing that he had so deplored in Grytviken, he said, "All that the whales need is to be left alone for a hundred years."

The Murphys lived out their lives only a few miles from his boyhood home. He traveled the world and was active until the end, lecturing to the Linnaean Society only one month before he died suddenly in 1973. He had gotten up early that day to prepare Grace breakfast in bed as he had done for most of their married life. Without warning of prior illness, his heart apparently stopped. His death became front-page news in the *New York Times* and elsewhere.

Murphy led the graduation parade, at his alma mater, proudly displaying on his gold watch chain the Phi Beta Kappa key he had earned as a young man.

Grace died a different sort of death, her flame fading quietly over the next two years until finally flickering out during an attack of pneumonia. In accordance with their long-standing agreement that if he died before she, they were both buried in Providence among Grace's forebears. Had Grace's death preceded his, they would have been placed near Bob's origins in Mt. Sinai ground.

The harpoons, scrimshaw, and whaling memorabilia he had collected over the years are on exhibit in various museums. His journals and papers are archived in Philadelphia at the American Philosophical Society, of which Murphy was an active member. His letters include those from Eleanor and Franklin Roosevelt, Walt Disney, Amelia Earhart, Helen Keller, Rockwell Kent, Clifford Ashley, John Masefield, Margaret Mead, Rachel Carson, Nelson Rockefeller, Emily Shackleton, and many others.

Incised on Murphy's gravestone is an albatross in flight.

ACKNOWLEDGMENTS

Grateful acknowledgment is made to the following individuals and institutions for their permission to reproduce illustrations in this book:

American Museum of Natural History: photographs by Robert Cushman Murphy: cover (negative 228024s), and pages 25 (228004s), 91 (228302s), 160 (227999s), 198 (228025s), 203 (228270s), 204 (228017s), 205 (228020s), 209 (228028s), 210 (228032s), 217 (228039s), 230–31 (313303s), 233 (228069s), 234 (228058s), 237 (228307s), 253 (228276s), 255 (228331s; 228335s), 266 *top* (29285s), 267 (228058s), 269 (29343s), 279 (29367s), 291 (228277s), 293 (228063s), 344 (227983s), 346 (218340s).

American Philosophical Society: pages 5, 23, 24, 69, 107 *top*, 117, 129, 130, 156 *bottom*, 161, 183, 188, 196, 222, 228, 241, 247, 272, 337, 345.

Christopher Mathews: page 35.

Whaling Museum at Cold Spring Harbor: 6, 26, 27, 33, 37, 41 *top*, 42, 63, 65, 68, 80, 81, 82, 83, 97, 99, 100, 101, 102, 105, 107 *bottom*, 114, 141, 143, 153, 156 *top*, 167, 177, 206, 215, 280, 313, 316, 323, 339.

The Long Island Museum of American Art History and Carriages: frontispiece "A Dead Whale or a Stove Boat!" by Clifford Ashley.